# THE AFRO FUTURIST EVOLUTION

## CREATIVE PATHS TO SELF-DISCOVERY

### YTASHA L. WOMACK

Lawrence Hill Books
Chicago

Published by Lawrence Hill Books
An imprint of Chicago Review Press Incorporated
814 North Franklin Street
Chicago, Illinois 60610
ISBN 978-0-89733-455-6

Library of Congress Control Number: 2025930495

Cover illustration: © John Jennings
Cover layout: Jonathan Hahn
Typesetting: Nord Compo

Printed in the United States of America

*For those who wonder as they wander
and become the marvelous along the way.*

*And special thanks to Jewell Ryan-White,
Joan Lewis, and Nona Hendryx.*

# CONTENTS

# INTRODUCTION

WHEN I BEGAN WRITING ABOUT AFROFUTURISM some time ago, I saw myself as a person on the periphery of an exciting worldview fueled by visionaries and creatives while I was charged with documenting the culture. However, I too was transformed by the inquiry into space/time, and the introspection it prompted reordered my world. Afrofuturism, this electrifying paradigm, gathered disparate parts of myself, imagined spaces, spacetastic culture, vision, and memory into a cohesive mainframe. As I began writing, I quickly realized that the writing itself, along with the creative story ideas that swept me off all landing pads, was evidence that Afrofuturism is also a practice that moves through and with us; one prompted by chili-peppered inquiry and honed with imagined worlds made real in music, dance, myth, and life. A sauntering down space/time theory lane coupled with a foray into the creative is where the Afrofuturist magic happens.

I champion Afrofuturism as creative practice, a futures practice, and a rotating lens to make sense of our collective relationship with the universe. Future visions we craft and adopt shape us just as the lack of a future vision can impact us, too. The shaping of an Afrofuturist lens requires openness, community-centric values, and constant checking in with the universe. I'm a cheerleader for optimism, for a mind-set that urges us to find the space "of inspiration" to move out, through, over, under, and beyond.

I'm writing this book because I've learned new ways of thinking about Afrofuturism since my initial trek down the yellow brick causeway to alter-destiny. I've encountered people who were noting their blocks around futures and also witnessed the watershed clearings that lead to deep insight. Through the juxtaposition of space-tinged and mystical ideas—some of which collapse times—revelations occur and visions are revealed.

## A Spacetastic Reading

Afrofuturism is nuanced; a living, breathing paradigm with shapeshifting energy. Afrofuturism is charged by the realm of the imagination. Imagination is a futures tool, a human need, but also a present action. Future visions leapfrog us out of the stuck space and shape practice today. This present action is a legacy tool that connects us with those of the past whose actions we build upon, and those in the future who will create from a comparable wellspring. Afrofuturism can help us connect to the many streams of "we." It can help us connect to those many streams now.

There are some who view Afrofuturism as another version of the great by-and-by—an untouched heaven, a protopia world to one day reach, a moment of the past that was somehow lost and encoded in story, but not one tied to present practice or being. Marie-Lydie Nokouda is an actress and creative director in Copenhagen. When Nokouda first researched Afrofuturism she had a hard time grasping it. "I was stuck on the aesthetic," she said, thinking of space garb and interstellar worlds. "Then I realized it's not about the aesthetic. It's about me, how I see time and space now. How I see the future of Black people in Denmark." Although Afrofuturism is riddled with theory, Afrofuturism is also an embodied experience echoing a worldview fired with optimism and wonderment, driven with determination to support worlds that value humanity. Afrofuturists are charged with being and perceiving the future in the present moment. Therefore, Afrofuturism is now.

With that, I'd like to provide some context for our Afrofuturist sojourn. For starters, nothing about it fits neatly into Western notions of reality or the English language I use to write. The languages we speak have inherent frameworks, and I'm aware of both the potential and limitations of the language I use in talking about concepts, some of which derived outside the Anglophone world—concepts that words don't aptly define. As a result, there will be aspects of this reading that will feel like language benders or will challenge your proverbial ground floor of reality. The objective isn't to have you tumbling amongst the stars (not in totality), but such experiences metaphorically occur when we are assessing the ways we've been socialized to see the world around us and expand our worldview. Afrofuturism is an exploration of outer space, the symbolic great beyond that hovers beyond the mental, emotional, and physical boundaries placed upon us. It is also an exploration of inner space, our subconscious, our dreams, and aspirations.

I define Afrofuturism as a way of looking at futures or alternate realities through an African/African Diasporic or Black cultural lens. However, I think it's important to note that not all cultures within the African Diaspora or on the continent of Africa identify as Black, yet they may be informed, shaped by, or live from indigenous African values. Therefore, a culture can be African and not necessarily Black. A culture can be African Diasporic and not solely Black. A culture can be heavily influenced by the continent and diasporic cultures and not be Black identified. Sometimes when we use these terms they are interchangeable, which isn't always accurate but is important to note.

That said, there's an array of cultures within this pantheon of Africanness and Blackness. Whoever discusses this subject, regardless of where they are, is by default often centering on the culture of Blackness they grew up with or are most familiar with. This isn't necessarily a bad thing, but it is something to be aware of.

African/African Diasporic people around the world live different lives. This may be a fact that goes without saying, but I've found it necessary to repeat. My experience as a Black woman in the urban Midwest of Chicago is not the same experience as a biracial trans woman from the favelas of Bahia or a Black gay man and son of immigrants from Guinea-Bissau in the Eighth Arrondissement in Paris, or an Akan cis man in East Legon, Accra. My experience is not identical to that of an elder from my African American culture living across the street from me, either. Yet, these lives aren't inherently opposing experiences. Afrofuturism is at its best when it recognizes the synergy in African/African Diasporic cultures and how they align with cultures around the world. I've found that some have a tough time recognizing the diversity of Black and African cultures and experiences. This lack of recognition is usually because many aren't exposed to a wide stretch of Black cultures in our media or possibly in day-to-day life. In other cases, we are exposed but don't know how to frame the tapestry. Much of the progress of people of African descent in facing daunting inhumanity has been overcome through unity of politics. However, seeking uniformity in politics for human rights does not negate diversity in culture or experience.

Moreover, many of us aren't accustomed to talking about culture. We may be familiar with how we grew up and the music or entertainment that our circle of friends or family consumed. We may know our communal traditions, language, slang, and shared interests, particularly if they are reinforced by pop culture or family norms. "Doing it for the culture" is a popular phrase invoked to imply that an action is pure in its intention to elevate the relevance of how specific people gather or create. However, we don't always know the full context or the history undergirding the principles that fuel the culture. We know some of these things but not all of them. We may know one aspect of the culture more than another.

Moreover, we are quite defensive or protective of the lens of culture we know or adapted to. Sometimes this can be a block that complicates, for example, talking about how cultures change while simultaneously retaining their core, or discussing how something can differ without that difference causing feelings of alienation.

I've also found that some can confuse Black cultures with pop culture. Although pop culture is a lens to understanding some elements of Black cultures, the totality of African and Diasporic culture is not pop culture. Just because one element of Black culture is celebrated in pop culture does not make those which are not unimportant, irrelevant, or unimpactful. Black cultures exist outside of pop culture. Moreover, one can be very familiar with the language of social justice, be an advocate of human rights, be familiar with the struggles that Black people have faced in history, but not know Black or African cultures. Recognizing the difference is important as grounds for being open to understanding Afrofuturism.

African/African Diasporic cultures are bound by overlapping politics of resilience in the midst of histories that have undermined their humanity. Yet, they also exist in spite of the histories of dehumanization. Sometimes I hear people talk about Black cultures being shaped by enslavement, Jim Crow, or colonialism but not about how they survived or thrived in spite of these interruptions. We are also bound by complementary philosophical approaches to life, space, and time with African origins. But these approaches are not born in isolation nor are they identical. Some intersect with ideas that are not African alone.

All cultures have a relationship to space and time that speaks to how a culture sees itself within space and time, how it experiences space and time, and how this relationship shows up in cultural creations. These philosophies are evident in the art we create, the design of our neighborhoods, our fashion, our poetics, our education systems, our politics, our architecture, our music, how we commune as well as our communal values. Although most people don't think of themselves as philosophers, we are constantly engaging with systems and objects that reflect a belief in what one should value or how they should live.

Afrofuturism is a reminder that there are relationships to space and time that evolve from the lived experiences, cultures, histories, spiritual beliefs, and creations of African continental and diasporic people. Some of these ideas are quite ancient and reflect observations of the stars. I think of the ancient Egyptian goddess Nut, the essence of night who birthed the sun, who is depicted in the yoga position downward facing dog just as the black sky arches over the universe. She stands as a symbol of night and deep space, as a feminine protector who births life by creating the sun and its progeny. The night and deep space are maternal and to be harmonized with, not symbols of the unknown to fear or conquer.

Other perspectives are newer iterations that reflect a shift in the values of the times, such as doing cosplay at comic book conventions to value play and reinvention. Although these perspectives differ, they typically overlap and serve as complements in a fluid tapestry of ideas shaped by geography and need. They respond to and fulfill a human craving for ritual, connectivity, meaning, and community. Within these complementary cultural ideas on how one engages with space and time, there are core themes.

1. Time is nonlinear; the future, past, and present are one and multidirectional.
2. Mysticism and technology are intertwined.
3. Intuition is intelligence.
4. Race is a technology.
5. Cultural memory exists in body and mind.

Afrofuturism intersects imagination, liberation, technology, mysticism, and African, African Diasporic, and Black cultures. In another sense, it's much like a pinwheel, with all spirals leading to a center. Each form a dynamic center we call culture, which radiates both inward and out. African/African Diasporic cultures inform these trajectories as much as the trajectories inform culture. This makes Afrofuturism synergetic. Thought processes or artifacts that engage most or all of these ideas simultaneously can be framed as Afrofuturist. Because people of African descent live in an array of places, Afrofuturism functions both within and without Western paradigms, in and beyond African paradigms, Indigenous, Latine, and more, adapting and expressing based on need and location. This is key. Afrofuturism is inherently malleable, adaptable, and fluid.

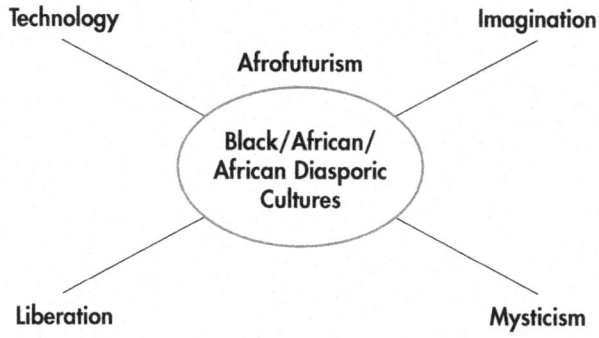

Afrofuturism as an artistic aesthetic is evident in music by Erykah Badu and Andre 3000 and films like *Black Panther* or TV shows like *Raising Dion* and *Watchmen*. However, Afrofuturism is also a practice and a method. For many who wrestle with the role of the imagination in their life or with their role in the future, Afrofuturism is a healing practice. I've met people with PTSD who were raised in the West Bank or survived Hurricane Katrina who shared that reading my book *Afrofuturism: The World of Black Sci-Fi and Fantasy Culture* helped them embrace a future. They spoke of feeling like they were on a hamster wheel. The book was a reminder that they had a future, that it was OK to dream about a future, and that it was OK to take steps toward living for one in line with their best self. It helped them off that wheel onto a new path toward that future.

We have agency. We make decisions based on what we believe is possible in our futures. We make decisions on who we aspire to be based on our own past, our culture, or the voices that shape our lives. We order our lives around our beliefs about time, its duration, and our role in what can be both finite and infinite. We traverse the space around us, choosing to take up space, shrink, or activate it based on our ideas about where and how we can be in our world. We thank ancestors, those with insights into humanity, because we believe there is a shared space both visible and invisible where we communicate.

For those who've been cut off from, are uncomfortable with, don't know, or devalue African/African Diasporic philosophies, Afrofuturism is a healing tool. Afrofuturism can serve as a practice to help people connect with their humanity by contemplating other ways of engaging with space and time, some of which may challenge conventions. Connecting with these ideas deepens our understanding of ourselves, our world, and our future. We make decisions, create, and plan futures based on these insights.

Sometimes, futures are presented as outgrowths of tension between those that benefit the few versus those that benefit the masses. Other times, futures are presented as outgrowths of tensions around whose worldview will determine the nature of the economy and public life. These options are often presented as binaries. Presenting futures as emerging out of a tension of binaries prevents us from seeing the trajectories of time and sometimes the participants in change.

We are a rainbow of streams, a quilted interstellar tapestry of histories, wisdom systems, projections, lived experiences, and dreams. Not falling into a binary should not be grounds for dehumanization nor a placeholder for a perennial state of being misunderstood. We are human, we are beyond human, we are interconnected. Afrofuturism is feminist, Afrofuturism is queer, Afrofuturism advocates for the healthy development of Black men, and for the safety of children. Afrofuturism advocates for humanity.

In this book we will explore Afrofuturism as cultural space/time relations, vision, dance, rhythm, and story as present pathways to reveal futures thinking and being. *The Afrofuturist Evolution* is a combination of studying and making; an evolution that is part contemplative, part creative. I have found that a personal creative practice, from journaling to beat making, is a big part of attaining a deeper understanding of ourselves, the world we inhabit, and the futures we hope to shape.

I'll include symbols, some ancient, some iconic, and some I've created that symbolize ideas and feelings. Weaving stories, myths, exercises, and guideposts, this book provides road maps for using Afrofuturist creative approaches to craft new works, new futures, new visions; to challenge conventions; and to rethink (remix) identity. This book is as much about your own insights as it is the information I'm sharing. Together, we're crafting a trail between inner space and outer space, a heartened focus that spurs new futures, new visions, and a deeper sense of being. This book aims to assess space/time wisdom from African/African Diasporic spaces, adding to the global toolbox for building a brilliant future and future now. Cheers to the refresh!

# I

# SPACE
# AND TIME

# 1

# THE O'CLOCK HOUR

## From Cultural Histories
## to Black Futures

WE STAND AT THE NEXUS OF HISTORIES AND FUTURES. We are both a product of our personal decisions or occurrences in our lives and the result of a host of geopolitical currents, family decisions, national events, global movements, and cultural beliefs that predate our birth. We are actively creating futures for ourselves, our families, our communities; for people who will be born decades, centuries, perhaps even a millennia later. We stand as a mobile junction of these times. We are creators or cocreators of these new futures whether we are conscious of it or not. We are in dialogue with times on all sides, whether we are cognizant of it or not, forwarding beliefs and agendas into a tomorrow that was born yesterday or anchoring new wisdom today for the next era. We make decisions birthed from visions of a probable tomorrow, a future sold to us in stories or advertising, a protopia we create as a North Star, an intuition harkening from a future.

Futures

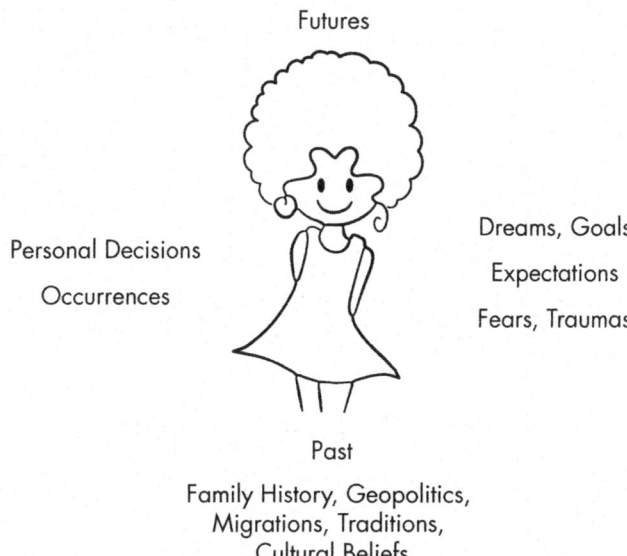

Personal Decisions

Occurrences

Dreams, Goals

Expectations

Fears, Traumas

Past

Family History, Geopolitics,
Migrations, Traditions,
Cultural Beliefs

Perhaps you spot patterns easily and the future feels like a familiar map with a few untread green areas or mountains. Perhaps the future feels like diving into the abyss, murky and unpredictable. History may tint your future dreams like an unescapable shadow. Some of us are immersed in the matters of today, not thinking too far ahead and leery of being weighed down by an unknown past, fearing guilt or traumas will lurk. In the absence of knowing much about either, many of us look to the imagination to make sense of worlds we don't know. Looking across time can be uncomfortable; however, a reconciliation with time and self can foster a deeper relationship to our own humanity.

I'm fascinated by thinking of myself and our world as a nexus of time, a synergetic crossroads that can be the gateway for our own unfolding. In this moment in time infinitum, we stand as a focal point of synergy of histories past and our relationship to these histories. The nature of our conscious relationships to these histories enables us to perceive a shifting kaleidoscope of future possibilities. This relationship helps us to hone a mission in life, a purpose that transcends the routine and laser focuses our actions. It spawns a litany of responsibilities that we have in community, if we in fact value humanity and life's many forms.

I feel comfort in thinking of inspired people in our so-called past whose work buoyed me into spaces they could only dream of. I feel dynamic when I think of myself as working in community with people who will explore shared subjects in future times. It makes me feel bigger, part of something more than what may appear before me. I am not alone. I feel in community with those exploring inspired ideas in other times and spaces. This nexus point can help us shake up or reinform our own narrative and how we think about ourselves in time and space.

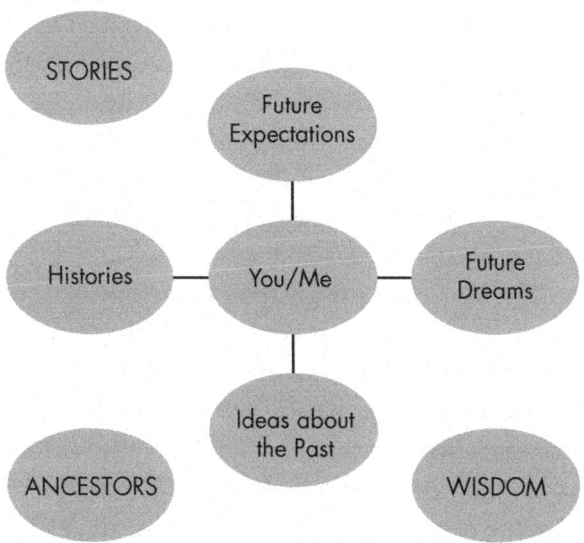

Self-narratives are an interesting lot. Many of us have a narrative about how we came to be that we tell ourselves and others. We have stories about why we chose a certain profession, why we have our political beliefs, our morning habits, our hobbies or lack thereof, why we maintain friendships with one set of people versus another, why we moved from one city to the next, why we left the old neighborhood, remained or returned, why we have children or don't have children, why we travel or why we don't. We talk about the options we had or didn't have, the ones we were aware of and the ones we weren't. We talk of the story of our birth. We talk of the things that family said or did when we were growing up and how it made us better people, or harbor anger, or feel empowered, or crafted our work ethic, or fostered insecurities. Then we have stories about who we are because of these decisions or happenings and the values, choices, and beliefs we make because of them. We talk of the responsibilities we have. "I grew up working poor and my family told me I was a princess. I wanted more and therefore [input outcome]." "I have advantages my childhood friends didn't have and therefore [input outcome]." "I wanted to be a lawyer but my mom said lawyers were unethical and therefore [input outcome]." "I grew up in the rural south and therefore [input outcome]." "I'm a first generation immigrant whose parents gave up a life for me and therefore [input outcome]." We speak of these outcomes, these narratives, as if they were a result of climbing up a hill or ascending from a valley. These outcomes, despite challenges, were inevitable, noting both a cause and an effect that form our story. This story has a theme that either makes us unique or empathetic or a victim or a hero or magical. This theme can form a bond with those who listen, establish a positionality in relationship to the listener. But ultimately, this story always justifies some means to an end. We seek to know ourselves. We select impactful moments of significance, some grand, some minute, collapsing times and space to make a point about who we are. This narrative justifies our existence. It gives our foibles, happy moments, mishaps, choices, and lack thereof meaning, a meaning that undergirds the aspects of ourselves that we use as our defining character traits, who we are and how we want to be perceived in a surface world that all too often juggles a handful of boxes for us to fit in.

Sometimes the narrative is a protective shield, warding off others' false projections onto us. Sometimes the narrative is a talisman, both proclamation of belief and mystical protector. Other times, it's a medal of honor from personal wars past. The narrative can be a rallying call, a badge of shame, a warning, a drum pattern to identify who we are. The narrative can be crafted with the best of intentions, but the cause and effect rationality may be plucked from a limited range of awareness, pulling from isolated moments in time, and therefore the resounding reason for the narrative as shield or talisman or stop sign may be off, much like a flashlight pointing near the right direction but not at the right subject, or rather a prism that provides framework by selectively ordering streams of light.

How far are we stretching the time line in this narrative? Are we including themes from our parents' lives and the lives of those who raised us? Where are these themes coming from? How are they assessed? Are we pulling from a cultural arc? When we include these elements or choose not to, when we pull one story versus another, we inform or alter our chosen fixed self-narrative.

It's easy to get stuck in our own narratives, the stories we tell ourselves about how we came to be, where we come from, and where we're heading. Some of us are married to these narratives. But narratives explaining the whys of who we are shift when we pull from a different set of isolated moments in time, a different data set from the same life, memories, and the geopolitical mappings that shaped it. Thinking of oneself as a focal point sprouting from a myriad of times remixes the present and shakes up our often-static perspectives—perspectives that can be the basis for our story or the story itself. We cling to static perspectives in our narrative because they provide a false sense of stability in a world that is ever changing, one where the attention economy can make us feel like we are hurling into socially mediated futures that require narrative shields. The flow of life requires a fluid lens with core values and flexible application. Therefore, the story is more of a prism with refracted light strains than the light itself. If our story, our self-narrative, is a prism, a focusing agent to assemble and disassemble streams of time and space, then we are forever being informed by time lines past and present with the changing of the prism's angle. We, you, I change the prism. We change how we assemble the elements in the story, how we choose to look at the tapestry, but the elements, the time lines and spaces of the past, are ever informing. We commit to the refreshed prism to get a deeper meaning of who we are, why we are, and our relationship with this grand universe because conceiving of all time lines and spaces simultaneously, is, well, difficult—or at least something we attribute to the great mystics. Thus the prism, the refreshed prism, and our new understandings of the self-narrative help us to perceive the bigger picture.

We're a nexus of threads of time; some we are more aware of than others, some feel more relevant. The time-stretching story we stand amidst is one that perpetually reveals itself; pouring through our inspirations, our dreams, our chance encounters, our research, our creations, and our insights. This axis, mind you, exists because of and in spite of our day-to-day decisions. Yet, the vantage point of thinking of myself and others as each a nexus of times keeps me on the path of inquiry, a trail of revelatory spurts. I live for the glee of connecting the dots, finding the missing threads in the tapestry, uncovering the lost puzzle piece, or reassembling the picture. I like the refreshed focal point of a new prism, new streams of light. I find joy in the path, one that balances the dips, turns, and mighty winds that blow. But it is a trippy ride, nonetheless. In this chapter, I would like us to think about the prism and the time lines and spaces we assemble. I'll begin with a prism of my own.

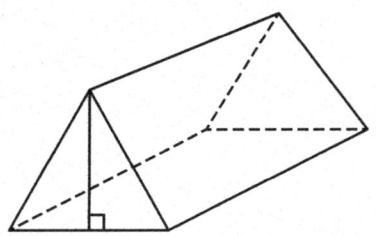

## The Story as Prism

A prism is a three-dimensional shape with two identical sides and a shared cross section. When light passes through it, the light refracts and the many colors of radiated frequency are revealed. This radiated light follows an order. This light, I will use as a metaphor for time, and the prism itself is a metaphor for story or framework as space.

## *The Story*

A few years back, I had what can best be described as the week of Afrofuturist epiphanies. These epiphanies were very present experiences of times and spaces, my own past, a lineage across time and locations, and the juxtaposition of futures all occurring over the course of two speaking engagements in the American South. The trip involved a train ride, a spooky mirror, a sage, and an Afrofuturist origin story. It was the day before my speech at Clark Atlanta University (CAU), my alma mater, the same campus where W. E. B DuBois likely wrote *The Princess Steel*, a short work of speculative fiction centralized around an all-seeing megascope that jettisoned though time. Dubois's imagined instrument would become an apt metaphor for my week in the making.

My talk was a big moment and I had packed a swank leather jacket. For added effect, I also had knee-high lace-up boots with motorcycle vibes. I was returning to the place of my Afrofuturist genesis, and I had to embody the swankness that such a return demands. Up to that day, whenever someone asked me how I got into Afrofuturism, I'd tell a story—my Afrofuturist origin story. I'd recall chatting with a fellow honor student my freshman year whose verbal gymnastics between quantum physics, ancient African technologies, social change, funk, and hip-hop led me to ask a prescient question: "What is this?"

Neither of us knew the term *Afrofuturism* to anchor his theories and we dovetailed into a framing of metaphysics as a foundation,

because we'd read some of the same texts of New Thought philosophy. By the time I wrote my book *Afrofuturism* in the 20aughts
I noted that this encounter was a moment. I was struck that in
asking "What is this?" I would come to answer my own question
by penning a book on the answer and the very moment itself.
It's a neatly packaged story. It's a true story. But as I would soon
discover, truth can run in many directions.

As I was in my Atlanta hotel room going over my speech in the
mirror the night before my return, prepping to present on Afrofuturism in the spot where it all began, a lightning bolt struck. What if the
"What is this?" question wasn't a genesis at all. What if my future
speech at CAU was the genesis point and my question as freshman
year me was the answer? What if my desire to ask the question was
prompted not from the student's verbal breakdown but from me
giving the speech years later on that very topic? What if the question
was a future whispering of the work to come in Afrofuturism? What
if tomorrow was the beginning? Was freshman year me feeling the
future? Was today me informing a past?

Did this thread in time explain why this freshman year memory
was more vivid than say, homecoming? Was I, in my contemplation, standing at the intersection of dialogue between a so-called
future and a past?

Having an epiphany while staring at your reflection in a vintage southern hotel mirror with an antique frame doesn't inspire
*Candyman* fright, but it's not a fairy-tale moment either. I felt elec-
tricity course down my spine. This cross-pollination in time, which
I spoke of theoretically and wrote about in story, was presenting itself as a fourth-dimensional possibility. During my speech,
I recounted this mirror moment, wholly aware that I was likely
sending thought waves to freshman me. Let's just say the inquiry,
this wonderment of beginnings, inverted the prism. It changed the
framing or the space of the story. When a prism is inverted, the
light that passes through refracts in a different order. Same light.
Same prism. Same times, same space.

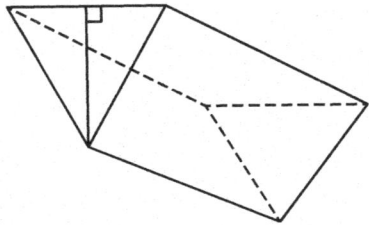

I was speaking to a me of the past, but I was also speaking to an audience of students and professors in the present. I was in the same space, the CAU campus, but there was a dialogue between at least two times, me speaking to a past me and vice versa. I could only guess at the other time dimensional occurrences happening simultaneously, because there were more. Fortunately, this future speak insight didn't go over my CAU audience's heads. Some of these students would integrate these insights into their own and press forward to create informed futures. Clearly, I would come to write about this occurrence in a future as well. This space/time awareness was noted.

There was a synergy in this moment. But it wasn't a closing of the loop of thought paradigms, but rather a spiral, a crazy-eight infinity symbol embodied by the Akan Sankofa symbol, which embodies looking back to move forward. The Akan symbol, often depicted as a bird looking at an egg on its tail, resembles the loops also evident in the English math symbol for infinity. The bird looking back, the egg of future's promise and new beginnings upon the tail, the feet facing forward are a reminder that you can always go back, and that the new beginning is born from the lessons of the past. These joined loops connect the continuity of futures speaking to the past and the past speaking to a future. It is one of over one hundred adinkra symbols, all representing concepts from the philosophy of the ancient Akan people, a philosophy held so dear that it is evident throughout Ghana today, where the Akan are most populous. Adinkra was a fabric stamped with the power symbols created by the Bono people, who are part of the Akan, and was originally worn by royalty and spiritual leaders at special occasions. Although the oldest existing adinkra cloth was found in the early 1800s, it's believed that the symbols and concepts go back to an earlier time. Sankofa is one of the most popular adinkra symbols, along with the commonly found Gye Nyame symbol for God. The Sankofa symbol is in fabric, textiles, art both ancient and contemporary, business logos, architecture. It's impossible not to be immersed in the symbol if you're in Ghana. Sankofa, both the word and the symbol, are iconically used in Pan African ethos and can be found in the names of organizations or themes in Black neighborhoods throughout the Americas and the United Kingdom. Sankofa is the creative and philosophical source for many Black cultures, especially in the United States. Morena Mariah, founder of Instituto Afrofuturo, a Brazilian organization that works with Afrofuturist ideas in Brazil, champions the symbol's reminder of reconnection. "It's never too late to recover what's left behind," said Mariah.[1] When it comes to discussing Afrofuturism, Sankofa is the crux of the art form's space/time collapse.

So, my moment of time loops felt like Sankofa as a synergy of time. That's the way I processed it. On one level, this awareness was personal, but on another level, it wasn't personal at all. This multipronged dialogue in time was in the context of the campus as space and informed with communication nestled in community.

Sankofa

Infinity

Another version of the Sankofa symbol is a joining of the curvature of two birds that appears to form a heart. This S-shaped curvature also replicates the curve of an elephant's trunk, a popular power symbol in Ghana. In fact, this version of Sankofa is ubiquitous in Ghana, almost more so than the bird and egg. Enslaved Africans brought to the Americas who were originally blacksmiths by trade put the symbol in metalwork, gates, door fixtures, and stair railings throughout the United States and Caribbean, a fact that colleague and film curator Floyd Webb pointed out to me. The symbol is literally hiding in plain sight, becoming a fixture in metalwork design. It wasn't until I returned from my first trip to Ghana that I realized the symbol was in the metalwork of my entire Chicago neighborhood. In fact, I grew up with it in the fixture of a swinging gate in my house. As I talked to friends in L.A. and New York, they spotted it in their homes, too. The symbol's pervasiveness was a testament to the enslaved who asserted the value system of the epic return to move forward, but also a reminder of how deeply embedded the symbolism is in culture. I like to think of it as two sides of time, future and past, thus forming a present synergy.

Double Sankofa

John Jennings, professor and artist, was among the presenters that fateful day in Atlanta, along with professor and archivist Clint Fluker. A few of my college professors also attended (to my delight).

After the presentation, the panelists were chatting offstage when Dr. Isabella Jenkins, the legendary head of the honors program, appeared and broke up our small circle. "Vodou," she shouted. Everyone stopped speaking. "Vodou," she repeated. I didn't know how to respond and neither did anyone else. We waited, respectfully, for what she would say next. "How can you talk about Afrofuturism and space/time, and not talk about vodou?" she asked. A New Orleans–born scholar, she was challenging us on how we were framing Afrofuturism in space/time. I was familiar with some elements of vodou, but I hadn't grown up with it enough to give hearty specifics and told her so.

"You need to understand vodou, especially New Orleans vodou," she said. Jennings, who had a better grounding in the practice than I did, agreed. We all vowed to better integrate African influences and spiritual practices to inform ideas of a possible future. Let it be noted that only at a Black college will someone check you for not framing your space/time explorations in one of the most maligned practices to have emerged from African worlds. But she was right—African/African American cosmologies, vodou specifically, and their space/time insights on interdimensionality and communion with ancestors, are essential anchors. As an educator who was always looking for the teaching moment, Dr. Jenkins was underscoring that African/African Diasporic spiritual practices were a theory and practice of a relationship to space/time.

Voodoo, vodou, or vodun has a complex pantheon and belief system that invokes ways of thinking and navigating beyond the here and now. Early practitioners had an awareness of quantum dynamics and a relationship to it long before the quantum nature of things became established as a focus in Western science. Haitian writer Reginald Crosley, a physician of internal medicine and surrealist poet with a theology background, grew up practicing African traditional religions and vodou. His book *The Vodou Quantum Leap: Alternate Realities, Power, and Mysticism* bridges the philosophy and metaphysics of vodou with quantum theory.

"In the Dahomeyan and Haitian reality, we exist simultaneously in different dimensions or parallel universes and we have consciousness also in both realities or dimensions," writes Crosley.[2] Crosley outlines the similarities between voodoo philosophy and multiverse theories espoused by astronomers seeking proof of universes beyond our own. The practice began with the Fon people of modern-day Benin and was also retained and adapted by enslaved Africans brought to the Americas, taking hold most notably in the French colonies of Haiti and the American city of New Orleans. The veves, ornate designs drawn on the ground at vodou ceremonies or religious spaces, are sometimes described as ritual geometry; a "synthesis of space, the astral, and their powers through Legba."[3] Legba, also called Papa Legba, a deity in the faith who opens doors for experiences to occur, has a magnitude that Haitian historian Milo Rigaud described in the early 1900s as the solar system itself.

Papa Legba Veve

The veve designs reflect three astral planes: source, light, and the visible world. It can be argued that the rhythm in the illustration is an articulation of time. While the veve speaks to literal space, the drumming that accompanies the ceremonies is a commentary on nonlinear time. "In Vodun, the drum beats connect you to an unbroken chain in time," says Fabrice Guerrier, a

Haitian American creative and Afrofuturist. "All people who heard those beats, you are connected to them." When the rhythms aren't designed for healing or transcendence, they can spark a sense of interdimensionality. Luther Gray runs the Congo Square Preservation Society in New Orleans, maintaining the sacred grounds where enslaved Africans were permitted to play music on Sundays and continuing the tradition today. "Drumming activates the mind, body, and soul," he says. "Drumming is a language."

However, vodun and voodoo's association with the Haitian Revolution, when the enslaved Africans kicked out their captors, and its proliferation of liberated women icons, including New Orleans's Marie Laveau in Victorian era, made the practice both exoticized and feared by the mostly Christianized Western mainstream for centuries. The denigration led to the common offensive practice of using vodou as a horror trope in media of all kinds. The core principles of the practice were either ignored or misunderstood by nonpractitioners who didn't get what drumming, symbols, or animal sacrifice had to do with science and a philosophy on one's relationship to space and time. Years later, I would see my man-in-the-mirror moment was aligned with the practice's take on the many-worlds quantum theory. Dr. Jenkins's statement stuck with me. I would think about her charge as I headed off to Mississippi.

## Cultural Memory Lane

A day later in this saga of space/time revelations, I hopped an early morning train bound for Jackson, Mississippi, where I met a very interesting man who ran a New Orleans ghost tour trip and had the theme from the *Halloween* horror flicks as his ringtone. I was headed to Jackson State College for the first Planet Deep South conference. Organized by professors John Jennings, Rico Chapman, and Reynaldo Anderson, the event gathered scholars to think on the Deep South and Afrofuturism. This time I was on my way to

Jennings's alma mater, his birthplace, and a state significant in my own family history. The trip felt weighted. As I rode on the train through wooded areas, stopping at small towns dotted along back roads off the railway, the fog of Southern history hovered as an ever-present reminder of a past that wouldn't be forgotten. Those backwoods trees had stories, as did the shadows that descended from them. If I hadn't had my man-in-the-mirror moment, which was rather empowering, I could've felt overwhelmed by the creeping history of Southern pasts not so long gone.

Some people are empaths. They can feel what others feel, they can absorb the feelings of the collective, taking on feelings that aren't their own, later parsing out what is theirs and what isn't. A writer friend of mine believes that all writers are empaths, enabling us to tell stories of lives we haven't lived. I believe that many humans have this ability in varying degrees, heightened at high-frequency moments, moments when our thoughts and feeling are vibrating in resonance with those who stood in the midst long ago. Although I wouldn't describe myself as an empath in the same way as friends I know, I do think I have a heightened awareness of spaces. So, if there's a term for being a spaces empath, or a location-based empath, that might be me. I do feel histories or maybe futures in spaces with heightened resonance. Although I can't say I feel what those abiding in such spaces felt in times past, some spaces are charged with an energy. Something happened—unresolved emotions, a chaos, a resolve of tensions—a resonance washed away, whose tentacles still have resonance.

There's research on inherited traumas invoked by sights or smells or fears, people who feel the residual pain of ancestors several generations removed. There is also a rich folk history of such traumas taking shape in physical form. Toni Morrison's work *Beloved* comes to mind. The epic novel follows a mother who escaped enslavement in the antebellum South but is haunted by the child she killed when she was at risk of being captured. The protagonist killed her infant so that she would not be enslaved.

The child became an adult ghost, consuming the mother's home. Neighbors, mostly women, had to invoke prayers to get rid of this shadow of the past. An unresolved past emotion, especially a trauma, the ones we experience or inherit, occupy a space as well. From this point forward, I will refer to traumas as unresolved emotions, for the lingering effects are nuanced and not always the origin cause or initial emotion itself. Unresolved emotion can be walled spaces neither limited to location but not entirely in mind either. Such spaces are an assemblage of memories by an individual or collective that stand in perpetual motion, separate and apart from the event or incident that triggered them. In my week of trippiness, I won't say I experienced a familial or communal circling of unresolved emotion, but I did feel as if I were navigating through a minefield of them, with a bubble of resolve or a barrier of time, or ancestral well wishes, encasing me from it.

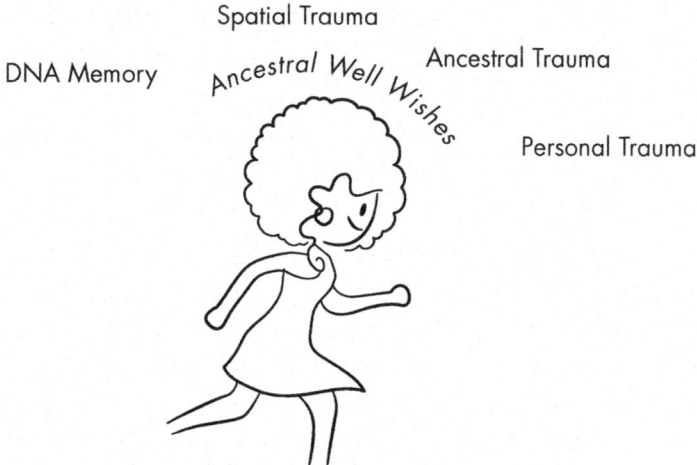

Spatial Trauma

DNA Memory          Ancestral Well Wishes          Ancestral Trauma

Personal Trauma

Jennings, who grew up in Mississippi, writes scary stories that he describes as "ethnogothic." His book *Box of Bones*, created with Ayize Jama-Everett, an Afrosurrealist and Afrofuturist writer, conjures stories from an invisible box of racialized hauntings, many of which were outgrowths of happenings in the southern back roads I was traversing. The book's characters include "the Nobody," a living wound whose knowingness is based in not remembering; "the Wretched," a sentient lynching tree; and "the Dark," the essence of Black servitude churned from the bowels of a slave ship. As I rode those slow trains through the backwoods of Alabama and Mississippi that rainy morning, I was reminded of where those characters come from. I couldn't help but think of my mother's recollections of one of her Mississippi-born aunts and her scare-the-bejeezus-out-of-you haunted bedtime stories. *Ghosts of Mississippi* was the title of a film chronicling parts of the civil rights movement, and although I didn't see ghosts on my sojourn and certainly didn't want to, the layered humidity was a blanket of otherworldliness.

There's no direct train to Jackson from Atlanta, or plane for that matter, so I rode to Meridian, Mississippi, where I could connect with a Greyhound bus. Meridian is a stone's throw from Newton County. Newton County is another beginning. I can trace my family in Newton County back to at least a generation or two before the end of the Civil War. It was the birthplace of my maternal grandparents. My grandmother's sister and her husband were currently living on a ranch there. Retirees who'd left Mississippi as young adults, they returned after running a successful business to abide in the town of their birth. The town where they abide within the county is what some people would describe as "the country." I'm not sure what counts as rural America anymore, but this town centered around farm life and was nestled in the woodiest of woods.

I got off the train, which was headed for New Orleans, and had lunch with my great-aunt and great-uncle. They were living out a childhood dream, returning to their home post–civil rights with land of their own. But my uncle lamented what he felt were policies slipping us into a state of resegregation. I'd visited the area several times before, usually for family reunions. Whenever I returned, I always felt like I should stay longer, not quite sure what an extended stay would reveal. Would I glean wisdom by connecting with the land or would I descend to find the Nothing from Jennings's stories, a mammoth being of past hauntings undetected by residents but who awaited curious visitors? I got the feeling that a mix of both was likely. It could all be dismissed as one's mind playing tricks except, well, the stories Jennings wrote weren't his alone. There's a collective memory many of us deal with around racialized, gendered unresolved emotions that goes unsaid—moments that, unfortunately, have touchpoints today. Location, being in the space of such memories, shoves these tales to light in a way that conscious remembrance or an old song does not. "That area is rural, deep, and dark," Chapman, a Jackson native with family in the area, would tell me later. He claims the feeling hits most at nightfall amid the trees. "Trust your fears," he joked, but it was also a warning. However, the short stay was a nugget of beauty. A reminder of love and family forged in ancient soils. My aunt and uncle's return was a victory, a reclaiming of a narrative. History aside, home was home, and they held their stake in the earth with pride. We had a fun time for our lunch. I boarded the bus for a short ride to the urban enclave of Jackson.

## Exodus Futures

I'm living in an ancestral future. You're living in an ancestral future, too. I'm a descendent of the Great Migration, among others. Never before had I been so conscious of being the descendent of an exodus as I was during this trip through Mississippi. While I was aware of White business owners and their frustrations with Black residents who moved north before and after World War II, I'd never thought about the impact of a massive emigration on Black residents who remained. This exodus wasn't so long ago, and the area was still recovering from the population loss and the racial violence that caused it. The sparsely populated towns I passed were once dense with poorly paid laborers, descendants of the enslaved and the disenfranchised Indigenous who worked the endless fields that bound one farm to the next. Although this passage is focused on my trip cutting through the Delta, any trip across America will reveal that most of the nation is wrestling with population loss and how to position themselves for competitive futures.

However, I was struck with the reality that I was walking in my ancestor's distant future and looking at the impact of their absence. Part of Mississippi's future took root elsewhere—moments from the creation of *Ebony Magazine* to the creation of *Soft Sheen* in Chicago could've all happened in Mississippi if "things had been different."

The Smith Robertson Museum and Cultural Center, once Jackson's first public school for Black students, is dedicated to the history of Black Mississippi. Conference attendees spent half a day viewing the collection of artifacts ranging from shackles from slave ships to work tools used on plantations. To my surprise, an entire section of the museum was dedicated to those who left and headed to my hometown. The museum's exhibit on the Great Migration, *A Quest for New Futures Among 20th Century Black Americans*, was treated with tongue-in-cheek humor to hide a frustration and deep sense of loss. The tour guide spoke of Chicagoans returning home to Jackson in the twentieth century's later half, adding that new northerners were "draped in fur coats all while living in tiny apartments" as a punchline. But she was also teary when she recounted how in the early 1970s her all-Black high school was fragmented by integration mandates and bussing, and students were placed in hostile all-White schools.

For the first time, I thought about the horror of residents watching family and friends leave, the disruption of coerced migrations on community, and the trajectories these disruptions created. They sometimes lead to sharp differences in job opportunities, mobility, or culture gaps. The migrant story was a variation of the immigrant story, which feels absurd because these "migrants" were moving within their own homeland.

Rapper David Banner, a fellow presenter at the conference, spoke of Black northerners who'd "forgotten where they came from." His criticism reminded me of stories I heard from immigrants recalling friends or family who looked down on their decision to make a home elsewhere. He admonished us for not giving back to our hometowns, looking down on southern ways, and championed the virtue of those "who stayed" to fight the good fight. Although I didn't completely agree with the sentiment—those who left in those days were leaving for a reason, often a life-saving one—there was value in this less-discussed narrative of resilience in staying in spaces with hostile histories. Although I had a relationship with my southern roots and had spent time in the Deep South, I was glad that Banner and the conference organizers were encouraging us to think on Black people and futures from the vantage point of residents in smaller and rural southern towns. Much of Afrofuturism's creative wellspring in its American iteration is urban centric, northern leaning, often viewing urbanicity as the future. Rural towns and smaller cities, sometimes the South in general (Atlanta's ATliens, Houston, and New Orleans aside), sometimes aren't integrated as they should be into lofty visions of Black futures. The same can be said of rural places around the world. In some cases, they aren't adequately framed in the present for their innovation or discussed as spaces with the potential for radical change or examples of new futures in the making.

That said, Mississippi is now. It is not a harbinger of another time. Jackson State University is an oasis. A beautiful campus and widely celebrated HBCU, it's a river of resilience in Jackson's evolving sociopolitical landscape. The Planet Deep South conference took place in the school's COFO Civil Rights Education Center, the same space where Fannie Lou Hamer organized the Mississippi Freedom Democrat Party and groups from SNCC to the NAACP launched voter registration drives in the 1960s. The conference aimed to bring Afrofuturist scholars together to present work and think on Black futures in the American South. Horror and mysticism scholar

Kinitra Brooks, who would later create a reading list for Beyoncé's southern mystical video *Lemonade*, discussed traumas as horror; Regina Bradley spoke on southern hip-hop rhetoric; Kiese Laymon highlighted Black male southern identity; Reynaldo Anderson spoke of the Black Speculative Arts Manifesto; and Erik Steinskog deconstructed the Birmingham circa Saturn–born jazz legend Sun Ra. This ancestral future, though broad in the cultural context, became very specific when I thought upon actual ancestors, thinking on grandparents' grandparents, and noting that I was standing very near where they once lived, sacrificed, and loved for at least a century. In my opening address on Afrofuturism I drew on the story of my own family in Mississippi. Again, I was swirling through the juxtaposition of eras, but this time it was via a family history. My great-grandfather once owned a sizable farm in the town I'd visited just hours before. He and his family lived off the land, selling produce and cattle and training horses. From all accounts they were a beacon in a community where the shadows of the antebellum South loomed large and Jim Crow laws were lethal. My great-grandfather's success and status sparked jealousy from neighboring Whites in the town. A peril unfolded that isn't always discussed. Much of the land was sold off. I remember going to a reunion and seeing "the land" behind a gate. Now I wonder if the Sankofa symbol was on that fixture, too.

For much of my childhood, there was a desire among family, his children included, to learn more about this mystery man and his complex ancestry. His passing away, which wasn't discussed in detail as far as I could tell, did not evolve into a generational stream of unresolved emotions, despite the questions we can't find answer to. Although I, like many descendants of enslaved Africans, have an aversion to farming, it has less to do with my great-grandfather and more to do with the centuries of unpaid labor before him. If anything, the potential for generational unresolved emotions around his passing was erased by a celebration of his life and the love of family. I benefited, two generations later, from a healing as later generations sought to get a greater grounding on how my great-grandfather came to be. That healing came through a biannual family reunion established in his name, stories passed on, genealogical research uncovered, DNA tests, scouring through old documents, and gatherings. No one ever said "and we are seeking a healing"; however, our commitment to family gatherings, storytelling, and the quest was a form of unspoken resilience.

Delivering my speech in the COFO Center was a return and a real-time recognition of standing in my ancestral future. To speak of this family history in the very place where Fannie Lou Hamer worked, a short drive away from where Medgar Evers, who I later discovered was a family friend, lived was conjoined with a cultural history that was broader than my own family's trajectory. I was standing in a place where ambitious people worked and died to create space for me to even talk about Afrofuturism freely. Their work was Afrofuturism in action, and I was a beneficiary.

As for my family, biannual reunions and family tree analysis mitigated the need for locality and addressed the yearnings of a large family that spread across the country to always know one another. Home was the love and legacy we shared across time and space, not great-granddad's land. Yet, I was aware of my relationship to Mississippi as a heartened "space" where a feeling of exodus ran deep. The "we were here" was prescient despite the fact that I had family currently living there. This relationship to space was a complex history of enslavement, pride, secrets, mystery, and family anecdotes with enough gaps to fill the Delta. I was proud of that Black Mississippi culture, the resilience, the food, and the relationship to family and how it shaped me. As a child, I thought most families were from Mississippi, that's how entrenched my Chicago world was in the state's Black descendants.

## Consciousness Junction

There's another level of depth to interrogating Black futures and speculative fiction in Mississippi, a wellspring that runs to the core because of my relationship to the space and its tumultuous history. Despite its long and notorious history, Jackson isn't a city mired in a past, although the layers of time are evident. The space of resilience that's seeded in the land and the community is a real-time healing and transmutation of space. Jackson is making serious moves. I loved the mix of traditions, radical politics, bohemian vibes, old tensions, complex histories, and a devotion to education. I enjoyed thinking of Mississippi's Black culture and how it stands apart from other cultures in the American South. The fact that some conference panels were held at Offbeat, a well-stocked comic bookstore, was a particular highlight.

But this mix of history, and my wading through the waters of time, wasn't over. As I took the train home to Chicago, I literally felt that I was retreading the path of my ancestors on the Great Migration, driving beyond Chicago into deep space. Trippy doesn't begin to describe the moment.

So here I was racing from Atlanta to Jackson, giving two Afrofuturist speeches in two places, one personal, one familial, where futures began. Two places that spoke to a past and present. Two places where I was a walking intersection of futures and histories. But this intersection was no accident and my thoughts on memory, space, and time were refined. Something was healed in that journey. There was a release that had very little to do with me and everything to do with me being in an ancestral future.

In Mississippi, I was part of a somewhat conscious dialogue between ancestor and progeny, whereas in Atlanta there was a two-way conversation between a past and future me. Here, I realized that our relationship to Afrofuturism can shift and be shaped by location, an experience that would be reinforced as I traveled. Space, literal space, can be embodied. In other words, the unresolved emotions or aspirations that take shape in a given space over time due to the actions of people in the space can be experienced in the body by people who are moving through the same space, whether they were present for the occurrences that defined the location's nature or not. Space can be a multipronged communication device, bringing time, bridging selves.

## A Lens Shift

I'm writing this, ironically, the same weekend that my brother held the first family meeting for our first ever family trip to the African continent. We were in discussion about where we wanted to go, identifying countries to put on the family ballot. A few hours ago, my aunt on my paternal side called and asked if I would help her assemble a family history packet for the branch of my family with Texas and Indigenous roots. The ancestors are speaking across time. What does this arch of communication mean? How does it speak to a future? What wisdom do they hold?

There are reconciliations to be made with our pasts, both personal and ancestral. There are opportunities for healing, and lessons or warnings to heed in building new futures. Having a healthy relationship with these streams of time helps us to recognize that we are not ordinary, but rather extraordinary people who have a responsibility to aid humanity. Some of our relationships to time and space are an amalgamation of where our lineage or the lineage of people who've shaped us sprung from. The spaces they occupied inform us.

Looking at the past can be murky, uncomfortable, frustrating, and angering—but it can also be inspiring, revealing, and enlightening. All things ancient and traditional don't have to be the building blocks for the next world, but we do ourselves a disservice when we choose not to acknowledge or give space to what these streams of time mean for us, or when we don't make space for insight. These pasts are speaking to us. The wisdom and warnings of the pasts are speaking to us. Whether we're open to the insight or not, it likely hangs within your home, at your doorway, like a Sankofa symbol elegantly affixed on a metal gate.

Acknowledging a past doesn't mean this past defines you, but it can inform us and provide context for the world we find ourselves in. But one's perspective is not fixed. Your respective lens is not destined to be a pupil-sized hole as if you're eying a big world through a bombilla stick. The lens does expand, as does one's positioning, if we acknowledge and allow it to do so. This lens on life requires that we rotate, shifting the lens, flipping the prism of our story to get a full view.

## Long Time

The beauty of DNA tests is that they reveal an older story of migrations, of people crossing national borders and oceans by choice or by force, due to war, enslavement, or opportunity. Such tests stretch the time line and place our lives in one that extends beyond family memory, neatly entrenching us in complex histories of tensions and encounters between ethnicities. The challenge in DNA testing is that it reveals a story of bloodlines and origins, but it can't map the cultural shifts, unearth missing names, or map the reason behind decisions. The tests resolve some questions and raise others. Only a historical deep dive can make any of it make sense. Yet, there will be stories of lives we must turn to scattered facts and our imagination to resolve. We are mapping backward through spaces and places whose dynamics have radically shifted from the times our ancestors lived. This variation of memory in blood cells is another space/time revelation; one that reveals a story that may interconnect with ancestral memory.

In my own case, I am a Chicago-born woman; I grew up very urban but I have a healthy relationship to my southern and African roots. I am African American. I am Black, but my perspective on that experience stretches beyond the side of town I live on and the nation in which I reside. I met an African American man once during a busy lunch hour who, when I told him about a trip to Africa, remarked that his tribe was Chicago. I understand wanting to anchor in the here and now for orientation purposes. Sailing through unknown ancestral pasts is a rocky ride in disorientation. Yet, there's a peace to be found in the scant data, histories, and guesswork we quilt. I am cognizant of a DNA-revealed history that fused ancestors who likely came from as far away as Madagascar by way of the Austronesian migration from Taiwan on a fifteen-month journey around the Cape of Africa to America's shores, along with those from the western side of the African continent by way of Gabon to what is now America. I've seen interesting data linking ancient relatives who likely trekked through parts of the Sahara to Mali as Amazigh. My lineage of experience in America is as American as it is a result of global geopolitics across Europe, seventeenth-century colonies, morphing African empires, and Native American resistance. Nearly every European colonial power that existed is evidenced in the data. There are places that pop up that reveal unexplained migrations in the Americas. Does Amazigh ancestry explain my attraction to Tuareg jewelry, unique pieces by a group within the Amazigh lineage? Does a possible family life in Madagascar explain my fascination with African islands? I wonder if our interests are whispers from other times making themselves known and surfacing as pastimes, hobbies, fields of study.

Many say that DNA tests are all hogwash with a 50 percent chance of identifying any tangible African ethnic group. Point noted, but it is a direction, an arrow toward something, which is more than what I began with. These revelations for some can be confusing. Extending the time line always boggles the mind. But these histories create awareness of streams of time and interlocking, far-flung spaces.

I'm influenced by many regions of the Black diaspora and beyond. I seek out these influences, and when found they feel organically a part of me. In some cases they are missing pieces of a puzzle. My Blackness was taught to me as a global experience enriched with regional reasoning. All of the ideas and institutions that shape me are not purely outgrowths of the Black canon of thought. However, they don't exist apart from it either. Perhaps part of my interest in the synergy of futures is in part a mapping of the intersections that led to my own existence. I think of this interest as an act of reclamation, recovering what was lost or unveiling that which is always with me.

We must acknowledge the things that shape us, those thought lineages that inform our thinking and the ways of life we were born into. However, we are not limited to these thought bubbles. I think of Malcolm X, who sought to write a book about the schools of thought that shaped his evolving beliefs, not the autobiography released after his death. A man open to transformation, he was aware of the beliefs from Garveyism to Pan-Africanism that formed his identity, but he was also open to evolving beyond those beliefs or discarding those which no longer applied in the liberatory futures he aimed to create. To acknowledge these ideologies and institutions allows us to dissect the experience while recognizing the vantage point of others without assigning judgment or inflecting class-based hierarchies. If I'm in denial of my urbanness, I can't recognize the uniqueness of a rural view of the world. If I'm in denial of my American-ness, I can't see the worldview it provides or the perspectives that shape Black identities and futures in Senegal or Brazil. If I ignore history, I don't realize I'm a product of its many streams, some of which I can be unknowingly carrying forward.

The Sankofa symbol is a reminder that to go forward we must go back. It's OK to go back, to retrieve and assess the lessons of the past, then build futures upon those insights. The point in assessing the past isn't to stay mired in the entanglement, one that can spawn guilt, fear, or anguish. Nor is it to swim in nostalgia, romanticizing a time that never quite was, held as a mantle that can't ever be reached. We go back to find the gold nuggets of insight, to connect with those streams of thoughts and actions that valued humanity. The go back doesn't have to be a physical trip. The go back is awareness. All pasts aren't purely streams of conflict. There's a reservoir of joy, care, and humanity. We are aware so that we can heal and use that refresh to live forward. We become aware of the lesson. We are aware to find a space of gratitude. We are aware to be consciously present in our lives and in the crafting of our futures. We are not AI, repeating patterns that take us to uncanny valleys. We are conscious, breathing beings. We are conscious breathing beings in community with one another.

## The Mega Lens

In W. E. B DuBois's fantasy story *The Princess Steel*, the all-seeing megascope shows viewers distant worlds, past, present, and future—a narrative with a lesson for the perceptive. The tale is a recently discovered work that showcases DuBois's use of the fantastic as societal critique. In the story, a couple peers through a "megascope," a time-defying telescope that could see in all times and spaces. The fictional megascope was created by a Black sociologist similar in temperament to DuBois himself. Through the lens, a winding tale of the Princess Steel unfolds.

The princess hails from the Pitt of Pittsburgh. A daughter of the Dark Queen of the Iron Isles, she was snatched from her home in Africa and her lover was killed by the Lord of the Golden Way. The woman encases her lover's body in "burning breathing silver," mummifying him in her own silver hair. The Doomsday Lord realizes the value of her hair and forces her to create mills across the world, forever enslaving her to an industry bound to her body. The fable is about the perils of capitalism, industrialization, technology, with a bit of Rumpelstiltskin thrown in. *The Princess Steel* evolves into a commentary on the dehumanization of people working through unresolved emotion whose healing tools, such as the princess's silver hair, are capitulated for profit. However, the husband in the story, the sociologist who sees the narrative through the megascope, doesn't know what to make of it. The wife isn't able to perceive the princess at all and only sees "clouds and the rising moon."

The tourists, the husband and wife who viewed the story through DuBois's lens, missed the point. How often do we gloss over the point, ignoring insights into futures and histories? In my travels through history's futures across southern cities, a trek through time was revealed. Unlike DuBois's confused visitors who were befuddled by the images through the all-seeing telescope, the pixels of time on my sojourn formed a clearer vision. The dots of stories past were aligning. The dots for stories past and future are aligning for us all.

## Reflection Questions

Let's take a few deep breaths, inhaling the beauty of the moment and exhaling stress and tensions. Become aware of your space, your mind, your body. You are present. In your presence you are also an intersection of histories and futures. Your own decision-making aside, you are the product of a history and your present connects to a future. You are bigger than the present moment, connected to people across times, and yet you are of these unique times. In this sense, you are synergetic, a nexus informed by a future, and also informed by a past, yours and others. Let's take a moment to answer the following questions. You can write them in a dedicated journal or note the answers in your phone. I prefer writing longhand, because it forces you to slow down. However, recording yourself as thoughts come to you and listening to the answer can be worthwhile as well. Repeat the question and then answer it.

1. How does it feel to think of yourself as being at the intersection of times, futures, and histories? Are there historical moments you feel you are a product of? What are they?

2.  How do you feel about history? Do you like feeling connected to the past? How do you feel about futures?

3.  Can you think of a moment in your past that felt like a whispering to the future? What was this moment? How did it speak to the future? How does it speak to who you are today?

4.  Can you recall a family narrative that's often retold? What is this story? Does this story connect to a broader moment in history? If so, what is that moment? How do you relate to this narrative? How has this story shaped you? What is the significance of this story to your family? Will you pass this story on? Why or why not?

5.  Have you visited a city, country, or neighborhood connected to your family lineage? Did you feel a connection to this space? Why or why not? How does this space or your family's history to this space inform how you see yourself? How does it inform your future?

## Exercise: Letters to Your Future Self

You can do this exercise alone or in a group. I always think it's ideal to do with a cup of tea. But a glass of water is more than sufficient. Take a deep breath and dig in.

1.  Imagine that you are peering at or experiencing the worlds in DuBois's megascope, a device that can project and capture all times and places. What do you see, feel, or experience? What world appears before you? Describe the experience and write or sketch it out.

2.  Write a letter to your future self, a letter of well wishes and desires. Your future self can be five years out, ten years out, or as many years as you'd like. You can even write one from a future lifetime if you like. Be sure to include advice or things you'd like your future self to remember.

**Take a brief break or return
to the next questions the following day.**

3. Now imagine that you are that future self. Imagine what that world looks like, what your life looks like. Pay most attention to how your future life feels. Now read the letter you've written as your future self. Now, as your future self, write a letter to your present self. What advice do you have for your present self? What do you want your present self to remember?

4. Do you notice any themes in your letters and megascope experience? What insights do you glean? Make note of them.

5. Draw a symbol that expresses how you or humanity in general sits as a nexus of histories and futures. Jot down or discuss what this symbol means to you.

6. For the next few days take note of any new insights you glean. Jot them down in your notebook or discuss them with the group.

# 2

# LIMINAL REVELATIONS

## Finding Ourselves in a Liminal Period

AFROFUTURISTS LOVE A TIME BENDER for self-reflection. Before we go any further, we need to readjust our time lines. All future pasts, aka today, are not evenly distributed. The apocalypse, the post-apocalypse, the liminal, and the idealized utopia can exist simultaneously and yet not be experienced by all universally. How does one survive in spaces that feel fixed? How does one thrive in spaces that shift? How does one shift time lines? In the yet-to-be future, as cocreators in our world, we ideally aim to create equitable futures. But a belief that equitable futures are possible or essential is key in the evolution, as is recognizing where you are in it.

We'll readjust our time lines several times, recalibrating our clocks and travel gear. So, stay ready.

The adage goes that if you want to know where you're going you need to know where you came from (yes, Sankofa). But if you're lost or unsure of your whereabouts in the immediate moment, you need to know where you are or *where you're at*. Remember a time you visited a sprawling venue, a college campus, a state park, or

a zoo, and found the large map with a red arrow pointing, YOU
ARE HERE. Upon spotting the arrow, you look around, assessing
directions to see how the YOU ARE HERE lines up with where you're
actually standing. You look back to the map for your destination
of choice and then twist about to ascertain how the map aligns
with your location. The challenge with these YOU ARE HERE markers is that you don't know what direction you're facing. Are you
facing in the direction of the red arrow or are you turned about in
the opposite direction? You can describe your location, you know
where you want to go, but you don't know the spatial relationship to the buildings around you nor the course to take. You are
finding some orientation, a grounding, so that you can go in the
right direction. There are times in life when we, too, are looking
around to assess where we are, emotionally, mentally, in relationship to the swirl of life happenings around us. We chart a course
through time and space that sometimes sends us through the land
of poppies. Are we anywhere near where we aim to be? Have we
arrived at our future or is the future yet to be?

## Straight Out the Apocalypse

Cyberpunk, the reigning sci-fi aesthetic moving into the twenty-
first century, asserted that the world was in or moving toward
an apocalypse. In the cyberpunk edict, systems were collapsing,
technology was taking over, and humans were feeding the beast of
capitalism run amok. *Welcome II the Terrordome*, *The Matrix*, and
*Blade Runner* were chockfull of leather-clad protagonists, sometimes with wire or metal accoutrements, seeking to be plugged
into or unplugged from a diabolical system. The aesthetic captured
popular imagination because it countered the prevailing narrative
that technology fuels progress.

After the Berlin Wall fell in 1989, marking the end of the Cold
War, political science writer Francis Fukuyama claimed that the
Western world had reached "the end of history." The world was

on a fast track to the highest form of government, so he said, a Western liberal democratic government. Such governments were the ideal, and it was just a matter of various countries achieving this end. There are some sweeping assumptions with this one. However, Fukuyama argued that this period was the height of achievement and therefore the end of a time line. The notion of an "end of history" was jarring. What wasn't so clear was what the new time line would be or how the prospect of change could be navigated.

Afrofuturism, simultaneously, was named in the 1990s, around the same time that both the End of History and cyberpunk's grim moody chic came into vogue. Like cyberpunk, Afrofuturism, too, dealt with a system to be hacked. From a fashion standpoint, the bold colors and space funk look of the 1970s, most associated with the space jinks of George Clinton's funk groups Parliament and Funkadelic or Labelle, eventually morphed into street fashion fueled by the ghetto fabulous—a blend of a wide array of elements: fur, bamboo earrings, unlaced sneakers, oversized jeans—a look that came to define hip-hop in its rise.

But in its early years, the hip-hop aesthetic was best captured by the group Grandmaster Flash and the Furious Five in their classic video *The Message*. The crew are walking through their neighborhood—one wrestling with urban decay—rhyming about the pressures, ironies, and struggles. They wear spiked wristbands, chic leather caps with fitted jeans, sweatpants, and dark sweaters. While the societal ills and the frustrations are part of the point of the song, the song in both beat and temperament isn't inherently relishing in the end of anything.

The chorus, "It's like a jungle sometimes / It makes me wonder how I keep from going under," is prescient. The artists wonders how, in this space of trial and tribulations, are they surviving? While this isn't pure optimism, the song is a testament of sorts. If you look at the abandoned lots or the crowded NYC streets in the video, it's clear that the more troubled sights are in the aftermath of something. It's also clear that this isn't a film set. The aesthetic is real.

Whereas Afrofuturism, too, acknowledged some of the issues in cyberpunk narratives, the time line differed. Afrofuturist takes on progress differed, too. In the Afrofuturist world, the apocalypse happened a few hundred years ago, marked by the transatlantic slave trade and colonialism. This period is known as the interruption. The evolutions of liberation that followed placed us not in a trajectory toward an apocalypse but rather of moving out of one. Although 1980s era Bronx had its challenges, it was a marked evolution some years removed from the cataclysmic interruption, though reeling from some of its continued fallout nonetheless.

We are a few years shy of moving on from a global pandemic, and the growing concerns about climate change, war, and political divisions are serious. Nevertheless, Afrofuturists look at present challenges as the nature of a turmoil that arises from moving out of a major apocalypse. I once had an opportunity to visit Cape Coast and Elmina, two of the slave castles/dungeons the enslaved who were brought to the Americas survived. Dante's nine levels of hell have nothing on these dungeons; those who had to march there forced to abide in their holes of filth and torture for several months, only to be shackled at the bottom of a boat ride of death, to a place of never-ending work and abuse where you have no control over your body, your whereabouts, your time, or your progeny.

The nature of time they experienced in their homelands was unlike the nature of time in plantation life where time was measured by labor and production. According to Ghanian beliefs, those who didn't survive the dungeons shifted from human form to the spirit world of the ancestors, a world that is interconnected with the living. One tour guide at Cape Coast said that those who passed away, joining the realm of the ancestors, became a part of the force that helped the living survive. The shift in form and space, one often coerced in extreme choice, was arguably a choice to occupy another space and function as power or life force in another dimension.

Amílcar Cabral, who led liberation efforts in Guinea-Bissau and Cape Verde, wrote that colonialism placed subjected communities into a time line that erased histories and neutralized agency over a future. "The colonists usually say that it was they who brought us into history," he wrote. "They made us leave history, our history, to follow them, right at the back, to follow the progress of their history."[1] With the interruption as the cultural reference point for the lowest of lows, anything else is a step up and navigable. In other cases, it's a course correction, sometimes a hard fought one. This perspective is born of a communal historical narrative and experience forged in the heat of the interruption with the aim of moving forward. The course can be a rough one, and steering away from danger is an art, but you are on a course away from the most dire of calamities in the human arc of time. This shift implies a forward motion buoyed by a tidal wave of lessons. That said, just because you're out of the frying pan, so to speak, doesn't mean all is rosy, and thus songs like *The Message*.

## You Are Here—the Post-Apocalypse

Generally, in Afrofuturist time lines, we, as in you and I, are in an aftermath. This vantage point explains the difference in temperament of Afrofuturist creations. Systems already collapsed. Human bodies were already enslaved, monetized, consumed. So with this lens, the transhumanist predictions of some horrors of the future have already come to pass. The current debate of AI replacing human creativity and human work at large is both a cyberpunk fear and a twist on times when humans were treated like robots, working nonstop and discarded with little regard. The idea of assessing humans as commodities, or robotic consumers, or worthless when they are neither, is a tension that's ebbed and crashed in recent centuries. Such experiences are not an unknown tragedy we're hurtling toward but one we've been propelled, through our own agency, out of and away from, and yet each generation in recent centuries must contend with another dynamic around the tensions of how to sustain humanity, that which keeps us connected, in the face of those who value the humanity of some over others, or don't value humanity when our connectors can't be commodified, or value that which can be produced but not who produces it, or treasure the land the people live on but not the people themselves.

There are other cultural perspectives with narratives comparable to the interruption. Each is different in how inhumanity was deployed or functioned, but nonetheless an inhumanity is the inflection. These atrocities disrupt lives, are revelatory, and shift experiences of time. The adaptations humans made some centuries ago to reconcile with the interruption of enslavement and colonization on African people (and the reboots and tweaks from life's navigations that followed) have morphed African/African Diasporic life into something akin to being a human cyborg in the liminal space. W. E. B. DuBois spoke of double consciousness, of being both Black and American and the conflicts that poses. Frantz Fanon spoke of those emerging from colonial rule, vacillating between differing, often contrarian value systems. The reconciliation between these perspectives is much like that of a cyborg who is both human and machine, human and the adaptation to a society with conflicting demands. Cyborgs are the apex of human integration with the machine or with systems that value people as commodities. Cyborgs claim humanity, finding beauty in adaptations born of survival to thrive in new spaces. DC Comics' Cyborg, an African American character whose existential crisis was determining whether he was man or machine was given new life with Morgan Hampton writing the series. Hampton told a crowd at San Diego Comic Con 2023 that he shied away from Cyborg's existential crisis and framed him as a human with a prosthetic. He is not human and machine. He is a human adapting.

If one is a cyborg, the ultimate adaptor, they are connected to the ancient and the future, or to differing value systems, while becoming an entity of their own. Cyborgs always wrestle with two ways of knowing. This positioning can move one forward, keep one conflicted, or keep one in a state of perpetual motion. I think of a person jumping double Dutch. Double Dutch uses two jump ropes and has two people turning both ropes simultaneously. Each "turner" is alternately swinging one rope counterclockwise and the other rope clockwise. A person jumping in the ropes jumps over each rope in syncopated motion. The speed quickens, it slows down, the turners can lift the rope over your head, and the jumper is charged with keeping tempo for when the rope lands on concrete again. The turners can flip the game by turning the ropes in reverse. The jumper is jumping on both legs alternately, both together, or one leg. There is an interesting mix of moves you can do. Jumping rope, said by a woman who prides herself on being shaped by the rigors of jumping double Dutch in thin-soled sneakers on concrete sidewalks for hours in ninety-degree weather as a kid, is not easy. But if we think of one rope as old wisdom and ways of doing things and the other as new wisdom and ways of doing things, the art of jumping over both is a test of adapting at rapid speeds with hefty swag as people sing along, taunting and cheering along the way. All hail the art, but this doesn't mean that even the best jumpers among us don't get caught in the rope (or end up with sore ankles). The rapid adapting without reflection and a break can cause disorientation.

## Liminal Living

In any aftermath, there's a bit of disorientation, a string of highs and questions, and a desire to give it all context and meaning. But the liminal space isn't purgatory. I think of the liminal space as a fog that people are trying to see through. The fog from the calamity is clearing. Some are fanning the fog to cause confusion. In some spaces it's more dense than others. Perhaps the fog changes colors, marking confusion around whether it's fog or something else. Assessing location and direction, or getting a clear view, in an ongoing fog of misinformation and disinformation is a perennial challenge.

This post-apocalyptic state is very much a liminal space. Liminal spaces are places of transition or the ominous in-between. In essence, you feel as if you are between two spaces, both more tangible than the present. The perceived instability in the liminal space can be hard to define. In our personal lives, a liminal space can be a season of job hunting. You were downsized from one job and are interviewing for a new one, but haven't started the next job yet. Both the period with the previous job and the future with the job to come feel like spaces that have more constants than the present. The last job could've sucked. The potential job has promise, but the present state, this in-between, neither completely mirrors the past nor the idealized future state.

While there's a good dose of patience to be mastered in such periods, you are not inactive. The liminal space can be marked by nervousness, excitement, frustration, and hopefulness. Perhaps you take on a new hobby to relieve stress between interviews. Maybe you're freaked out by dwindling savings. There can be achievements and pitfalls. If you have not found the job you're looking for, markers of progress feel off. The reactions can run the gamut in the liminal, but generally you're riding the waves of change in a moment that's temporary, and making the best of it.

Iyanla Vanzant writes about liminal periods in her book *In the Meantime* and says they are a "time to get clear, get real, and heal yourself" in preparation for the next. It is, she reasons, a moment to assess and determine what one truly wants.

However, how does the liminal feel if it lasts for a decade, a century, several centuries? Life can be amplified. A sense of hyper-reality or an oversensitivity to an overstimulating environment emerges. Perhaps a numbing to an increasingly layered environment becomes a norm. Some will desire escape into other realities. Or maybe the new space feels like a substance-induced state. The Last Bath is a commemorative site by a Ghanian river where the enslaved bathed before being marched to captivity. It also doubles as a space of return for descendants of enslaved Africans who step into the river for healing. A guide at the site leads visitors to step into the water, pray, or sing, acknowledging the ancestors and symbolically standing as them in their return. The guide also speaks of those who weren't captured in the trade—of them not knowing what happened to loved ones and friends who were kidnapped, a pervasive feeling compounded by centuries. Finding life and vision within this pervasive fog of loss and yearning is a form of a liminal space, too.

Liminal spaces, short term or otherwise, can be off-putting. There's joy and there's danger. Childish Gambino's video for "This Is America" comes to mind. Gambino, an Esu-like figure, snakes about empty spaces—a parking lot, a church—standing ebullient between joyous dancing kids and intense violence. Esu is found in a pantheon of African/African Diasporic religions and is a deity who stands at the crossroads and opens the way. This alternate world of joy forces its way through a world that feels like a string of temporality.

For some, both the past and future feel out of reach in the liminal. The present can feel ominous, and a sense that there was nothing before or after can set in if the lack of motion, or nature of motion, feels perennial. But this is a feeling, not an existential state. Life is in motion, even when it feels as if all is static. When we capitulate to this sense that there is no relevant past or future, we don't claim our agency in the moment. We are not present. We are not consciously aware.

Poet D. Scot Miller, a Bay Area–based culture writer and theo-rist, wrote the "Afrosurreal Manifesto." In the vein of Amiri Baraka, he says liminal space gave rise to what he dubs the Afrosurreal. In the lens of the Afrosurreal, fluidity, ambiguity, dandyism, excess, and sexy gods abound. With the settling of the post-apocalyptic dust, the fabulous arises. A new world, a new future, is bursting forth. This fabulousness is currency and agency.

"Afro-Surreal presupposes that beyond this visible world, there is an invisible world striving to manifest, and it is our job to uncover it," he writes. Afrosurrealism centers on the hyperre-ality of the present in this Afrofuturist arc. Although we may be navigating through the fog, it is our responsibility to find evidence of the brilliant future now in progress. The future now that values humanity is present and hiding in plain sight. This perception is based on a knowing. This knowing is awareness. This awareness is a source of joy and action.

We experience ripples and waves of transformation individu-ally and collectively each day. The brilliant evidence of the future in progress is all around us. Our charge is to perceive it. As we spot evidence in the form of kindness, fabulousness, serendipity, synchronicity, or innovation, we think upon streams of time and look to Sankofa. When times are tough, we look to these elements of potential futures as evidence for the humane world we yearn to exist.

## The Space Refresh

African spiritual systems state that there are two realms of existence, the physical and spiritual. However, these two worlds are always in conversation with one another. Nigerian writers Oghenechovwe Donald Ekpeki and Joshua Uchenna Omenga call writing that speaks to these intersecting realms *Afropantheology*. "These stories though they are from African lore are not wholly imaginary," they write.[2] The term aims to "assert the right of Africans and African descended people to tell stories of African deities and mysticism in the proper manner," adding that missionaries who came to the continent ushered in a culture of dystopias where Africans were "storiless." Afropantheology is a reminder that African religions generally view these worlds either as two dimensions operating in one space or two different dimensions where one has access to the other. I think of it as two cylinders, or circles, stacked on top of one another with energy spiraling between them.

This view of space changes the nature of the world we navigate, asserting that we are always in dialogue or share presence with the invisible. African spirituality asserts that we are abiding in a fluid state of change where change is the constant. A fluid liminality is not an in between, but rather an expanded space where a transformation is a natural space. A fluid liminality is empowered with guideposts where change is evolution and spirits are constant.

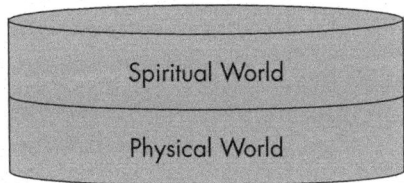

With their film *Mascon: A Massive Concentration of Black Experiential Energy*, the Otolith Group, composed of Kodwo Eshun and Anjalika Sagar, explore the "gestures, geometries, grammars, and geographies" in films by icons Ousmane Sembène and Djibril Diop Mambéty only for an intertwined world of spirt, humans, and memory to emerge from recut images. Faded images of characters atop lush Senegalese landscapes, women rubbing divination beads, shared gestures, money exchanges, and the temporal nature of open and shut doors of paths and opportunities, are interlocked as "the borderless imagination of the cine-Sahel" unfolds.[3] Who is a spirit? Who is human? They assert that we are always in conversation with what was, what is, what will be, for the spirits abound.

The human life and the spiritual are bound much like a spider web. Ananse the spider is a central figure in Akan lore and wisdom. Stories of the great spider were carried into the Americas. In the Americas, Ananse became more of a trickster who overcame power imbalances. Among the Akan, Ananse was a mediator between Nyame, or God, and society, transcending spiritual and physical spaces. He is wise but is also an arbiter of chaos. Ananse knows the webbed worlds. Seminal writer and teacher W. E. B. DuBois spent his last years in a newly independent Ghana. He is enshrined next to his home in Accra in an edifice with a ceiling that replicates a spider web. DuBois was honored as one who knows the web. Ananse, much like the orisha Esu in the Nigerian spiritual practice Ifá, is a transformational figure. Although Ananse is multifaceted, dancing between binaries that he obliterates, the web stands as a symbol of an interdependent world of dimensions. We stand as transformational figures in an interconnected world.

A webbed world of spiritual and physical realms

## Changeland

Octavia Butler aptly wrote "God is change." Change becomes a norm in the liminal space, but the indicators of this change are relative. As we change, morph, and adapt, our viewpoint shifts. As the collective of shape-shifting people funnels change, society shifts and us with it. We aren't leaves blowing in the wind, but there are breezes and storms of our collective making that swirl about us, and carry us with them. The post-apocalyptic dust is a fog always ascending and receding, but what is revealed? There are lessons in change that help with the next moment. Through the liminal we uncover another level of understanding about riding winds and setting course. We orient, finding balance in spaces where we thought there was none. We move deep within our souls, we go high as we're lifted by gusts of wind unknown. These ripples and waves are on an upward stream, not a downward one. As the fog of interruptions past clears, you realize you're not on land at all, you are on water.

I'm on water?

I can remember a liminal period once. I was a journalist tossed out of the jostling comforts of a full-time job into the sea of freelancing. It was before the blogosphere and social media fully evolved, and publications were still debating just how or if having digital counterparts was profitable. It was a period of deep change in the industry. I remember feeling like I was juggling assignments, writing everything for everyone, but doing it while running full speed up a hill in a mudslide. Running full speed and feeling behind is an unsettling feeling. I was running as fast as possible, slipping, but gaining traction. At some point, it felt like things had stabilized and I was in full takeoff mode. I'd reached level ground; the mudslide had ebbed. If I kept the same pace or even slowed down, I was able to cover more ground than I had when I was heading upward in mudslideville.

The stabilizer for me was a book I wrote, one born of the myriad worlds that freelance writing placed me in—a book I likely would not have written otherwise. I'd gained a heap of insights during this mudslide period, some that prepared me for the next. One takeaway from this arduous period was that I now knew how to run up a mudslide, a skill set I didn't have before and didn't know I needed. As other mudslide periods presented themselves, I felt confident in navigating the tumultuous change because I had found a way through once before. Although there were other hills to climb, the sun was shining and the mud was no more. I would never forget that feeling of wondering both what was going on and why each step didn't feel like a marker of progress. But in total, despite sliding and gliding around, I'd covered ground and made progress. Sustaining oneself in a mudslide is progress.

## The Change Wave

In thinking about Afrofuturists and space/time, your YOU ARE HERE marker is pointing on a continued trajectory in the aftermath of an apocalypse; on an upward stream of waves of change, each wave landing at a new destination, new worlds, with a better one in the making. My sojourn into the freelance world was not the apocalypse. Your YOU ARE HERE is ever in motion.

In looking at your map, you aren't merely seeking to know where you are. You want to know where you are within the upward stream of change. Perhaps we can think of each wave of change as having its own liminality, with a before world and after world; with each arc and flow, a new sun rises.

Upstream is upstream, nonetheless. One can sail onward, the forces of nature pushing one smoothly forward, or the ride can be as rough as a class V rapids. The dance between new world and old can feel like hopping over land mines at a carnival. Who keeps fanning the fog of confusion and disorder? Maybe it's best to think of it as a residual undercurrent from the apocalypse and that which caused it.

The stabilizing force in this realm of liminality, constant change, and new suns is the Akan principle of Sankofa. With Sankofa, you assemble and collect things from the past and reassemble a new artifact that rides these waves of change and jettisons you forward. The artifacts are the reward, but the lessons are the gift. This process of Sankofa is your operating system, the engine in the motorboat headed upstream, and these artifacts, the guideposts on the map of time.

## Reflection Questions

Let's think about liminal spaces in our lives, their nature, and our own resolve.

1.  Can you identify a period in your life that felt like a liminal space? What marked the beginning of this period in your life and what marked the end of this period?

2.  How did the liminal space feel?
3.  What lessons did you learn about yourself or the world around you from this period in your life?
4.  What joy did you find in this period? How did you sustain a healthy outlook?

## Exercise: Circles and Blocks

1.  Draw a circle that symbolizes this space. You can give the circle a name, call it liminal space, or label it as the emotion or color that best describes this period in your life.
2.  Now draw a second circle. You can label it INSIGHTS or a color that best embodies the emotions you associate with those lessons. Within this circle, write down all the lessons and insights from this period that enriched you.
3.  Review the insights in this circle and select your favorites. Do you remember building blocks that you played with as a child? The base level of the blocks was always the foundation for the playhouse or pyramid you were aiming to build. Take your favorite insights from the liminal period, the ones you believe are the best foundations for new worlds. Draw a picture of building blocks and label each an insight. Feel free to color and decorate these blocks as you like.

# 3

# ARTIFACTS FOR TIME TRAVELERS

## Symbols from Our Past for Our Future

IF THE STABILIZING FORCE in the river of change is Sankofa, a look back to move forward, how does one keep from getting whiplash? Riding the waves of change isn't always the easiest. Afrofuturists look for the opportunity or light in the change. Each time period presents a unique opportunity to grow and build. We find elements in the moment that are life giving and keep us moving forward. We find artifacts, uncover avatars, create new ones, and remix them to ground who we are, where we're headed, and what to value as we get there.

I once heard a political candidate reference to a situation that he described as "building the boat and rowing it at the same time." This doesn't sound like the ideal scenario, but how often are we presented with the ideal scenario? Perhaps the moment is uniquely suited to talents we don't yet know we have. The one who must build the boat and row it is likely neither a maker of boats nor an expert rower, but they use what they have because urgency necessitates that they "find a way or or make one," as the Clark Atlanta University motto says.

I think of this boat-building metaphor as being similar to Sankofa, but with urgency taking precedent. The Sankofa bird looks backward at the promise of a future on its tail, but its feet are facing forward. Going back to move forward can be rationalized as two conflicting actions. Yet these actions, as a unit, are essential to creating healthy futures. Constructing a boat and rowing it at the same time are actions born of necessity and urgency, but they are essential to achieving the goal—reaching a place of safety. Building and rowing can feel like two actions that are in conflict with one another, yet a symmetry is found. Building the boat is supposed to precede the boat's send-off, a past action with a future aim. Sankofa can function out of necessity and urgency, too. Yet the process of Sankofa necessitates that this look back and look forward occur, much like the building and the motion of the boat, in one full swing. It requires dexterity, balance, and focus on the future in the same way that building a boat double time while rowing forward is an act. You don't build a boat and row it because you want to, but rather because the time and urgency of the matter demand that you must.

Connecting the dots gets my synapse firing. Connecting the dots clears the post-apocalyptic fog. Sankofa as creative and thought process weaves seemingly disparate moments with loosely threaded ideas into a quilt of cohesion.

I spoke with a journalist who didn't understand why Afrofuturists referenced the past so frequently. I reference the past not because I'm mired in it but because the process of building a new future now is informed by interrogating what, if anything, in the so-called past can be a building block for healthy futures. What are the lessons learned? We are always living in someone else's future. We are living in our own childhood future. We interrogate the past also to recover practices that sustained us, uncover stories and historical moments that inspire, and build a relationship with those in the past who laid groundworks for worlds that value humanity. We can also assess what not to do. What roads to avoid. The interruption in Black cultures lends itself to an ongoing Sankofa practice: recovery, assessment, and building the next, passing on the story, repeat. This Sankofa practice, as symbolized by the odd bird looking at its tail, the old "get back and fetch it" as it literally means, runs at the core of many Black cultures.

So, this looking back process isn't just about dusting off cool memorabilia to put in a glass case. You are in a constant state of creation of moving lessons learned forward into both action and as a living resource. Sankofa is a creative tool.

I think of Octavia Butler's acclaimed book *Parable of the Sower* and the living document assembled by the story's protagonist. *Parable of the Sower*, first published in 1990, became more popular during the 2020 pandemic when people saw parallels between the story's political chaos, climate change, and calamities and the global uncertainty of 2020. Some wondered if Butler was a psychic, predicting future dynamics. However, Butler, who passed away in 2006, had said that she was a student and observer of the times. The main character, Lauren Olamina, is a teen navigating intense change in a world turned topsy-turvy. The book is her journal. For Olamina, her notes on lessons learned, observations, and wisdom from the past become the basis of the Earthseed belief system. The belief centers on change. This document was the basis for cultivating a belief that helped Olamina and her community navigate, survive, and sustain, one with ties to their collapsing world and the new one they are stepping into. Perhaps Olamina was building a boat and rowing at the same time. I'd argue that Earthseed, and the journal, is Sankofa in process.

The Sankofic process is prompted by an urgent need. This need takes the form of questions: Where am I? Who am I? How did I get here? How do I move forward? Such questions lead to data collection, looking to histories, stories, practices, or beliefs. These data become the pieces in a larger puzzle. The Data Thief in John Akomfrah's documentary/fictional essay *The Last Angel of History* serves this function. The Data Thief, a time traveler clad in sunglasses and wide-brimmed hat, collects artifacts on a quest to understand Afrofuturism.

You, too, can be the data thief. Rather than assembling the pieces to complete a picture of the past, the pieces are aligned to form a collage, a fresh, spinning tapestry that speaks on how to move to a future or is, in fact, an artifact of the future itself.

## The Artifact

The most obvious example of this collage in creation is sampling in hip-hop. Hip-hop was born in the 1970s from musically inclined youth in New York City schools with redacted music programs, who turned turntables into instruments and used breakbeats from sometimes rare funk and jazz songs as the sonic and emotional rhythm pattern to punctuate their poetics.

I think of Public Enemy's song "Fight the Power," voted by *Rolling Stone* the second-best song of all time. The socially conscious song is in the vein of Pan-African orators or activists before them. Musically, the song has so many layered samples, scores of which go unidentified. One could listen to this song and hear a new sound every time. The song is finely woven. Producer Hank Shocklee of the Bomb Squad, Public Enemy's dynamic production team, told 247HH.com that members of the team were assigned to look for different sounds. They, too, were data thieves. Chuck D, the group's lead, would look for Black empowerment catchphrases and poetics from other eras. Others (Keith Shocklee) would search for guitar licks. Eric Sadler would create the musical time frame, and Hank Shocklee saw himself as adding "the agitation" and created a story as a background for Chuck D's fiery bars.

Shocklee wasn't just putting random quips and sounds in a blender. There was a message, a mood, a tone, an intention. These seemingly disparate sampled elements, all from varying times and art forms, were zapped from their respective contexts and placed in a fresh one. The aim of the music was to empower by fusing messages and sounds.

Hip-hop heads adore samples because they compel listeners to research sounds and songs, thus becoming a unique ode to music or philosophical histories. In Shocklee's case, his data thief approach resulted in putting together some of the first music of its kind. These nods to a past are essential, not for legitimacy but as acknowledged language components for a story that speaks to a future but is eternally present. Music producers J Dilla, King Britt, and Ras G warped speed soul sonics in directions that completely reimagined the originals, creating unique sounds that speak to the present, and sometimes stand as sounds of a future world.

If life is a vibrant song, then we are the chords and harmonies. We are often given a song to play, a tune not of our making. Our perspectives of life necessitate that we craft a conscious sampling of understanding. We reassemble to move forward. We make use of dissonance and unused tones, sounds from junkyards, phrases from speeches, and breakbeats from dusty 45 records to create new keys of life. These discarded, lost tones are invaluable parts of ourselves and of humanity that some entity dismissed as having one purpose only. These samples are in need of being recollected, remixed, and re-understood.

Nina Woodruff-Walker is the executive director of the Museum of Children's Art in Oakland. The museum hosts the Community Futures School, an urban think tank grounded in Afrofuturism and including Indigenous Futurism and Queer Futures. We frequently talk about this notion of feeling we must recover lost and devalued practices in culture. This feeling is a preoccupation in the African Diaspora and many others who've felt some forced separation from life-sustaining ways of being. Our roundabout conversations with some cross-cultural pollinations have led us to this conclusion. We haven't lost as much as we thought. To the extent we did, much was recovered.

"We are much more connected than we thought we were," Woodruff-Walker told me. "How we live our daily lives is much more connected across the diaspora and continent than not. Our daily practices are much more connected to the continent than not, although some of us are hundreds of years away from being there. It made me feel good and hopeful that our Africanness still lives with us today and is very much alive. The beauty of who we are, we've been taught to deny that."

The realization is life-changing. "We thought we were lost and disconnected and we have found that there are so many ways that we are connected. That's the beauty. That couldn't be taken from us. All the tactics used to take away our history our culture, it is empowering to know it's present in all of us."

## The Panther

When the Lowndes County Freedom Party ran its slate of Black candidates in 1964, they needed a symbol. Abiding in the segregated American south, the candidates were taking a stand by running and registering voters, a stand that asserted their equality and citizenship in a place that suppressed nonwhite voters. It was a stand that put the candidates' and voters' life at risk. There was deep fear in being both a candidate and voting. But backed by the Student Nonviolent Coordinating Committee (SNCC), the candidates stepped forward.

Because rural Alabama had a low literacy rate for people of all backgrounds, candidates were encouraged to use a symbol to identify their slate. The freedom party selected a black panther. The panther was a protector, strong but also nimble and focused. This symbol would later be used to inspire Marvel's first Black superhero, the Black Panther, along with the liberation party of the same name. The use of the panther symbol stretches back to an all-Black regiment in World War II, and further to the Ancient Egyptian goddess Bast. Film curator and historian Floyd Webb says that the panther was a "liberation avatar." This avatar is a reminder for people far and wide that they are protected and imbued with power as they surmount inhumanities. From the Bantu cultures of Central and Southern Africa to Kwame Nkrumah's consciencism theory, there's a general African belief that all entities, living and inanimate, have a phenomenon aura. Avatars and Sankofic creations are no different. I think of an avatar as a beacon of inspiration that cuts across time and space. There are a number of avatars in Black cultures, from the Egyptian Eye of Ra to the Black Power fist. Here are a few that recur regularly:

- Sankofa
- Elegba or Esu
- Black panther
- Motherships
- Ankh
- Black fist
- Pick
- Afro hair, especially on women
- Lion of Judah
- Eye of Ra
- Black star
- Red, black, and green
- Rivers, water, boats
- North star
- Crossroads
- Ark of Bones
- Bottle Tree (symbol of protection)
- Haint Blue
- Afrohorn
- Anansi

## The Avatar

Avatars are multidirectional. Much like the nonlinear time tenants in Afrofuturism, cultural avatars often reach through time, pulling ideas forward. We can point to those who reframed the symbols in the past century through a book, or piece of music, or social justice movement. We may have a harder time pinpointing who originated these symbols and their ancient meanings, or who preserved them over the years. Avatars can have deep meaning for individuals and also for communities of people. They are created with intention, articulate a series of values, and serve as connectors. They are usually inspiring and encouraging, and they function as reminders of why you're here. They are comforting and protective. They urge us to recalibrate our actions, to course correct, to be a better self. Some are affirmations of a future state of being.

I've selected five avatars or symbols to explore and think about as interdimensional objects with symbolism across times and locations: The Mothership, the Ahnk, the Pick, the Black Woman with an Afro, a Rooted Tree, and the Crossroads.

## The Mothership

Funk pioneer George Clinton has pragmatic reasoning for his mothership metaphor. When Clinton's bands Parliament and Funkadelic came onto the scene, the doo-wop era of his Motown dreams was fading and Blackness felt commodified, he said. After reading the cult classic book *Chariots of the Gods*, a college circuit favorite that speculated on the technological advancements of the ancients, Clinton adopted the space motif. He launched *The Mothership Connection*, a classic album of funk utopia. He adopted the moniker Star Child, and the album cover pictured him hurling out of a funktastic spaceship, adorned in a silver suit and giant sun goggles. Clinton said he was returning to reclaim the pyramids. The funk Clinton sang of was that which undergirds life. The

Mothership was the interstellar protector arriving to course correct humanity. The follow-up album, *The Clones of Dr. Funkenstein*, marks the return of the Afronauts, interstellar superhumans returning from the celestial realm to bring funk to all galaxies. The funk was hidden in Egypt's pyramids, awaiting humankind's readiness with the pharaohs. The Afronauts were cloned from Dr. Funkenstein, the greatest Afronaut of them all. "Funk is its own reward," Clinton says in the album's intro. The Mothership brings funk, life force, to the masses. It also brings a life force that enhances those who value humanity while enlightening those who seek to connect to the universal web (think Ananse) of life. It's a sonic transport, healing the world with high vibrational frequencies. The life-size mothership that descended upon the stage during Parliament-Funkadelic concerts now sits in the National Museum of African American History and Culture. The Mothership is referenced in countless songs, from Erykah Badu's "On and On," where she states that the "mothership can't save" the unconscientious, to Gonjasufi, who chants on "Afrikan Spaceship" that he "came to Africa on a spaceship." The anthology *Mothership*, edited by Bill Campbell and Edward Austin Hall, is a major sci-fi short story compilation that references the mothership as "the bringer of knowledge." Comparisons can be made to Marcus Garvey's Starline fleet, ships his organization was raising money for in the 1920s to facilitate international trade between the African Diaspora and Continent and to usher a return of those in the diaspora to "the motherland." Lee "Scratch" Perry, Jamaica's dub music pioneer, named his studio the Black Ark, an homage to the interstellar sky travelers.

These spacecraft avatars have parallels with indigenous African origin stories that source the first in the community as descending from an otherworldly plane. The Serer of Senegal state that their first humans, a woman and man, boarded the ark of Yaabo-Yabo after the creator god, Roog, brought them to life. They departed from the Empyrean Heaven and sailed the ark to Earth. The Ancient Nubians and Egyptians said that the goddess Bast would sail in a sky ark each day with her sun god father, Ra. The ark pulled the sun across the sky. Vusamazulu Credo Mutwa, a Zulu shaman, writes of the "flying egg" that descended to Earth holding the first beings. Afrosurreal writer Henry Dumas's short story "Ark of Bones" speaks to a boat that sails into the sky, housing the ancestors.

The Mothership in its contemporary iteration is a reminder that we are one with the universe. Our humanity goes beyond Earth's realm, and music is an otherworldly healer. The Mothership brings love and peace, guiding us to our cosmic core and Earth rooted joy. This bringer of joy is a protector.

## The Ankh

This symbol of life permeates Ancient Egyptian and Nubian culture. Worn by pharaohs and deities alike, the ankh is a reminder of life force. The round upper portion is said to symbolize the womb, while the stem symbolizes male fertility. This union creates life. This four-thousand-year-old symbol can be found in ancient and contemporary art, murals, clothing, and jewelry across the African Diaspora. The symbol doubles as a key of life, with the shape also serving as a tool to unlock consciousness. For many in the African Continent and Diaspora, it's a reminder of a major African society, one shaped by those further south, who then shaped ideas in Ancient Rome, Greece, and the Western world, as well as deeper into Africa itself.

Erykah Badu, X Clan, Dawn Richards, Sun Ra, Beyoncé, and countless others have adopted the ankh as a key symbol in album covers, logos, clothing, and jewelry. Adorning the ankh is a reclaiming of Ancient Egypt's role in the world. Although some look at the pyramids and elaborate burial ceremonies as a preoccupation with death, they are actually entrenched in preserving abundant life. The ankh that appears in royal tombs, temples, and statues can also easily be found on murals in Oakland, California, and the

National African Burial Ground in New York. This symbol of life goes beyond mortal time lines, asserting an eternal life force, or eternal soul, that lives always.

## The Pick

As a kid, I always saw the pick as a utilitarian tool to detangle curly hair. It was especially essential for those who wore Afros or natural styles. The handle's tip sometimes had a fist, an homage to Black pride. The pick, as symbol, was a key icon in the Black Is Beautiful cultural movements of the 1960s and '70s around the world. Spotted on art and fashion alike, it's a staple in Black beauty stores. Some people with fluffed styles would wear the pick in their hair, a reminder of beauty and nonconformity. Nevertheless, I thought of it as a modern invention.

When I was in college, I went to an Atlanta museum to see precolonial African art and saw ancient picks with an array of decorative handles. Picks with ornate handles were found in Egyptian tombs, a reminder of the importance of maintaining beauty in the afterlife. They are ubiquitous among the histories of curly-haired people. Among the Akan, the pick is also art. People adorn their walls with an oversized wooden pick whose handle is a delicately carved woman's face. For the Akan, the pick is an older symbol that represents beauty or a reminder to make time for beauty and grooming.

Today, images of a pick can be found around the world on T-shirts and hats denoting Black cultural pride. It's a symbol of the beauty of tightly curled African hair and also embodies strength and resilience.

## A Black Woman with an Afro

The Black Is Beautiful movement also popularized the iconic Afro. Women stepped away from straightening their hair and embraced their curls, cropping them into a neat circle. Human rights activist

Angela Davis was known for her advocacy and recognized by her hair's billowing silhouette. Actress Pam Grier was as idolized for her action hero roles as she was for her striking hair. The hairstyle's evolution was a stark departure from previous styles Black people wore in Western or colonized spaces that valued straighter European looks over curls. At various times, the Afro style was viewed as radical. But the style's evolution was part of a reclaiming of complex hair textures as beautiful. The style also denotes a future forward woman who's comfortable with herself. Other times, the symbol denotes a woman connecting to her goddess energy, an ethereal sense of self.

Beyond C'est (an homage to Beyoncé), the towering Black woman/interstellar alien who appeared in HBO's *Lovecraft* series, was adorned with a shiny purple near-metallic suit and an angular Afro. She's a goddesslike figure who urges an aspiring Black woman scientist to claim who she wants to be.

Over time, the symbol of a Black woman with an Afro adorned fashion and merchandise. The style, which isn't the easiest to achieve, became a symbol of beauty and strength. This idea of femininity as strength connects deeply with warrior woman energy and goddess energy.

## A Rooted Tree

On *Finding Your Roots*, a popular PBS show hosted by scholar and professor Henry Louis Gates, Gates maps out the family trees of celebrities. This notion of roots and trees as a symbol for life and lineage has a long history. The book *Roots* by Alex Haley was released in 1976. The saga of an enslaved family and their aftermath was brought to the small screen a year later to great acclaim and was remade in 2016. Historian Floyd Webb says that Haley pulled the term from Black folk culture. Phrases like "you can tell he came from good roots" were sometimes used in passing. "Families are considered to be the progeny of strong roots," says Web.

*Roots* sparked a new interest in tracing family lineage. At the end of the book as well as the show's second season final episode, Haley encouraged people to do family research, as he had. This arduous task was complicated for families interrupted by enslavement, during which families were often torn apart and sold away from one another. Piecing together family histories was part of a healing and recovery process for some who thought various names were lost to the wind. Family reunions and researching family histories grew in popularity in the show's aftermath. The use of the term *roots* to reference family or social consciousness grew in popularity, too. To "go to your roots" was to go to where it all started, the root of soul, the root of family, the root of what sustains. The hip-hop band the Roots is a modern outgrowth of this movement. They promote an earthy, socially conscious music and host the Roots Picnic festival in Philadelpha each year.

There are a host of African proverbs that center trees as family, wisdom, or strong ethics. Proverbs abound and speak to the Sankofic value of return: "A family is like a forest, when you are outside it is dense, when you are inside you see that each tree has its place"; "A strong tree will always grow from the roots and not the seeds"; "Though a tree grows so high, the falling leaves return to the root."

In many African and African-derived spiritual practices, trees are central in worship and belief. Trees house spirits. You can find baobab trees in Senegal hosting offerings of money and jewelry. In Cuba, enslaved Africans identified the ceiba tree as being similar to the baobab and used it as a centerpiece for their spiritual ceremonies. The creation story for the Serer of Senegal and Gambia begins with a series of trees. Mutwa writes of an intense mating between a woman and tree that created living beings on the Earth.

This notion of the roots in a tree running deep is a reminder of the importance of family, fictive kin, and knowing family history as a life-generating force.

## The Crossroads

In 1997, Cleveland-based hip-hop group Bone Thugs-n-Harmony won a Grammy Award for their song "Tha Crossroads." The song is a good-bye to loved ones who passed away and a reminder that they would meet again at the crossroads. This metaphor of the crossroads as an intersection between the seen and unseen stretches into many folk cultures and African spirituality. There's an old legend about the bluesman Robert Johnson, a fast-rising blues star with an enviable career. He passed away young, shocking fans. Rumors persisted that his fast rise and early death was because he sold his soul to the devil at a crossroads. The legend is debated to this day. Film curator and Afrofuturist Floyd Webb, who was raised near the highway where Johnson allegedly made his pact, has another theory. "He didn't sell his soul to anyone," said Webb. "People who honored Elegba, or Esu, would place their offerings at a crossroads. Those who didn't understand African religions or were afraid of them looked at the practice as devilish." Mystery solved.

The crossroads, this notion of a place with a thin veil between the seen and unseen, pops up as both metaphor and music. The horizontal line in the ankh is as much about creation as it is life morphing from the invisible world to the visible one. Historically, the Amazigh and Tuareg cultures were nomadic, often travelling across the Sahara Desert. The Cross of Agadez, a popular adornment in Niger by the Tuareg that's often worn as a necklace, is a reminder that strangers, lovers, or new friends will find one another again. It's a reminder to be kind to those you meet for you will see them again. This reacquaintance as a supernatural destiny is symbolized as a crossing of paths.

## Modern and Future Avatars

When thinking on newer symbols, I found myself thinking of brands and logos. Some of the symbology that once evoked cultural values today is more often than not catering to brands and entertainment: hip-hop groups, tech companies, superheroes, fashion, start-ups. The more popular ones are aspirational, encouraging us to take on the qualities that the product promises to provide. The Air Jordan symbol that features basketball legend Michael Jordan flying through the air in his epic dunk posture is a symbol of excellence or reaching the heights in your field. Luxury goods have the same appeal. Harlem-based fashion designer Dapper Dan established a bold new look in fashion in the 1980s by taking luxury brands and patterns and completely reinventing them for hip-hop savvy customers. He took new fashions aimed for luxury clientele and repurposed the status associated with it for an audience the brands weren't thinking of reaching, creating a new way of thinking about fashion.

Although some of these branded symbols can be inspiring, they are ultimately designed to sell products, to encourage us to take the future action of buying the product. Some symbols are exclusionary; they mark a territory, establish hierarchies, or gaslight fears. But the avatar powers I'm referring to are always centered around valuing humanity. Avatars "go back to the root" and in the Sankofa creation process, articulate a series of altruistic beliefs that have helped society or can help society as it moves forward. Lonny Brooks, an Oakland-based Afrofuturist and professor, designed the game *AfroRithms from the Future* (ARFTF) to help people design future artifacts emerging from tensions and opportunities. The game helps people to think about what they value and what insights from culture are future forward.

We can create artifacts, avatars, wisdom devices by pulling from insights or experiences in our own life. We can pull quotes from sages and loved ones, historical moments that have deep meaning for our understanding of humanity, or daydreams of futures to create a symbol that helps us unlock new futures and connect with ourselves. In some ways, we do this all the time, updating our views of the world or assessing what strategies work for us. However, we likely don't set aside time to note to ourselves the things we believe, what we value, or the streams of times that serve as reservoirs of inspiration for us. Giving space to sample or reflect just serves as a guide for how to think about life. Much like any guide, you can always add new insights or change it altogether. These insights aren't written in stone, but they serve as both markers of time and as an ever-shifting megascope-like lens in the highest Du Boisean order.

## Reflection Questions

Let's create an artifact centering the practice of Sankofa. This is an imaged artifact.

1. Think of at least three ideas, historical events, lessons, or memories from the past that you would like to pass forward in building futures. This message can be in a song lyric, a catchphrase, a figure in history and their symbolism, family wisdom, or an incident in the past. List them.

2. Let's think of at least three lessons from personal history that you want to use as building blocks. Feel free to pull from the building blocks you created earlier. List them.

3. Let's think of three expectations you have for bright futures. Maybe you expect clean water to be easily accessible for all or human rights to be fully protected. List them.

4. Do you note any themes between your selections? What are they?

## Exercise: Creating an Artifact or Avatar

1. Looking at the tapestry of ideas you've generated, create an artifact or avatar. You can draw this artifact or, if you work in another medium like clay or fashion, you can create based on your theme. It can be a symbol, an object, a fantastic invention, a fantasy creature, a building, etc. If

you're drawing the artifact, transfer your ideas from past, present, and future wisdom into the artifact by listing them within the drawing. Feel free to do this exercise as often as you like, playing with new combinations of ideas. You can add to your artifact or you can draw new ones with different combinations of future, past, and present histories.

2. As the days go by, see if Sankofa inspires you to write a poem, a short story, or a song; create a collage; take a photo; or undertake any other creative means of expression. Note if any ideas come to you.

# 4

# THE CRY OF JAZZ

## Unlimited Musical Improvisation in Limiting Places

CREATIVITY IS FREEDOM. The ability to take an idea from the realm of the invisible and into the physical is a high-consciousness activity. The old adage of changing lemons into lemonade highlights the resourcefulness creativity sparks. Creativity is a lifeline, a reservoir of life sustaining ideas. For creators who have societal limitations placed upon them, creativity can be a lifesaving practice, one that helps them break free of inhumane restrictions or self-imposed ones. For some Black creators, societal barriers have been both a resistance to their humanity and a wall to access and resources. The societal barriers, often invisible, were also a block to connecting deeply with one's experience of freedom and a barrier to connecting to an African worldview.

Sometimes, the quest for freedom through creativity takes one into the celestial realms of philosophical matters or Earthly matters beyond the familiar. Other times it ushers us into a holistic African perspective that in our day-to-day lives is undervalued or that we aren't overtly allowed to explore. Oftentimes, those who pursue these creative paths are guided to both. The new world, the celestial, and the African (which could also be celestial) are foundations for connecting broader ideas about life and the universe. The creative processes we explore to create the songs or art are also soul journeys in tackling mental and emotional obstacles. There are lessons in these quests that have produced some of the greatest music, literature, or art of our time, often created under duress and under the guise of low expectations. The very works themselves sometimes assert the artist's humanity in spaces where such a claim was viewed as threatening the order of things. Such works challenge convention not for the sake of coming-of-age rebellion but to level walls of ignorance, fear, and hierarchy. Leveling the walls was an act of expansion. Such works created room, in real time, for artists to create and operate from a space of being. In this space of creating, the artist could feel purely free. This feeling or experience informed their life, and lives of those who keep open minds when engaging with the works.

Many of us work through invisible societal barriers that prevent us from connecting to life-sustaining ideas that aren't squarely Western or acceptable. We push past barriers that push against us being our highest vision of ourselves. Many of us feel uncomfortable exploring sides of ourselves that don't evenly line up with what we're told leads to upward mobility. Many artists work through these ideas daily. There are life lessons to glean from their process and insights. You don't have to be an artist to build from their wisdom.

*The Cry of Jazz* is a groundbreaking 1959 film by director Edward Bland that features jazz icon Sun Ra and was shot in Chicago's South Side jazz scene. The story centers around a conversation about the nature of jazz. Bland, who also stars in the film, is most known for declaring that jazz is dead. But what gets lost is why Bland makes this declaration. Bland thinks of jazz as a societal mirror. His point isn't that jazz as an astute art form has run its course, but rather that the music is a symbol of Black people improvising a life within the limiting parameters of society's ideas about race. Jazz, according to Bland, is an art form born of navigating spaces of limitation. As societal barriers fall, the form of jazz will necessarily change.

"Melodic improvisation and rhythm conflict are the joyful freeing and present oriented aspects of jazz," he states in the film. "While form and changes [in jazz music] are the suffering, restraining and futureless aspects of jazz." According to Bland, jazz is a commentary on the limitations of the liminal space.

"Denied a future, the joyous celebration of the present is the Negro's answer to America's ceaseless attempts to obliterate it. Jazz is a musical expression of the Negro's eternal re-creation of the present." Bland continues, "Negro life as created through jazz is a contradiction between worship of the present, freedom, and joy, and the realization of the futureless future, restraint, and suffering which the American way of life has bestowed upon the Negro."

The more access the culture has to live beyond these parameters, the more likely the music will change and reflect new freedoms in society. Parameters will be obliterated. "Jazz is dead because the restraints and suffering of American life on the Negro have to die. The spirit of jazz is alive because the Negro spirit must endure." He further adds that jazz is a "transport of joy," like a spaceship or time travel device.

"Through melodic improvisation and the ever-present contradiction in rhythm, the Negro makes an art form that insists on the deification of the present and which, among other things, is an unconscious holding action until he has also master of his future."

Jazz came of age in a segregated, pre–Black Power America and unfolded as a spirit-seeking freedom of expression in a limited space. Jazz as a statement of the present condition, according to Bland, could not "make space" for a future. Although some may debate this, I'm most interested in Bland's use of jazz as a metaphor for a life force that creates beauty in finite spaces.

Bland's commentary about the creative spirit as resilience is compelling: "The Negro, or jazzman, must be constantly creative because that is how he remains free. Otherwise, the dehumanizing portrait America has drawn of him will triumph." He adds, "The jazz body is dead but the jazz spirit is alive." This sense of limitation in form as reflective of society may be why culture critics such as Amiri Baraka were champions of late 1960s experimental jazz by Ornette Coleman, Horace Tapscott, Cecil Taylor, Sonny Sharrock, Archie Shepp, Sunny Murray, Marion Brown, Phil Cohran, Sun Ra and more. These musicians wanted to break form, and doing so required that they embrace an African orientation or Africanized abstraction. What some called accommodationist was really a fighting within form which reflected limitations on how Black people could move and be in society.

This new era of jazz, circa 1968, was viewed as revolutionary music by the writers of the *Cricket*, a jazz-specific culture journal by Black writers. "The new Black music sees the future, it is the future of what we will be," writes Roger Riggins.[1] Critic Norman Jordan suggests that the future music must contain "a positive harmony on the physical, mental, and spiritual level."[2]

In the essay "Trippin': A Need for Change," writer Mtume says that Black musicians desiring to make future music must "be the antennae which receives the visions of a better life and time and transmit those visions to concrete realities through the use of sound and substance."[3]

While Bland speaks of an era of jazz reflecting a quest for freedom, Mwata Bowden notes that it's also a bursting forth of Africanized expressions. Bowden, former president of the Association for the Advancement of Creative Musicians (AACM), a jazz collective that had been cofounded by, among others, Sun Ra band member Phil Cohran, adds that the notes in jazz "go after those sounds in our African heritage. We bend and reshape notes along the way. We look for the sound that imitates a quarter tone." Even the evolution of jazz was an outgrowth, or a quest, to echo African sounds through musical parameters that weren't designed to allot for whole sonic worlds, thus forming a new one.

Connecting with the music of creators in African/African Diasporic cultures is essential in understanding Afrofuturism as a space/time experience. Some of this music is described in the context of Afrofuturism for its mind-expanding properties. The experience of listening in contemplation or living with the music as you go about your day unlocks insights when you have an open mind.

## Reflection Questions

Sometimes we find ourselves in spaces that feel limiting. The spirit of jazz is about finding ways to move within limitation but also breaking form.

1. Is there a space or place you're in that limits your ability to express yourself? Perhaps it's your place of work, a relative's home, or a classroom. Why do you feel limited in your expression? What do you do to alleviate feelings of limitations?
2. Can you think of times in your life when a set of limitations compelled you to be more creative in your problem-solving or art making? What did you do or create?

## Exercise: Jazz Immersion

We can all enjoy music for its great rhythms and melody. Music evokes emotion and can elevate and shift a mood. However, providing context around ideas explored when listening to a song can provide other space/time connections. Each song listed here was recorded before 1959, when *The Cry of Jazz* was produced. The reigning sound in jazz was bebop, a fresh modernist music approach at its apex.

*A Love Supreme*, John Coltrane's most popular album, is known for its musical circle of fifths. Coltrane's approach to music has been compared to Albert Einstein's approach to physics for its mathematical acumen. Coltrane aspired to connect with music's spiritual evolutionary potential. Ornette Coleman is among the great jazz innovators of free jazz, a controversial art form at the onset. His album *The Shape of Jazz to Come* is a predecessor to free jazz.

Coltrane, Coleman, and Clark were at the cusp of a change in music, one they would facilitate. Part of this change was a stretching of time and space dynamics to experience a freedom—or reach for one. This music also aligns with an acceleration in the American civil rights movement. As you listen to the songs, think about the stretching of space and time. Think of this musical acumen, with the alternating quick tempos, as a metaphor for people navigating shifting spaces, sometimes finite, while maximizing joy and finding self. Jot down any thoughts that come to mind.

1. Listen to one of the following (or all of them):
   *A Love Supreme* by John Coltrane
   "The Sphinx" by Ornette Coleman
   "Be-Bop" by the Sonny Clark Trio
2. The songs listed here are part of the free jazz experience. Listen to the songs. Each artist listed was celebrated by the *Cricket* for creating futures music. Each song was produced between 1968 and '69 when *Cricket* writers were exploring the notion of music as a future. Think about the scope of expansiveness. How does this music make you feel? Think of this music as the soundtrack or gateway to a future. Is it a gateway or future itself? How does it differ from bebop? What comes to mind? Do you have any thoughts of living life creatively?
   "Sound Gravitation" by Ornette Coleman
   "Bialero" by Sonny Sharrock with vocals by Linda Sharrock
   "Anthem to Eternity" by Charles Gayle
   "In Light of Blackness" by the Black Unity Trio
3. Watch the short film *The Cry of Jazz* and note the Sun Ra cameo. It's wonderous!

# 5

# SPACE IS THE PLACE

## Sun Ra and the Space of the Mind

SUN RA'S MISSION was to keep people of Earth in a high vibrational space. He aimed to do this through music and poetics. You can't be an Afrofuturist and *not* engage with the space/time ethos of Sun Ra. Sun Ra, born Herman Poole Blount, was one of the most future-forward musician philosophers of his time and ours. The nature of space in Sun Ra's world is multifaceted. His album *Space Is the Place* is a crash course in merging African/African Diasporic relationships to space as being potential and reality. A music deity, he was committed to exploring and to living with this awareness as practice. His life's work undergirds Afrofuturist reasoning. In a single album, he demonstrates how expansive the spaces we traverse can be. So, for this section, listening to the *Space Is the Place* album is a must. There's a movie that goes along with the album that brings Sun Ra's visuals to life. However, for the sake of this section, I'd suggest listening to the album first. The ride is all sonic ebullience. As we move forward we will think about the spaces we create, share, and abide in along with how they inform our scope of possibility and futures.

Sun Ra left Birmingham, Alabama, at a young age and eventually came to Chicago in the 1940s, abiding in the Washington Park neighborhood where he, along with entrepreneur Alton Abraham, developed theories on music, space, and identity. At some point early in his career as a pianist and bandleader, he had an experience that would come to change his life. Sun Ra had what could equally be an alien abduction or a spiritual conversion wherein he realized that the alienness he felt on Earth was due to his Saturn origins. He was on Earth with a mission. He joined the Thmei study group, founded by Abraham, to read ancient text, write new ones, and reimagine Black futures with music. He aimed to elevate consciousness with music.

Adopting the name of the Egyptian sun god, Ra, Sun Ra assembled a band to explore music's healing abilities and teleporting frequencies. He was among the first to use electronic elements and African instruments in jazz. He'd create a catalog of music that explored the outer realms, bringing us space utopias with wisdom of ancient Egypt. His penchant for pushing musical conventions and asserting other realities and free spaces for Black people beyond the stratosphere made him a unique figure in the Black Arts Movement and an admired one in the jazz world. But his albums were not just for entertainment, they were shapeshifting guides he believed would lead to self-liberation, a freedom he uncovered through community. His insights channeled a novel path of being and viewing the world, a path out of the limitations society placed upon him, to become a sun god avatar.

*Space Is the Place* is his most popular album. Although the title song of the same name is a swinging jazz tune, the album, created in 1973, doubles as the sound track for the takeoff and arrival, euphoria and inner conflict, of embarking on a "space" journey. The opus, an experimental blend of bebop, early electronics, African percussion, and space jazz, includes an invitation to join Sun Ra and his enriching Arkestra in the great space ways. There's a song with talking planets, an homage to Ancient Egypt, and soliloquies of life-inspired proverbs for those not ready to take the journey. Sun Ra is certain to capture the excitement, joy, and uncertainty of a sojourn through the cosmos. But any casual listen to the album will reveal that the musical deity, who claims Saturn as his ancestral home, is not merely talking about space.

What begins as an operatic saga to a far-off planet quickly shifts into a shamanistic journey, because space is not merely "a place." The first thought that comes to mind when hearing the chorus to the song "Space Is the Place" is that this is Sun Ra's jazz, hepcat speak for saying that the realms beyond Earth's stratosphere are cool. Space is swank like the best after-work spot to slide through or the island vacation to save up for. Therefore, space is the place to be.

But when I was asked to write the liner notes for the album's reissue by Modern Harmonic in 2023, I noticed another temperament in the title and song of the same name that served as the album's challenge to humankind. If space is the place to be, why aren't you there? Why aren't you where you're supposed to be?

The album title's assertion is an afront to the ego. But it quickly becomes clear that space may not be a destination only. There is a stature in life, one more closely aligned with how we see ourselves, that we have not attained. Space, in this inference, is not just a location, but a reimagined self. Space doubles as a state of mind. This state of mind is its own consciousness, a realm of perception achieved with intention and desire. I desire to experience peace, regardless of whether dynamics in my life are conducive to this state. The desire to experience peace is an intention that, once achieved, shifts my perception of the occurrences around me. This state of peace is experienced regardless of immediate events and is projected outward. How does one unfold into a new level of consciousness? The mystics of the world have presented ideas on the matter for centuries. However, Sun Ra believed that the high vibrations and intentions in music can facilitate the shifting from one state of consciousness to a preferred one. For that matter, he encourages us to be aware of the who, what, and whys around the spaces we abide in. So, when Sun Ra says that space is the place, he also means that an elated state of consciousness is the ideal way to experience or overcome the challenges of the world.

## Why Aren't You in "Space"?

There are some grounded reasons to explain why we aren't in outer space. Space flight isn't a norm—yet. Sun Ra's open invitation is complicated by the fact that we don't have a space shuttle to get there. This musical sun deity is asking us to do the near impossible to get to this oh-so-cool place.

But even if you did get the space shuttle, flying ark, or stepped through a magic portal, where exactly are we going? Again, I think back to our map and the YOU ARE HERE arrow. Where in space, exactly, am I supposed to be? Outer space is infinite. Simply rocketing off past the atmosphere isn't enough. Is there a specific space in the outer realms that we're aiming for? If such a space is swinging, where exactly is it and how do I get there?

But if the space Sun Ra is referring to is a state of mind, one where we express our highest potential, then saying that we should *be* at this exalted state poses some internal reflection. I can explain why I'm not in outer space with basic science. I know that I don't know where "there" is. But addressing why I may not be living as my highest self is another question altogether. Why aren't we shifting emotionally, physically, or mentally to a space that brings us joy? Do we feel that a state of exaltation is off limits for us?

But the album doesn't seek to answer whether space is a physical space or a higher state of consciousness at the onset. Instead, Sun Ra and his Arkestra assert that you, one who is squarely planted on Earth, are not "when" you think you are. "It's after the end of the world, don't you know that yet?" soloist June Tyson sings as the album's intro.

In the previous section, we introduced the interruption as apocalypse narrative, one that happened many moons ago. But

Sun Ra's revelation, minus this prep, is jarring nonetheless. No, Sun Ra and June, we are not wholly conscious of that reality.

This shifting of space is one that many Afrofuturist artists explore because it mirrors our human desire to have agency in the day-to-day spaces we inhabit and to live freely. Sometimes we seek to break free to emotional spaces that bind. In the same way that we questioned what nature of space Sun Ra is talking about, we can think of Prince's wondrous ode to lavender rainfall. "Purple Rain" is a song sweeping in emotion. Feelings of longing, nostalgia, and wonderment underpin the deep guitar chords. This emotion is a space itself.

In the song, Prince says he only wants to see the woman of his desire laughing in the purple rain. Taken literally, one can assume he's talking about a phenomenon in a physical location. There aren't too many natural effects that would give rain a purple glow. So, is Prince saying he never wants to see her again? Purple rain is an imagined phenomenon that, as far as we know, doesn't exist on Earth. Is Prince saying he only wants to see her in this imagined space or in his dreams?

Some argue that this is a breakup song, an ode to a woman who's chosen another partner. This is probable until Prince sings that his great love "wants a leader, but can't make up her mind." He then adds that he'll *guide her* to the purple rain. Is he ushering the woman out the door of his life or inviting her to embark on a journey in an imagined space?

This song reminds us of our own imagined spaces and their emotional wallings. What imagined spaces are we guided to? Which ones are rooted in love? As we rely on others to take us there, we uncover that it is we who must do the treading to this space of joy, one that may be a reach into our own soul and not necessarily a pairing with another.

Some say that the song is about unconditional love. Things aren't working out in the relationship, so Prince wants the woman to be happy. Purple is the color for the seventh Hindu chakra, an energy center seated in the center of our heads, the highest one before reaching ascension. She can only be at her happiest when she isn't with him, he says. In this sense, purple rain is a state of elevated consciousness achieved when the two former lovers are apart. So purple rain could be an imagined space, or the attainment of higher consciousness for the adored woman in question. Either way, it's an admission of moving on and self-love.

However, *American Songwriter* posits that the song is about reconciling with a loved one at the end of the world. It's poignant that the realization of self-love can feel like a world ender. This, much like Sun Ra's opus, isn't a question of what or where, but like Sun Ra's space/time quagmire, a question of when. In this case, it's not after the end of the world but just before the apocalypse. Prince has other apocalyptic narratives, most notably the song "1999," in which we were encouraged to party as if the world were ending. When do we claim this space of love? Before or after our shapeshift in purple bliss? Claiming joy, claiming love, reorders emotional space.

But this reminder about an end is also a launching pad for a new beginning, a shift in consciousness from one limited paradigm of how we view ourselves in the world to a more expansive view rich in possibility. Shifting from one space to another, physical and emotional, is a marker of change that can be difficult. But some shifts are essential in finding our happiness. Some people may not be able to tag along for the journey. Everyone, as Sun Ra will remind us, isn't ready for the ride.

## The Me in Space

You don't have to be a music icon or a mystic to have a poetic relationship with space. Our fluidity between digital, lived, and dreamed spaces is increasingly routine. Occupying multiple spaces is something we do effortlessly all the time. For example, at the moment of this writing, I am in an airport. I am physically in an airport in Chicago. I just finished eating a cupcake. I just spoke on the phone to a friend in L.A. and an astrophysicist in New Hampshire. In those moments of conversation, we are in a shared space, an audible one, not virtual. I have family who are simultaneously heading off to a wedding in Atlanta. I am in text conversation with them. We are in a shared space, arguably virtual. I'm not at the wedding party, but I am there in spirit with very clear images of what I think the wedding reception ballroom looks like. I could be wrong. But I can see myself, enjoying this space, although I am not there.

I am on my way to New York City. Shortly, I will be in a plane, flying across states. I am in the plane, although not technically in the states I'm flying over. I am thinking about what I will be doing when I land. I see myself in NYC hanging out with a friend.

Where am I? Physically, I'm in Chicago. However, my thoughts and those I'm communing with are in multiple spaces across the country. Although my thought isn't a tangible entity walking around my future New York, there is a part of me that's engaged with a future space where I will soon be, and a part of me that is imagining myself at the wedding reception where I will not be, and another part of me that's in the in-between phone space with people I'm chatting with. Where am I? All over the place.

For me, this isn't a question of where am I physically. Unlike the YOU ARE HERE, I know where I am. I know where I'm going. I know how I'm going to get there. I know where I'm currently sitting—in a chilly airport where I'm wearing a thick black hood to keep my ears from freezing. But these spaces beyond the physical are real ones that I also experience. Some are imagined, but these imaginings are not the worldbuilding we associate with fantasy and storytelling. The cities I'm imagining, I'm familiar with, although the locations I'm imaging are new for me, too. These imaginings aren't fantastic, but are rather ordinary day-to-day interactions.

In this example, it's not so much a reality of where I am but how I experience these spaces, however brief, often overlapping in the span of a few minutes. The common denominator in all of them is me. I become centered in my own world of images and communication. Collectively—the freezing airport, the wedding reception dance floor, the red-hued lounge with my gal pal, the voices in a phone call—these are shared spaces. Collectively, these spaces can conflict or align, but they are in conversation with one another, with me as the intersection. These spaces, all of which I occupy, inform me. Individually they inform me and as a neat fractal of puzzle pieces they inform me. Collectively, they can be a moment, unique to itself.

The feelings we have in these multitude of spaces can be spaces, too. I think of these gliding spaces as concentric circles, often overlapping. A song about love can put you in the emotional space of yearning romanticism. A song can spark a memory, a fantasy, or send you on a journey. An activity can put you in a space. A bike ride can dig up feelings of freedom or adventure.

Throughout the day, this web of overlapping spaces shifts physically, virtually, musically, emotionally, and imaginatively. Some we spend more time in than others. Some we are more actively engaged in than others. Some we are more conscious of than others. However, together, they form a map. There are imagined spaces that we occupy. There are spaces on Earth that we all occupy. And there's a way that we see ourselves in the space.

Oftentimes, when a person is in a physical space they'd rather not be in, they lean on imagined or nonphysical spaces for refresh, escape, levity, or to be informed. All of these spaces can impact how we engage in our physical spaces. If I experience empowerment in envisioning arriving in my destination, that feeling changes how I feel about waiting for hours in an airport. A phone call to a friend during which we're analyzing a think piece can make an annoying wait a purposeful one. In this sense, these nonphysical day-to-day spaces we occupy change how we engage and experience our physical space.

Ever think about the things you have to do for the day and feel tired? Ever think about the vacation you've planned and get excited? In these instances, we've sailed to these spaces and those feelings changed us in real time. It's always a good idea to be aware of what spaces we choose to be in, even if they're in our mind, and have an awareness as to why we are there and how we feel. This awareness is a reminder of our agency. If we don't like a space we're in, a mental or emotional space, we can acknowledge so and choose to shift, move, or adapt. We don't have to be anchored to the emotional resonance of a space, physical or otherwise. If we're in a dynamic we can't leave physically, we can shift mentally and emotionally. When I'm sitting in an airport imagining a wedding, I am conscious of the wedding space, not my immediate surroundings. My mind is not present, and one could reason that my lack of present awareness is akin to me not being there. My emotions from this imagined space remain when I shift my awareness back to the airport. I bring the emotion with me.

Imagined spaces can be a form of release, escape, refreshment, and curiosity. However, these feelings in such spaces are not fictive. We experience them. These feelings can be indicators of an action we may need to take. If I'm imagining a wedding I can't attend, enjoying the glow of family fun and wishing I was there, perhaps I need to reach out to family upon my return or be sure to attend the next family function, or prioritize them more. If thinking about all the tough work I need to do makes me feel tired, maybe I need to reorganize how I want to approach it. Perhaps I can break the work up and add refresh interludes. Maybe I need help and shouldn't do it alone. Perhaps the task is one I need to rework so that I find some joy in it. Or maybe it's a big hint that a career shift is necessary. This emotion experienced in an imagined or projected space is a means of interrogating a future action.

Nevertheless, the emotions we feel in these projected future spaces, physical and otherwise, are revealing. We don't have to stay in these emotional spaces, but we do need to acknowledge and build from the insight. If you find yourself in physical spaces that make you angry, or emotional spaces that rehash guilt, shift first, and then take in the lesson. Create or claim a space that brings joy, imagined or otherwise, and anchor that joy in your physical present as a state or awareness that exists regardless of the space around you. Bring the emotion with you to the physical reality. The goal is to keep us in a high vibrational frequency.

Music is one way to assist on this journey. Shaman Malidoma Patrice Somé writes of all work on chores in Burkina Faso being accompanied by music. "Music is meant to maintain a certain state of fullness," he writes.[1] He adds that this sense of fullness is abundance and takes away worry. Just as we note the troubling feelings, we should also take in the spaces that bring us joy, be aware of those elements like music or other experiences that enrich it, and spend more time abiding there.

It's this ability to shift space, choosing to abide in spaces that bring joy, or bringing joy and peace with us from an imagined space to the physical, that Sun Ra views as a celestial ability.

## Place in Space

In *Space Is the Place*, Sun Ra chastises Earth: "Everything is in its place except you, Earth," noting that our planet and its residents must make serious changes for us to realize our fullest potential. Space is the place, the phrase and the album, obliterates boundaries. The word *place* is very loaded. When one is told to "get in place," a hierarchal order, one that doles out access based on how high one is in that order, comes to mind. To "stay in one's place" can mean one shouldn't aspire to much. To "get in place" infers that one is the odd one out or not conforming to an assumed order. That said, when Sun Ra says that space is the place we should get into, he is placing us in an environment with no known boundaries, free of being confined and fitting in. In boundless space, one can take up as much space as they like.

We, too, may feel that there is a place we are supposed to be, a stature in life that we are expected to attain, or an expectation not in line with our soul's desires that we are to meet. Such pressures may order our steps in a direction we don't want to go. What can feel like a pragmatic decision to fit in chips away at our very being each day. Conformity can become a value of diminishing returns, with rewards that never address our soul needs. Sun Ra's work implies that there is another way—a destined order of things where who we are is in concert with the celestial web of life. Our uniqueness in this universe of worlds is invaluable in achieving the harmony that keeps our Earth on course. We each play a role. It may not be Earth and its populace that's not aligned with its destiny, but us who are not expressing the fullness we desire. Chastising Earth about not being in its place is a reminder that we, too, are unique beings working in concert with a celestial community that needs our contributions. The larger universe requires us to "be in place," for we are supported by a greater cosmic arrangement that's dependent on us finding value experiencing the fullness that keeps our vibrations high.

In short, Sun Ra's space/time quagmire is the following: You are not where you are supposed to be, neither the space utopia of your free dreams, nor the grand cosmos. You are reconciling with the reality that you exist long after the apocalypse. Furthermore, you have placed yourself in or are abiding in the equivalent of a box, a limited space of existence, one whose frameworks must be shattered, if you are to go on to travel the great spaceways and occupy the space of joy as "your highest self."

All of this is supposed to explain, in part, the surreal nature of contemporary Earth life. You, like Sun Ra, are a walking myth, he says. This walking myth runs parallel to the "Afrosurreal Manifesto" and its take on the hazy nature of the present. However, being a myth does not mean you aren't real (although Sun Ra did tell a group of teens so in his film), but rather that you may not be real with yourself regarding the freedom and joy you want to experience. Sun Ra's mythmaking reminds us that we are an architect in a story of our lives. On the other hand, if we think of Afropantheology, and the spiritual world intertwined with ours according to many African spiritual principles, then being a myth takes on a multidimensional temperament. You are more than you think you are and have the capacity to be more, as most myths indicate.

We should aim to be conscious of this creation and space shifting to create freedoms and experience fullness. Either you're celestial or you aren't. Either you have a purpose or are on a journey to discover one. Although you don't have to name yourself after a celestial god, you may have to step out of limitations you've been socialized into so that you can be in place. Your work, words, and actions have impact beyond the day to day. People are affected by the things you say and do; they carry it forward. This impact, big or small, shifts the celestial web of life. This means there is some responsibility that comes with the things we say and do. Not too dissimilar from the classic deities of our stories and spiritual pantheons, we do have impact in our spheres of influence and possibly beyond. We don't just occupy space, we shape it. We define it.

Sun Ra's space-time quagmire is the rabbit hole. This classic disorientation is one that many Afrofuturist works pose. The unveiling isn't one to be feared but one to embrace in anticipation of the great cosmic journey to come. Sun Ra synthesizes these messages all before a listener gets to track two.

## The Alter-Destiny

Space, to Sun Ra, is a land of many faces. The philosopher/musician is adept at flipping the nature of space. In one song we're invited to go on the great spaceways, heading to a destination that we assume is a physical one. Perhaps we'll go to Saturn, where we can live in the alter-destiny. Arkestra chanteuse Tyson sings that the alter-destiny is "a place that's really free. There's no limit to the things that you can do."

Sun Ra adds an extra left turn in our understanding. He also proclaims that *he* is the travelers' destination. "I am the Alter-Destiny, the presence of the living myth," he says. Being or existence becomes space, an imagined space of utopic dreams that Sun Ra asserts with imagination, pageantry, and belief. We, too, are the destinations we aim to reach. We are the potential of the dream. We are the dream in manifestation. So, if you go back to your map, you are reminded that there is a journey that brought you to this space. You have arrived at a destination before you began. Perhaps the place you are looking for, the peace you seek, the future you desire, you are anchored in the seedlings of. This implies that the alter-destiny isn't so much a where but a "we" or a "be," symbolic of a state to evolve to or an embodied state to become.

If we, like Sun Ra, can become "the space to be," then as the alter-destiny we are both place and arrival point. If the destination is higher consciousness, then one could achieve that state, physically, right where they are. So the travel through the spaceways is an existential one, us soaring through the concaves of our soul. In essence, we are the potential of that we wish to become.

This archetype for freedom is a common one. In "Purple Rain," Prince switches from being a human talking to his great love to being a deity (again, I'm thinking of Sun Ra). As this deity, he ushers the woman and others who follow from one world to the next. This trek is a shift in consciousness.

But Sun Ra's *Space Is the Place* as blueprint is not through with us yet. In the song "I Am the Brother of the Wind" the musical deity morphs into the elements of air that sustain life as we know it—the same elements that occupy livable spaces. "You cannot breathe without the wind," he reminds us. This self-evolution, this experience of joy, is fostered by being in community with people and nature. In our shifts and evolutions we must make time to connect with nature. How often in our shift from one space to the next do we overlook the miracles of a sunrise, the changing leaves, or a fresh rain? Our ambitions can take us through many worlds, but we must take time for nature's beauty for it, much like music, adds the fullness of our experience. Nature is life sustaining. Communing with nature, thinking of ourselves as being in community with the elements, trees, lakes, rocks, and rivers around us reminds us of a presence that is always rejuvenating.

In counting, Sun Ra identifies space as three states of existence: a physical location beyond Earth's atmosphere, a metaphysical one, and an element. As the album nears completion, this place to be shifts again. The space to be is also in Earth's past. Again, we are reminded of Sankofa. Sun Ra redirects us to Ancient Egypt or Kemet. As the album concludes and we're seemingly zapped back to Earth's present, listeners are addressed as if they hadn't just sailed through the cosmos at all. "In some far-off place, be like years in space, we'll wait for you," sings Tyson in an ode to those who aren't willing to embark. The Arkestra and friends will build a world. The alter-destiny is one to be created. We create our alter-destiny, sailing through points of awareness, as we evolve to who we truly are in harmony with a life-sustaining community.

## Reflection Questions

1. Afrofuturists think of experiencing space in a multitude of ways. A single location can metaphorically occupy many spaces. What ideas come to you as you think about a single space being experienced in many facets? Does this idea feel empowering? Uncomfortable? Jot down your thoughts and feelings.
2. Can you think of other songs, stories, works, or your own experiences of space where locations have multiple meanings?
3. What does joy as a space look or feel like for you?

## Exercise: Your Space Is Your Place

1. Reflect on the spaces you engaged with today. List all that you can.
   - Physical spaces
   - Phone calls
   - Virtual spaces
   - Imagined spaces
   - Thought spaces
   - Story spaces
   - Music spaces
   - Emotional spaces

   If any other spaces come to mind, list those, too. These spaces are a fabric of your world.

2. Jot down any feelings you have about this snapshot. This world can change.

3. Follow up later to reflect on these spaces:
   - Which space was a conscious choice?
   - Which space would you like to return to, imagined or physically?
   - Which space would you rather not engage?
   - How would you describe your ideal alter-destiny?

# 6

# SONIC COMMUNITY AND BEING THE SPACE

## Shaping Community Spaces with Intention

I WAS A JUDGE FOR A DIGITAL AFROFUTURIST ART COMPETITION during the COVID-19 pandemic in 2020. The goal was to keep artists, some of whom were out of work, or creating in deep isolation, inspired. The artists were charged with creating idealized futures. A typical survey of futures art depicts people in some form of isolation—a lone spaceship or encampment, an astronaut researching the nature of space alone, a counterculture figure with asymmetrical hair and slick fashion standing in cool postures, facing the windy Martian sands by themselves.

But one of the greatest insights from the river of lessons of the year 2020 was our need for community. From the casual interactions with strangers in the grocery stores to the deep conversations with friends, our interactions reinforce connection. When we are not together, we become siloed, are easy targets for misinformation, and lean on a tendency to magnify fears. This showed up in most of the images created for the competition. Very funky futures people were depicted at parties, all kinds of parties—clubs, house parties, day parties, all-ages barbeques, dancerama skyscapes, DJs rocking worlds on other planets. One image depicted an uncle of the future manning a high-tech barbeque grill with an interstellar chef's hat, music pulsating in the background. Most of these celebrations centered music, family, and friends.

The greatest epiphanies are not only solo occurrences. Although there are paths to evolution that can come from withdrawing from culture, being in silence, or stepping away from the world, there are other ways of knowing that come from shared culture-making where music is an energy source, sound is a ground floor, and creating is access and a path to mastery. The sound can be thunderous: The voices loud, the art splashed across brick walls in rainbow colors, the dancing otherworldly, and the voices booming.

We form communities so that we can understand ourselves. We form community because we need one another to survive. Much of our identity, our approaches to life, and our scope of possibilities are formed in communion with others. Sound-centered communities with parties and cocreation as a modernized ritual are no different. They are ontologies, a way of knowing formed by sharing with others.

The Cape Coast School for the Deaf and Blind is known for their innovative practices in Ghana. Among their prized performance teams are their dancers. The dancers are hearing impaired. They perform highly complex, rhythmic routines backed by rows of towering drums—they can feel the bass and talking drums reverberating in their bodies. They can also feel one another. So, a sound that is not audible for them is one they can feel deeply enough to be in synch or in harmonic motion with those around them. This feeling of connection ushers in joy and deeper communion, along with a healthy dose of pride.

I'm excited by communities where sound, music, and creativity run at the core. I'm excited by spaces that believe that music and creativity are lifelines for communities at large and value the lessons and collective good that come out of such gatherings. I have a newfound appreciation for people who create such spaces. I think of Eric Williams, who hosted the long-running Silver Room Block Party in Chicago. In the beginning, Williams wanted to throw a customer appreciation party. His store sold eclectic jewelry that attracted a mix of artists. The store became a hangout spot for customers, so Williams assembled an annual party in the store's alley where the customers created the vibe. Some were DJs, others were painters, some had bands, some were entrepreneurs. As the customer base grew, so did the nature of the performances. The party moved from the alley to an empty lot and later a portion of the block the store was on. When the store moved from one side of town to the other, customers followed. As the customers matured and had kids, events for children were added. Until finally, Williams had a full-on street festival, still primarily composed of customers with three full stages, live painting, installations, vendors, and lots of dancing. Performers ranged from blues and gospel acts to cumbia, reggae, Black rock acts, tap dancing, African dance, and hip-hop, all culminating in a house music party with multiple DJ sets. The event grew to accommodate thousands of attendees. Although the initial desire was to launch a customer appreciation party, the joy that emanated spoke to something much larger—a need for shared creativity and community. For nearly twenty years, the collective was held together by a spirit of community (and a lot of organizing).

However, events like the Silver Room Block Party aren't just environments with good beats that people vibe to. There's an intention at play, an intention to create a space of joy and communion. The audience isn't just an audience. They are participants, too. Whether they are dancing on speakers or walking art scapes in body paint, they are joining in the spirit that music, creativity, and community matter.

Space is infinite. The intention shapes it in the imagined and physical world; how you show up in the physical space activates it. Creation is an individual and collective sojourn of shared energy with shared intention.

The spaces that evolve out of these musical communities allot for communal and individual expression. The DJ, MC, or primary performers are conduits for energy or help facilitate the exchange, but they are not the carriers or purveyors. In music communities, everyone plays a role in sustaining the intention. These roles are fluid, open, and reflect an exchange of shared energy, where no one person is the sole focal point for long. We are a part of a group, but we can be our own unique self within it. The interplay between the two has unique lessons for thinking about being in community and forming communities.

We are at a point in our world where stressing the value of real-life interactions is a new battle cry. Our social devices have become extensions of ourselves that can serve as valuable connectors across long distances, especially when people cannot be together physically. They are connectors for our disabled communities. They are also communication forms that frequently morph as we outpace algorithms trying to find one another in our desire to connect. However, the shared insights we gain from one another as we connect physically cannot be underestimated. Attending a party or a festival, or forming a cipher, creates spaces through which people connect with themselves and recognize their humanity in others.

## Sound as Dimension

The Asante Empire of what is now Ghana came into power in the 1700s. Known for their fighting prowess and multilayered culture, among their many beliefs was the power of sound. When the Asante went into battle or felt under threat by unsavory forces, they used the Asante horn. It was believed that this ivory horn was imbued with a spirit. When the horn was blown and the thunderous sound echoed, it did two things. For one, it created a protective barrier, or a "barrage of sound" around the community. Two, the sweeping sonics were a clearing, ushering the way for the ancestors to join. The combination of the thunderous wall of sound and the ancestral presence was a protective forcefield.

In this sense, sound was three-dimensional. This wall of sound was molding space. The horns' thunderous call shared intention. Although the wall was not a physical one, the intention and action served as a demarcation. The horn's roar created space, a safe space, while simultaneously fostering empowerment.

In sound cultures, the sound is both a foundation and a protector through which identity and ways of being are formed, values are shared, and guiding principles are centralized. Music cultures, in their highest form, can be joy generators, resources, with a sense of safety that binds us with others.

Just as space is multifaceted, sometimes visible and other times invisible, with varying emotions, the nature of the spaces created by sound can have an array of functions and create other spaces.

The music creates a space. The nature of the event where the music occurs is another space. Between these circles, an evolution occurs. The cocreation with the music forms a third space.

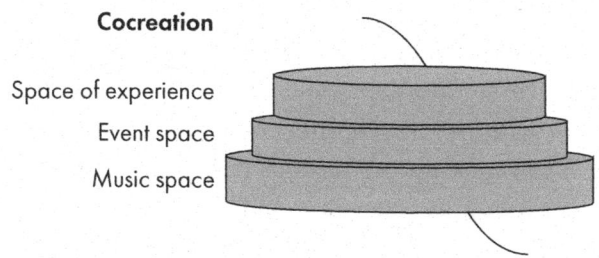

**Cocreation**

Space of experience
Event space
Music space

We are also constantly framing spaces, placing boundaries to restrict or expand movement, to shape engagement. The creation of a space of belonging begins in the mind first and is replicated outward.

Spaces can be created. We make our apartments homes by decorating them and entertaining. We make our events welcoming by offering snacks and playing music. Usually when creating a space there's a conscious intention. This intention refers to a reason for the affair or place, something we hope to achieve, a feeling or information we want those who partake to leave with. The space is usually created to address a need, one bigger than the initiators' own desires. This need becomes a theme that reflects a community need. The intention in the space dictates the space. How we show up in the space sets a tone as well.

A friend of mine often remarks that there's no community anymore. She feels that, generally, many people aren't in spaces that are neighborly or that value care among one another without monetizing interactions. I shared this with my mom once, a woman I'd describe as being a community shaper, and she said something that I now repeat often: "Either you're a community person or you're not." In other words, *you* bring community to the space. When you engage with those around you or find purpose or meaning in the space, the element of communing comes alive.

## Hip-Hop as Space

Hip-hop is a community formed foundationally by sound with intention. Those who align around it are part of the culture. Cultures are created spaces. Hip-hop, by and large, is a culture. Originally, if you took up the ways of rapping, deejaying, breaking, tagging, or B-boy fashion, you would become a part of this culture whose origins go to the Black and Brown communities of the Bronx in the late 1970s and early '80s. Kids, as always, were looking to define themselves. With music being stripped from schools and underinvestment in neighborhoods a prolonged norm, people like DJ Kool Herc used public parks and Jamaican sound system culture to bring people together with purpose, as an alternative to floundering in street life. DJs and others created spaces for people to express and channel their frustrations and joy.

KRS-One is one of hip-hop's legendary MCs. Born Lawrence "Kris" Parker, he hailed from the South Bronx, hip-hop's land of origin, and formed Boogie Down Productions in the early years of the genre's creation. As a teen he lived in a group home and later in a homeless shelter. But his love for hip-hop and tagging was the genesis of his quest to understand the mystical wisdom of the world. His interest in ancient texts and uncovering histories would become the subjects for his raps. Hip-hop saved his life.

Knowing the transformation that comes from speaking truth to power, KRS-One embarked on a mission of community uplift. He saw a need for the creativity that saved him to be prioritized in the culture. He advocated for the kind of empowerment that spawned his growth to be a core creative tool for all who participated. He was dubbed the "teacha," a moniker that works in concert with his acronym Knowledge Reigns Supreme Over Nearly Everyone. His spirited raps and work of building hip-hop as a "kulture" (the k in homage to Ancient Kemet) centered around education, love, community, and inspiration. In May 16, 2001, the United Nations, UNESCO, KRS-One, and a contingency of supporters declared that hip-hop was a world culture. This declaration was a major statement. There were still people debating whether hip-hop was an art form. How can a music born of samples, graffiti, dancing, and words from an underserved community become a global kulture?

In KRS-One's *Gospel of Hip Hop*, he writes about the philosophy of the hip-hop kulture. The book, published in 2009, is written in chapter and verse, much like the Christian Bible. He identifies hip-hop as a metaphysical principle. Metaphysical principles are tenets that frame or serve as guides in understanding the nature of reality. They interrogate space and time, identity, change, or possibility, often situating these ways of thinking as helpful ways to understand the universe. KRS-One, too, was thinking about hip-hop's ability to slice through space and time and build community.

It was a theory he'd lived. Making a special point to separate hip-hop history from the history of rap music entertainment, KRS-One goes on to describe hip-hop—not the industry but the kulture—as a syncretized kulture, a way of life with guiding principles. "For us real Hip Hop is a transformative power that has its beginnings at the genesis of human awareness." Acknowledging the griots as rappers and hieroglyphics as tagging, he adds that "Hip Hop is the return of the ancient ways, the healing ways, the natural ways, the way of God."[1]

In this sense, hip-hop is a kulture and a knowledge system that reclaims ancient practices for the postmodern era. "We are truly the return of an ancient people with the ancient skills rooted in the earliest experiences of human consciousness."

Sun Ra's community of musicians shaped the collective's beliefs on space and time by living and experimenting with music together. Just as Sun Ra expressed a way of breaking past limitations, KRS-One thinks of the joint community of hip-hop as serving the function of helping one another elevate consciousness as a collective. The wall of sound in hip-hop and the ways of participating in the kulture charge an energy, both ancestral and protective, like the Asante horn, that has the potential to shift our experience of reality.

However, KRS-One, much like Sun Ra, says that he is hip-hop, thus hip-hop being a higher state of consciousness, one achieved through the quest for knowledge and, in his case, the mastering of the MC craft. "I am Hip Hop and, in my time, I have mastered myself." He later says, "The fact that we create ourselves points to our divinity." He, too, like Prince and Sun Ra, compares hip-hop to $H_2O$, or water, symbolized by the two $H$s and the single $O$ in the genre's name. He further says that the $P$, as phosphorus, which when mixed with hydrogen and oxygen can create phosphoric acid that is used in fertilizer, is a metaphor for enriching the soul. Even the words *hip-hop* are the practice of breathing, "hip (inhale), hop (exhale), as an essence of life."

This kulture has property, nine elements he identifies as 1) Breaking, breakdancing, freestyle, or street dancing; 2) emceeing or rapping; 3) Graffiti art or tagging; 4) Deejaying; 5) Beatboxing; 6) Street fashion; 7) Street language or verbal communication; 8) Knowledge, elder wisdom; and 9) entrepreneurship. Conventional hip-hop only identifies five (dance, emceeing, graffiti art, deejaying, street fashion). I've read of others who suggest comics. I, personally, would add hip-hop journalism. However, in KRS-One's philosophy he reminds us that while there are many ways to participate in a community, ideally no one way is higher on the hierarchy scale than the other. Yet, music is the glue.

As such, hip-hop is a sovereign nation. "We (Hip Hop) have a unique opportunity to join the World's peace process and establish the sovereignty our parents envisioned without violence and war," he writes. He identifies hip-hop as a culture, a nation, an element, a higher state of consciousness, a way of being with the aim of self-mastery. Hip-hop becomes a "sovereign space" in community with those of like minds. However, KRS-One doesn't talk about the kulture as destination, one to hop a sky arc to. He speaks of hip-hop as a living, breathing nation abiding in the present, a kulture with no geopolitical boundaries.

I think of the word *sovereign* in this instance not purely as a self-governing one but also as a reminder that communal spaces can be self-sustaining. Does the space meet the needs of the community and is it flexible enough to adapt while staying true to the theme? The Silver Room Block Party was amenable to expanding physical space and accommodating anyone who was in the spirit of the community. The participants were accommodating and had a nonjudgmental temperament. As we create spaces with intentions, are we open to how that intention expresses itself? Are we open to cocreation established with intention?

This idea of music with intention building a nation that celebrates peace can be thought of as a real-time creation of Sun Ra's alter-destiny; culture and principle evolving from thinking of sound as a three-dimensional entity, a possible protective space; a space that generates space and transformation.

## House Nation

House music, much like hip-hop, spoke of itself as a nation in its early years. The genre, spawned by Frankie Knuckles's arrival to Chicago, was named after the club, Warehouse, where Knuckles fortified his blending dance euphoria in 1977. The House Master Boyz and the Rude Boy of House's "House Nation" was one of the genre's early classics. It underscored that the nation was spawned by people who cherished community, the music, and freedom. But in house, the method for elevation, or self-mastery as KRS-One would say, was the spirit of dance.

As the music industry turned away from disco, DJs began looping soulful R&B and adding quick tempo tracks to the melody, creating a new sound to replace the old. Initially, the scene was a haven for queer people looking for spaces to be themselves. The new sound then became the backdrop for the competitive ballroom scenes detailed in documentaries such as *Paris Is Burning* and dramas such as *Pose*. It also became the music du jour for a frenetic youth scene. As the music quickly expanded, house became a unique space of connectivity through dance and love of the spirit of the music and the freedom to simply be.

Techno, Detroit's reigning sound after Motown, is neither a world nor culture but rather a technology to transport one to a future space, writes techno producer/writer DeForrest Brown Jr. It calls to mind the way that Bland spoke of jazz as a transport, too. Techno music can double as both the soundtrack to a future world and the gateway to get there. When Afrofuturistic artist Abdul Qadim Haqq designed the cover of Brown's *Assembling a Black Counter Culture*, a book about techno culture, he did so with the understanding that techno is an advanced vibrational technology. Just as George Clinton of Parliament-Funkadelic spoke of funk as life force, techno views its reigning sound as an application of a science of music that induces futures, disrupting one world in the formation of another. In fact, early creators said that techno would infect the world much like a virus in a mainframe, a term that doesn't go over as well these days. Although techno lovers didn't think of themselves as a nation, they did think of their music as the soundtrack of a future world. I think of the Asante barrage of sound, in this case as both carving out a future and serving as transports to it. Whereas the Asante horn called the ancestors from one realm, perhaps the techno sound ushers us to another.

Both house and techno genres centered around the DJ and extensive hours of music play. The DJ becomes a musical shaman, a conduit for the flow of life force energy coming from music. This life force seals the space. The appeal of sound communities is the revelry and community. The sound itself shifts time. The feelings of joy, traveling to new worlds, and escape are a function of the music and the towering speakers it pours through. This sound shift sometimes induces a trance. When I spoke with King Britt, a DJ/producer who now teaches Blacktronika, a course on the contributions of Black creators to digitally created music for University of California San Diego, says that DJs are storytellers who transcend time. "My longest set was thirteen hours in Japan and I could've gone another five hours," he said. House innovators such as Frankie Knuckles, Tony Humphries, and Larry Levan all often played twenty-hour sets. That's what made them so great. "When you spin, you put yourself in a trance," said Britt. "As a DJ, you're a storyteller, and it's an endless story that you're weaving."

The spirits of hip-hop, house, and traditional African rhythms are threaded through South African amapiano and the Botswana house kwassa scene. Events from Everyday People day dance parties to the Chosen Few picnics are among those that celebrate the culture. DJs including Black Coffee, DJ Moma, DJ Reborn, DJ Rae Chardonnay, DJ Honey Dijon, DJ Hard Hittin Harry, DJ Duane

Powell, DJs Lady D. & Ron Carroll, and so many others continue to build community with house.

I think Afrofuturism, as a community-centric lens, isn't so much about the individual expanding their aura, a tactic that some energy writers suggest, but about the individual being aware of communing and bringing that idea of community with them. In aura expansion exercises, one imagines themselves with a ring of love surrounding them or within them that expands out. However, in music-centered communities, the awareness of communing is accentuated with the music. The connection to the music charges the energy. Our task is to be present and aware of shared connectivity and to share like-minded energy. Bringing community to a space doesn't mean literally bringing friends and family (although you can do that, too), but rather there is a sense of bringing a conscious recognition of shared humanity with you. Recognize that when you show up, you are in a relationship with the people, Earth, ancestors, and those who share your intention in the space. This sense of communing projects outward. Yet you are also receptive to the sharing of energy. If this was an old cartoon, you'd have antennae on your head, receiving transmissions and sending them out. This sharing of energy approach doesn't mean that when you show up, everyone's your friend, but it does mean that you acknowledge you are sharing space. Perhaps you are also sharing space with those who valued community in that space in the past or will in future times. You are, in one sense, communing with that spirit of community, even if no one speaks to you. You, by bringing community with you, by acknowledging you are sharing a space with others, activate the space.

Activating a space is an intention that you set in a space. Generally, event creators have a mission they want to achieve, one that sets the tone for the affair. However, you, being your own ball of energy, activate a space by having an intention and serve as a receptor for how you would like to experience the space. Broadly, you may say that you would like to dance and enjoy yourself—that intention gives you some direction as you stay open to how joy can express itself. The challenge is that people can step into a space with no intention, or they dillydally without being receptive. I have to note that being an observer is not the same as being present in community. The balance between the two is a circus act. If you have no intention, you can blow in the wind of the direction of the one who has the strongest intention, which may not be aligned with your own. If you are not receptive, you cut yourself off from the enriching experiences that are unique to the space.

In this dance of energy in motion that communities become, you recognize that this space is part of a human family of unique people. I like to think of myself and others as being in that space for a high vibrational reason. If there's music in the space, it likely charges the energy, so be aware of your emotions when you are in community with others. Stay aware of the feelings you are bringing into the space and the feelings you are taking on from those around you.

There's a great deal of conversation about creating space. I understand the intention of crafting a space where conformity isn't a norm and care is preeminent. Afrofuturists create spaces, from comic cons to art shows, all the time. Sometimes I hear people talk about creating space as if you somehow aren't occupying a space unless someone makes room for you. But you are present, wherever you are, whether someone acknowledges you or not. You are a soul, in a body, in at least one space, one dimension, or possibly two.

## Reflection Questions

Afrofuturist approaches to music can view the music as space and assert community in its sonic intention and world building. Care can assert community. We can bring a sense of community as we show up in spaces familiar and unfamiliar by being conscious of connectivity.

1.  As you traverse through stores, work, public transportation, or various events in your day, do you think of yourself as being in community with those around you? Why or why not?
2.  What makes a space feel welcoming? What makes it feel like a community?
3.  If you could bring an emotion in a space (work, home, or otherwise) that all could experience, what would it be? Why?

## Exercise: Commune

For the next few days become very aware of the physical spaces you enter. Try actively thinking of yourself as being in community with those who share the spaces you're in. Think consciously about acknowledging their humanity. Think this regardless of how prickly some of their personalities may be. Think about those who may have shared that space in the past or those who will visit in the future. If you're in nature, think of yourself as being in community with the life-forms around you. Jot down any observations that come to mind or experiences you have.

# 7

# TANGO AND THE BOX

## Taking Up Space with Your Fashion

Whenever one travels abroad (I'm speaking terrestrially) there's an adjustment process upon returning home. I remember coming back home to the United States from my first trip to Europe and having a heightened awareness of how young my country felt. There wasn't a single building in my Midwest city older than the late nineteenth century. In Paris, I was passing refabricated castles and churches that were centuries old. The sprawling Chicago downtown was a skyline in evolution, with most buildings representing the heights of late twentieth and early twenty-first century architecture. Normal streets and buildings I passed all the time were now beacons of a time within a hundred-year span. Younglings we were atop Indigenous land.

When I returned from Senegal, I had a similar experience. My first few days in Dakar, I was immersed in the enchanting aesthetics. On the edge of the Sahel, the soil is a yellow sand and casts a yellowed palette to the environment. The city is along the ocean so there's a vibrant culture of surfers and fishermen. Bright colors and elaborate patterns are the norm. Most people wear bespoke clothing. Rather than go to a clothing store, many people go to the sprawling market, pick out a fabric, and have a tailor design their outfits according to the customer's vision.

Because this is part of the local culture, most people have a healthy relationship to color. If you're designing the outfit, from color to cut, chances are you are always going to look good. At the very least you're going to feel comfortable. Senegalese generally aren't afraid of brilliant color or mixing bright patterns. Although most buildings are white or match the shaded sand, pops of color spring forth throughout the city's design. Billboards are bright. The buses are adorned in multihued paint. Even the fishing boats are uniquely designed with rich color patterns to set them apart from each other. As a result, I say Dakar is one of the most fashionable cities in the world. Everyone, from the woman selling bread on the corner, to the security guard, to a high-level government employee, has an impeccable sense of style. So, when I returned home, I became aware of the lack of color in the Western environment. Many public spaces were a range of beige, browns, or washed-out blue. Fortunately, I live in a city with a lot of public art and murals, which makes a big difference, and one that is speckled with people who aren't afraid of bright colors.

One day, as I was looking at people cutting through the rectangle parking lot full of cars fitting neatly in the painted lines, I was overcome with the feeling that we were all squeezing into our clothes. We were taking generic off-the-rack sizes that didn't fit exactly and making them work. We were wearing colors that muted our complexions. I became aware of how boxy our society was. Our cities felt like a series of lines and angles. All spaces, from restaurants to shoe stores, were shaped like a box or a rectangle. We were walking from box to box, many of which weren't built with the uniqueness of the community in mind, wearing clothes we had to squeeze into, and sporting colors that muted our skin. There were people I observed who had a fashion sense and were very intentional about how they put clothing together. I wondered if they could've achieved their looks easier if they could just go to a designer and tell them what they wanted.

Maybe the drab feeling I had that sometimes came with fall had to do with the fact that my color palette switched from rainbow colors to black. I had a refreshed appreciation for people who tricked their cars out, highly accessorized their wardrobes, or dyed their hair in crayon colors. I was among these people, as much as I was among those who were squeezing into boxes. We were trying to press out of this feeling of the literal box. No matter how many patterns we mixed, or hair changes we made, or new furniture we bought, we were still operating around a convention that defaulted to rectangles, minimalism, and beige.

Rectangles, boxes, and grids aren't inherently bad. Black, beige, navy blue, and mauve aren't the worst of the worst either. For many people, getting their clothes made is a luxury. But the metaphor of squeezing into clothing and abiding in homes not created with your uniqueness, culture, or range of expression in mind is a literal application of the term "fitting in the box." I would argue that George Clinton's lyric "here's your chance to dance your way out of your constrictions" was a reference to wiggling our way out of these boxes.

Sometimes we don't wear the things we want or decorate our homes in a style that best suits us because we want to fit in. We don't want the ire that standing out can draw, the harsh glare of the spotlight. Sometimes we want to be invisible. We don't want to take up space. We don't want to draw attention. We'd rather just get by. Sometimes we fear the adoration a new style could bring because of the expectation or hateration that comes with it. But guess what? You already stand out. People can already see you or feel your presence. You are not invisible. You take up space. You are not the box or its walled-in sides—and that's a good thing.

There are a lot of fashionistas in the Afrofuturist ranks. Although being fashionable isn't a requisite for thinking about futures, being aware of how you show up in a space is. The energy that pervades us from our glow up projects outward and into futures. It's also good to know what fashion items make you feel rejuvenated. Songstress Erykah Badu said she wakes up and wears bells on her ankles. I have another friend who designs jewelry for his long beard. So, claim your space.

## Reflection Questions

Sometimes our physical environments condition us to express in ways that don't best reflect how we see ourselves. Subconsciously, we can take on the expectations others have of us and dress to fit their norm. These expectations can be overt as well. Sometimes this may be necessary. Other times it's not. Regardless, you want to carve out space to dress in ways that best reflect how you want to express yourself or what's most comfortable for you. You want to be aware of what you're wearing and why. What we wear alters our mood, our comfort level. What we wear is interweaved with how we view ourselves. We want to allow ourselves to lean into our inner fabulous or superhero at our own choosing. Doing so is an intimate celebration. But it also establishes our body as a space of freedom. We are free within our bodies. We have control over our bodies. We are beautiful.

1.  What style choices do you make when you want to fit in? At work? At school? With family? With friends?
2.  How do these choices align with your personality? Do these choices align with your personality? Do they align with how you see yourself? Why or why not?
3.  What color would you like to wear more of but don't? Is there a style of clothing or hair you'd like to try out but are afraid of the response? What is it and why don't you wear it?

## Exercise: Step Out of the Box

1.  Pick a day and wear that color, bold pattern, or clothing item you're afraid to wear. Wear it in public or wear it in your home. Find a way to make the item work where it best suits you. Jot down your observations.

2.  If you're averse to bright colors, spend a week wearing bright colors or bold patterns. If you're accustomed to bright colors, select an accessory you'd never typically wear, like a giant hat, or ankle cuffs. How do you feel? What experiences do you have?

3.  Sometimes we decorate our living spaces to match the expectations of others, too. Is there a home décor item you'd like to buy but doesn't match your current décor or seems too outlandish? Maybe it's a mask, a wacky table-cloth, a lava lamp, or a poster from your favorite comic. This item doesn't have to match anything. You can select an item from a secondhand or vintage store. Place this item prominently in your home. Note how you feel. Does it clash? Does it speak to you more than your current décor? How does this new fandangoed item reflect you?

We now have a better grounding on where we are in time and space. Our relationship with time and space is a conscious awareness. We know how to stretch the finite and create space from the infinite. We know we can blow past the boxes of containment. We know how to commune in spaces, mindful of presence in our ancient to the future trajectories. We bring community with us, across time. Now we're off to contemplate how our imaginations shape our reality.

# II

# IMAGINE STATION

# 8

# THE FORTITUDE IN OPTIMISM

## The Courage to Expect More

DURING PRESIDENT BARACK OBAMA'S INAUGURATION, as the throngs of well-wishers lined DC streets and the motorcade went by, a reporter interviewed Congressman John Lewis. Lewis, a staunch civil rights activist who'd worked with Martin Luther King Jr. and fought against injustice, was remarking on the day's historic achievement. Lewis said what many people had said at the time: He never thought he'd see the day when America had a Black president. Lewis went on about the significance of the moment and his own emotion. Then the reporter asked him, What would King himself think of this momentous occasion? And without equivocation, Lewis said that King would say "I told you."

It was an interesting juxtaposition of perceived possibility. Lewis was emotional and in awe over a moment he'd never expected to see, despite wanting to believe it. King, on the other hand, saw it as possible, a half a century prior. I don't get the impression that Lewis thought of himself as a visionary in the way that Martin Luther King is regarded. King's fortitude, commitment, and ability to speak to a vision as he galvanized people to seek change is legendary. Although King's visionary abilities were established early in life, Lewis committed himself to a vision that at various points he couldn't quite see but yearned for deeply. Although Lewis didn't think of himself as a visionary in the traditional sense, he was open to embracing an evolving role he would play carrying forth a vision for a brighter humanity—one that stirred his soul.

SNCC strategist Ella Baker worked behind the scenes but was a visionary nonetheless. Baker's style of visionary work was evident in her mentorship of the next generation of leaders and her grassroots organizing of voting rights efforts, training college students to do the groundwork and carry the movement forward. She rose through the ranks of the NAACP in the 1940s and later joined the Southern Christian Leadership Conference (SCLC), where she shaped the vision and strategy for SNCC. Before working with SNCC, she'd worked with countless movements and causes organizing on ground levels. Baker assembled the strategy and cultivated the next generation on community-centric levels, a highly personable engagement with people of all walks. "Baker's message was that oppressed people, whatever their level of formal education, have the ability to understand and interpret the world around them, to see the world for what it is, and move to transform it," writes Barbara Ransby in *Ella Baker & the Black Freedom Movement*.[1]

In social justice movements, everyone doesn't have the same role, the same starting point, or the same background. They have different strengths, they may disagree on strategy, but they do ideally share in an aligned vision. King's strength was that he could touch hearts and minds with the vision and encourage people to take some action, step outside their comfort zone, and make a difference. He was willing to be the focal point for the myriad of responses to the vision. Baker's strength was that she could enact the vision and find roles for volunteers to play, creating a dynamic where all who participated felt valued in their push for change. Lewis would be a stalwart force who evolved from youth protester to movement organizer to congressman, working grassroots and later shaping legislation in politics. All were relentless in their commitment and determination. However, to work on a vison of any magnitude, you ultimately become the vision. You carry the vision forth. Whether you're the organizer or the volunteer on phone bank duty, your commitment makes you a carrier of the vision. This power of the shared vision in action helps the collective push past obstacles and fear. This motion is inherently optimistic.

"In the movement, we didn't know how history would play itself out," writes Lewis. "When we were getting arrested and waiting in jail or standing in unmovable lines on the courthouse steps, we didn't know what would happen, but we knew it had to happen."[2]

Although Lewis may not have been sure of the outcome, he was firm in that the injustices against humanity and widespread segregation needed to end. He wanted to see the vision. He didn't know the outcome in the way that a psychic would, where visions of the future are crystal clear. Maybe he wasn't always certain that the outcome would be optimal. However, he was firm in his desire that the inhumanity in the world *needed to cease*. This knowing, which wasn't one that gave him a vision of a future per se, at least at first, was one anchored in the need for injustice to end.

This knowing anchored him in the face of violence. It anchored him when he spoke new truths. When King was assassinated, the future that King spoke of did not fade. Lewis continued his work, working against injustice in times when it was less publicized, and eventually becoming one of the greatest congressman of his time. He is remembered as a stalwart reminder of the redemption "of the American soul." Other movements, from Black Lives Matter to environmental justice, would pull from the lessons of those before with many embracing nonviolent strategy, use of media, and Baker's ground-up approach to organizing.

This sense of knowing also fueled Hazel Johnson. Known as the mother of environmental justice, in the late 1960s Johnson was a resident of Altgeld Gardens, a public housing project in Chicago. Johnson got involved in environmental justice because she noticed high rates of cancer and respiratory issues among residents in her neighborhood, people whose families had no history of the illness. Her husband died of lung cancer. She went to the library and did research, soon making the connection that neighboring chemical plants, steel plants, and landfills were polluting the neighborhood. As many as fifty landfills were in the area. She started going to community groups and government regulatory agencies to push for change. In a televised public forum, she challenged journalists who questioned whether these businesses causing the pollutants should be closed. "Close all the industry down and relocate all the people," she said. "Human health comes first." She created the organization People for Community Recovery, a group that would change local, state, and national legislation. Johnson brought an ignored issue that was devastating neighborhoods to the forefront through diligent work over several decades. She was looking for answers to questions, and her quest expanded her capacity to become the answer to the questions she posed. Her work would be a game changer. Johnson's daughter, Cheryl Johnson, continues her mother's work. "The fundamental drive for her as she said was mothers are protectors for their families and their children. [She said] I'll die and go to hell before I let someone just poison my kids."[3]

## Commitment to the Vision

Although Lewis admitted to not having always seen the vision, he believed in the need for a society that fully valued humanity to be real. He was willing to work toward it becoming real, at great sacrifice. He was willing to devote his life to it. Over time, some aspects of the vision became clearer than others. Moreover, he saw himself as part of a continuum of people doing similar work both before and after him. His awareness of the continuum was empowering. "Ours is not the struggle of one day, one week, or one year. Ours is not the struggle of one judicial appointment or presidential term. Ours is the struggle of a lifetime, or maybe even many lifetimes, and each one of us in every generation must do our part," he writes in *Across That Bridge*.[4]

Lewis, like King, believed in nonviolence as a strategy born from an outpouring of love for humanity. This deep belief led to a type of optimism born of necessity. He needed to be optimistic in order to sustain the work.

"You are a light," he says in *Across the Bridge*. "Never let anyone—any person or any force—dampen, dim, or diminish your light. Release the need to hate, to harbor division, and the entice-ment of revenge. Release all the bitterness. Hold only love, only peace in your heart, knowing that the battle of good to overcome evil is already won."[5]

This optimism, backed with fortitude, recast what progress looks like, where a stumble, backslide, or all-out fall is a forward motion. Revered activist Fannie Lou Hamer devoted her life to registering voters in Mississippi, serving as the vice president of the Freedom Democratic Party, a party formed to counter discrimina-tory policies in the state's democratic party. Hamer was resolute in her fiery optimism. "If I fall, I'll fall five feet four inches forward in the fight for freedom," she said. "I'm not backing down."[6]

Optimism can show up as brazenness. Brazenness is not "bad girl" behavior for the sake of rebelliousness. Nor is it strength devoid of humanity or vulnerability. It is a willingness to defy barriers placed upon you, or self-imposed ones, that impede your connection with life and light. "Brazenness leaves the tyranny of needing to be respectable and people pleasing at the gate," writes Abiola Abrams in *African Goddess Initiation*. She points to Sitira, a dancing spirit of Buxton, Guyana, as goddess of brazenness. Sitira, popularized in the folk song "Sitira Gal," is spoken alternately as slur and deity for her unfeminine femininity. "Brazenness is asking,

'What would I dare do if I knew I could not fail?' Brazenness is courage topped off with faith in your own divinity and power," Abrams writes.[7]

Erykah Badu, the iconic neo-soul chanteuse—and one of the first singers I ever knew of to reference quantum physics or cell phones killing bees in a song—stands brazen in her creativity. Although her music continues the R&B love and hip-hop consciousness sensibility of those before her, she remains unique in her expression, fashion, and general approach to life.

"Creativity is freedom," she says. "Creativity is also the absence of fear. Not being afraid to approach something and be wrong or right. It's the absence of fear. I guess the braver you are, the deeper you go into your craft. I don't have any fears at all. I think at this point they've pretty much dissolved and it was a choice. You choose to be in your mind. Fears exist inside of your mind. If you choose to live in there, there are probably a lot of things that can scare you. Out here there's nothing. Human beings don't scare me at all."[8]

## The Inertia of Fortitude

Sometimes there's an assumption that the optimism in Afrofuturism is a light, fluffy, airy expectation. The imaginative insistence on fabulous doppelgangers and pink, puffy coat alternate worlds where steampunk tech resolves historical downturns is sometimes misconstrued as impractical. However, there's nothing wrong with the light touch or the fabulous infusion. As an air sign on the Western astrological charts, I find the light touch to be rather delightful. Every matter doesn't have to be forged like steel in the fire (no offense, fire signs). However, the truth of the matter is that optimism isn't solely a wish upon a star. (Note to self: Go wish upon a star for good measure.) Optimism is also a practice.

Optimism is a practice backed with fortitude. One may need to be courageous to create art from the African fantastic when

Black lives are asserting they matter and face resistance. It takes fortitude to be optimistic when there are no obvious signs of victory. It takes courage to expect more or seek out the best outcomes with unwilling parties. It takes courage to walk away from a project that is draining your soul and not know when you'll find a better one. It takes courage to think of the world as being abundant and not a space of scarcity.

Optimism is a deep commitment to finding peace of mind in turbulence. It is the practice of finding the dawning light so you can move forward.

Faith is a slightly different matter. Faith often interplays with belief. Faith is a rooted knowing that things will work out or a belief in a higher power or gracious universe that will work things out in part through your release of a situation and definitive actions. Sometimes faith is a deep belief in your own resourcefulness. There are plenty of testaments to faith, regardless of your belief system, to glean from. A well-known Christian verse about faith is that faith without works is dead. This teaches that the belief or expectation you have is sustained in part by the actions you take to bring it about. Faith can be like working a muscle in the direction of a pragmatic optimism. Naturally this depends on what you have faith in.

I think of optimism as creating an emotional environment of possibility that supports such actions. Optimism as practice is a commitment to finding the good in a moment or season. It is a commitment to uncovering the kind of peace that sustains you. It is a commitment to joy. You commit to maintaining joy in your life, finding gratitude despite challenges, and moving forward. Optimism is not allowing the behavior of others to disappoint you to the point of not valuing humanity, nature, or our vast universe. Optimism can nurture faith, and faith can nurture optimism.

My colleague John Jennings says that once he had a child, he could no longer afford to not be optimistic. He *has to* desire and work toward a better world because he wants his child to live in a healthy, happy one. Following the birth of her first child, superstar singer and fashion mogul Rihanna said the same thing. "Raising a young Black man is one of the scariest responsibilities in life," she told British *Vogue*. "You're like, 'What am I leaving my kids to? This is the planet they're gonna be living on?' All of those things really start to hit differently."

However, you don't need a newborn to shift your focus to better futures. We are present in a future partly of our own making, an outgrowth of an optimism forged for some who came before. If we search our own lives, thinking upon those who came before us, or others who assisted us in some way, or out of respect for those who sacrificed their lives in the name of improving the human condition, we'll find that a part of us yearns to be optimistic. Perhaps being optimistic is our natural state.

The challenge in being optimistic is simple. But it's not easy. We are clouded with information, news, current events, and other happenings that can make optimism seem futile. There are histories that frustrate the soul just to think about them.

In Childish Gambino's music video for "This Is America," Gambino, as an Elegba-like figure, snakes shirtless among elated dancing kids in school uniforms atop cars in parking lots. This fervent joy is interrupted by the mass murder of a church choir. The song continues. The dance continues. No time to mourn. The stark contrasts between joy and horror are alarming. But the persistence to find a modicum of joy, whether through denial or for human survival, between these catastrophes doesn't go unnoticed. How do we change this world Glover mirrors?

Pessimism is presented as pragmatism that counters childhood idealism. In fact, being pessimistic can be a bonding agent. One can always corral like-minded folk who can have winding conversations about the righteousness of hopelessness. Their reasons can be completely valid. Some strings of breaking news reports read like time tickers for the world's tumble into hell via handbasket. But there's also ample evidence of human kindness, stalwart joy-making, and collective action springing from love, and the grace of the rising sun or the beauty of a crescent moon that reminds us otherwise.

The problem with pessimistic thinking is that over time, we stop dreaming. We stop creating. And we wind up contributing to a consciousness of limited expectations—the same consciousness of limited expectations that encapsulates the things that frustrate us. It's usually posited as being realistic. However, realities change, and clearly everyone isn't experiencing the same reality. Pessimistic thinking undermines our own agency and tanks our expectations. Moreover, pessimistic attitudes encourage others to do the same. Such thinking leads to beliefs like "I can't do such-and-such a thing and therefore you won't be able to do it ever." Subconsciously or consciously, your focus goes toward not just seeing the world in a scope of limitation but also taking actions to make sure this limited scope remains for all who are around you.

Ayize Jama-Everett adapted *The Count of Monte Cristo* into an Afrofuturist-themed tale that takes place on a futuristic Earth riddled with climate change where the African continent is humanity's hope. *The Last Count of Monte Cristo* looks at narcissism and power in tumultuous times. Jama-Everett, who enjoys writing dystopias, is clear that optimism is embedded in Afrofuturist thinking. One has to be an advocate of humanity regardless of the circumstances. One has to be an advocate for Black people in the future, he shared with me. This assumes that you both believe there will be a future, and that you want Black people to thrive in it.

Optimism as practice doesn't mean you aren't aware of challenges. Optimism doesn't mean you walk around with a frozen smile plastered to your face and deny inhumanity. Alexis Aggrey, director of *Afrofuturism: The Origin Story*, said she had interesting dialogues explaining to curious folks that the optimism in Afrofuturism isn't an empty hope but rather one resolute in futures that value humanity—because they must value humanity. *Pitchfork* writer Sadie Sartini Garner wondered about the nature of optimism in Afrofuturist bandleader Kahil El'Zabar's album *America the Beautiful.* It was released in 2020, at the height of the COVID epidemic and Black Lives Matter protests. The US death toll was rising. The album begins with a drum. El'Zabar swings through a Latin, jazz, and funk fusion. The song "Freedom March," Garner says, sounds "like both halves of a jazz funeral happening at the same time, the dirge and the celebration coexisting in a way that's coherent, but not easy."

In his statement of purpose for the album, El'Zabar says: "Now's the time for us to collectively invoke a confluence of trust and imagination that will enlighten a future path towards ethical humanity." Garner is mystified by the optimism. "It seems strange, in the waning months of 2020, to have someone express hope for our country's future—to suggest that anything like 'ethical humanity' is still possible on a societal level. But then again, Americans have been guiding their country toward the light since the days of its broken birth. Most just weren't called 'American' at the time," she concludes.[9]

Be critical. Be angry about inhumane acts. Vent. Be disappointed in colleagues who don't speak out against injustice. I'm all for redirections, rethinking, pulling back to assess, or finding alternate paths, resting, and dreaming. I'm all for asking for help, researching, assembling new teams, self-care, and surrounding yourself with people who are supportive. But these actions, in the face of barriers, are forms of optimism in action, particularly when you maintain that the frustrating parties have humanity, too. In Martin Luther King's renowned "I Have a Dream" speech, where he articulates a vision for what racial harmony can look like, he's well aware of the difficulties. He urges the audience "not to wallow in despair" although some may be "fresh from narrow jail cells" or "staggered by the winds of police brutality." He asserted this in one of the more contentious times of racial segregation in the United States, that he has a dream of racial harmony, in spite of the laws and obstacles that forbid it. "So even though we face the difficulties of today and tomorrow," he says, "*I still have a dream.*" He states this *before* he articulates the vision in the speech he's most known for. Your fortitude and optimism could serve as prophecy. What actions will you take to step out of the feeling of despair? Optimism doesn't mean you won't have feelings that aren't happy ones. Yet, a commitment to optimism means you are focused on finding a resolve, finding inner peace, and moving forward. Scenarios and occurrences that appear as barriers won't define you.

## Beyond Expectation

I am deeply spellbound by Black American women artists who traveled abroad in the first half of the twentieth century. In the 1930s, Katherine Dunham, a ballet dancer, while in pursuit of her anthropology degree, was running a dance company. Through her study, she would later pursue what she'd call dance anthropology. By 1935, in the thick of the Great Depression, she was awarded fellowships that allowed her to travel to Haiti, Martinique, Jamaica, and Trinidad, where she engaged in local dance culture and spiritual ritual dance. The trip was fully immersive. She lived with the Maroons of Jamaica, the descendants of escaped enslaved Africans who'd formed free societies, becoming the first "outsider" to live among them. She learned the calinda, a stick fighting dance based on an African martial art form brought to Martinque and Trinidad by enslaved Africans. Much like Brazilian capoeira, calinda was a martial art hidden and practiced as a dance.

She had extended stays in Haiti, immersing herself into the culture, and became a voudon initiate to study the dances and practices. I just have to emphasize this for good measure: Dunham wasn't content with distant observations typical of the field at the time. She actually went through the process of a long-running initiation that lasted for days. Another anthropologist, writer Zora Neale Hurston, on a quest to collect Black folktales in the American South, would likewise go through an entire hoodoo initiation to both gather and understand the lore. These women had the drive of the gods.

Dunham often traveled, learning perspectives, languages, and dialects as research both to bring African Diasporic dances to the world stage and to forge a new style entirely. Dunham's work was a foundation of modern and contemporary dance. There were no African dance classes to attend when Dunham was coming of age. There were no Afro-Caribbean dance courses or performances touring the world. Ballet was the ruling high-art model. Although there were an abundance of dance styles and social dancing in America, Black professional dancers were steered away from ballet and often shunned by White dance companies. Other dance world options for Black professional dancers were limited and often demeaning.

Carmencita Romero was a Dunham company dancer in the 1930s. She recalled the hardships in the documentary *Free to Dance*. "If you were a Black dancer all you could aspire to was to be a shake dancer, a tap dancer, or a contortionist or an acrobat," said Romero. "That's all that was open to you." Dance scholar Halifu Osumare, a choreographer and professor emerita of the Department of African American and African Studies at the University of California, adores Dunham. She expounds in the documentary: "We needed to see another vision of what a Black dancer could be."[10]

While Dunham had some colleagues and supporters who thought her dance research in the Caribbean was a worthy pursuit, I'm sure there were many more who thought it was all a waste of time and that no monetary gain could come from it. There are people who would tell an upcoming dance ingénue to abandon her travel dreams today, better yet a century ago. Yet, Dunham secured a grant and the support of her professors at the University of Chicago and headed to the Caribbean with letters of endorsement in hand and introductions to strangers who were open to hosting her. She had a desire to have a deeper relationship with African/Caribbean dance aesthetics that fueled her.

Rex Nettleford, cofounder of the National Dance Theatre Company of Jamaica, understood Dunham's quest. In the documentary, he shared, "Dunham was tracing her own roots. Her own roots as a Black person, a person of African ancestry. She would've seen dance as a means of communicating, a means of expressing life and living itself. The European influence is also there. But the slaves and their descendants took many of the European influences and transformed them. That is what the dance is about."

Dunham's technique is central to the evolution of modern, jazz, contemporary, and African contemporary styles today. Fellow dancer Ruth Beckford recalled that the Dunham technique, developed based on her research in the Caribbean along with ballet, was the most difficult one Beckford had ever learned. It focused nearly exclusively on isolating all parts of the body, from neck to wrists to hips.

In the 1930s there was no precedent for what Dunham was doing. Dance anthropology didn't exist. Being a dancer and a scientist didn't exist. Being a Black American woman traveling internationally for research was virtually nonexistent. Being a Black American woman traveling alone for any reason was plain dangerous. To top it off, the nation was in a deep financial depression. Bread lines were circling the country. Swarms of families had lost their savings. Conventional wisdom would say that there was no money for nonexistent disciplines to be found. Yet, Dunham was awarded a grant.

Nearly everything that Dunham was doing would've fallen somewhere between "impossible" to "foolhardy." Even within the countries Dunham visited, her interest in going into rural areas and befriending practitioners of African religions was against the status quo, even the Black status quo, and often put those who hosted her at risk. However, Dunham says she never felt any sense of danger on these trips. She toppled convention with her bold actions. If Dunham had changed her mind altogether and stayed home in Chicagoland, no one would've questioned her. Yet, her work changed the course of dance history, with a young Alvin Ailey spotting her performance and rethinking his dance practice and later forming the Alvin Ailey dance company.

There's no way you can be a Black woman studying secret or maligned dances in foreign countries during the Great Depression without a healthy dose of optimism as practice. Dunham was also a visionary. She had little doubt that she could visit countries she wasn't familiar with, navigate them, and find acceptance. "I wasn't concerned about the hardships because I always felt I was doing what I had to do, what I wanted to do and what I was destined to do," she said. "I always believed that if you set out to be successful, then you already were."

During her first years of study, she wasn't always sure what she'd find, but she was open to the possibilities. She writes of her experience in Haiti in her book *Island Possessed*, a reflection of her life she wrote while in Senegal in 1969. "It is hard to describe to an uninitiated the process of becoming initiated. Harder still when one remains for years on a fringe border of belief and nonbelief, because the two are so close. A thing happens, you experience it often without seeing it, and it is true."[11]

Dunham's experiences as initiate challenged her own beliefs as a scientist. However, her devotion to research unearthed answers to questions she didn't know she had. In her optimism and fortitude, she remained open to new ways of thinking and existing in the world: "And when people ask me, as they do now, what of those mystic or occult experiences I believe in, or why I spend so much time in their search and research, I find myself answering as I did even as far back as those houngfor days, that I honestly do not know. I am there to believe or not believe, but willing to understand and to believe in the sincerity of other people in their beliefs, willing to be shown, to participate, and where the participant begins and the scientist ends, I surely could not say."[12]

When she returned to Chicago, she finished her undergrad and completed a master's thesis. She also used her dance company to re-create and introduce African Diasporic dance styles on the world stage. This decision put her at odds with her professors. She made a conscious choice to value her art and public presentation over a career in the ivory tower. She left behind what could've been a more conventional, widely lauded career as an anthropologist in academia, and reimagined her dance company to showcase the works she studied. She also fortified African American aesthetics, most notably in the performance *Barrelhouse Blues*, a dance performed as a flirtatious couple and homage to Black American dance in blues clubs. She presented the dances she learned of, studied, and built upon with the utmost respect for the originating culture and dancers in the face of being exoticized. Her drive emboldened her creativity, and creativity allowed her to see new possibilities in movement and ways to showcase her work to the world.

Optimism bubbles from a *knowing* that there are possibilities other than the ones that appear on the surface. Optimism forces one to find some granules of hope, to lift your spirits enough to actually find or think beyond scenarios that appear as barriers. Optimism keeps you open to something better. Optimism raises your vibration enough to connect with other possibilities. The belief that there are other possibilities makes other possibilities evident. Optimism, rooted in fortitude, *finds* a way—or admits that you don't know how to move forward but you can find joy. The joy is rooted in a desire to find joy in moments where circumstances are less conducive to the emotion. Optimism releases the fear, frustration, anger, and despair of not reaching a desired outcome. Optimism clears a path. Optimism is an expectation that informs actions taken.

I think about Beyoncé's line in her ode "Freedom": "Hey! I'ma keep running, 'cause a winner don't quit on themselves." While life isn't a sum game of winners and losers, connecting to your own light, finding a space of gratitude, always puts you in an emotional space to view things differently. That shift in perspective and approach may be just enough to open up other options in what was previously a narrow pool of finitude.

It's tough to perceive possibility, even if it's within reach, when pessimism is the reigning lens. If you call yourself an

Afrofuturist, you have to find another way. Creativity has given many a sworn pessimist a moment of escape, solace, and comfort. The creative process is intention, receptivity, and release. Creativity is a form of problem-solving with a higher calling. You desire to create a thing. Perhaps you have an idea or concept in mind. Perhaps you have a method or approach. You stay receptive to how the concept can be created. In the midst of the focused creation process, you release any attachments that don't contribute to bringing the idea to light. Perhaps you uncover a better idea or a better method. Options only unfurl in the midst of the creative process, not before. You can't see the possibilities until you're in the middle of the process. Creatives have to be receptive, push themselves to new heights to both conceive and create the images they imagine in their minds. That creative breath is enough to forge a fortitude in optimism. The ability to create, to move the invisible to the visible, is a reminder of possibility that fundamentally expands options.

Although optimism can be the gust of wind that keeps us lifted, our optimism isn't just for us. There is a future contingent on our decisions and our scope of possibility. Our own futures along with those of generations to come begin with an amalgamation of previous courses chartered. We are constantly creating new world dynamics, new ground floors, and new possibilities with our expectations, choices, or lack thereof. Whether we like thinking about it or not, there is a future counting on us.

## Reflection Questions

1. On a scale of 1 to 10, where would you rate yourself on the optimism scale? Why?
2. Would you describe yourself as a person who is hopeful for the future?
3. When you're feeling down, what are the little things you do to create joy in your life?

4. Think of a "turning lemons to lemonade" moment in your life. What happened? What did you do?

5. Think of a "when one door closes, another door opens" moment in your life. What was it? What occurred?

6. What can you do to create more joy in your life?

## Exercises: Generate Optimism

With these exercises we are looking to cultivate practices that help you work your optimism generator. We are also working our gratitude muscle. With each one, note how you feel afterward. Try doing the tasks for a week. Note how you feel. Over time, if you're feeling down, explore these tasks as a pick-me-up. Feel free to adopt them as practice.

1. Write three things you are grateful for.

2. Write three things you like about yourself.

3. Write three moments that filled you with joy.

4. Write three good things that happened in recent world events.

5. Create a playlist of at least five songs that make you feel good about yourself and the world. Why do these songs keep you inspired?

6. Carve out a moment for joy in your week. The task doesn't have to be cost intensive. Perhaps you moon gaze or play your favorite music. Perhaps you make time to see a performance or make time to have coffee with a friend you don't spend enough time with. Whatever you choose, this activity should be something that fills you with joy.

# 9

# BELIEVE A WORLD

## Imagining Our Futures

IMAGINATION IS A CHERISHED ABILITY. The world we abide in is composed of systems, designs, architecture, art, and more that groups of people imagined at some point in time. Are you walking in someone else's imagination? Absolutely. You are seated on a couch that someone designed. You walk the streets that someone designed. We wear clothing that someone envisioned. We participate in online purchasing sites which someone conceptualized. We order menu items that someone cultivated. We watch films that others conceived. And we are also, consciously or unconsciously, cocreators in the societies we are a part of. We decorate our homes. We throw a birthday party. We add content to websites with predesigned templates. Our jobs, and the meaning we bring to them, are all cocreations. We vote. We protest. We create or cocreate lived experiences as a fact of navigating our lives. We also contribute, affirm, are subject to, and respond to ways of thinking that are also born from someone or a collective's imagination. We interact with, respond to, and are affected by the creations of others as we simultaneously cocreate experiences ourselves. Social systems of organizing are technologies, too. They are also creations.

Clearly the conversation about whose imagination can play a part in the shaping of our world is one of the greatest tensions in our society. Flautist and composer Nicole Mitchell Gantt points to Marimba Ani's book *Yurugu: An African-Centered Critique of European Cultural Thought and Behavior*, which states that Westerners are entangled in the imagination of the Greek philosopher Plato. The revered composer, who uses the name Mitchell in her professional work, says, "With his imagination, he created a theoretical reality (his utopic vision) that eventually manifested into a future—our physical reality." Plato's perspectives, ones in which human intellectualism eclipses all other ways of knowing, are so embedded that it's hard to see beyond them. Mitchell, who is also a professor of music at the University of Virginia, contends with the tensions around ways of knowing, valuing dreams, the imagination, and nature as invaluable spaces of wisdom.

"In traditional African and other, non-western cultures, knowledge is not objective; rather, to know is to sense truth in every part of one's being," says Mitchell. "Everything is subjective because it is informed by real experience. Trees, places, and people are all living beings that are too complex to look at as objects. Plato, in his writing, makes the case that objectivity is the only true way to perceive reality, but—as Ani's writing illuminates—in fact (to use Spock's logic) objectivity itself is an illusion."[1]

## The Wonder Life

Stacey Robinson is well known for his Afrofuturist illustrations. A professor and half of the art duo Black Kirby, he speaks frequently on Black utopias, with Prince's purple worlds of luster among them. One day, we were in conversation near the University of Illinois in Champaign-Urbana's campus and he remarked that my presentations on Afrofuturism and optimism made him think of the Care Bears and Winnie-the-Pooh.

"I'm not sure if that's a compliment," I told him. I wondered if he was making light of my lens as cutesy wishfulness. But Robinson was sincere. He grew up deeply appreciating these stories of deep care and the lighthearted fare of a rainbow-streaked world of safety. He deeply yearned for a society where adults valued care and love in our interactions and policies. The value of hope that I sprinkle in my talks made him think of his childhood and the wonderment of cartoons. "All the Care Bears function with the help of the other. That's what makes them dope," he said. "We're taught to build utopian spaces as children and lose that as an adult."

The worlds painted by many Afrofuturists in their comics, narratives, and costuming often have a wonderment that reminds people of the innocence of childhood and unencumbered dreams. Childhood stories provide a space of safety to think about fear. "Life is magical" is the message that resounds. This mix of hope, cooperation, and the fantastic abounds. In the Afrofuturist mind, the imagination is a wonderment playground. This pixie dust sprinkling and cowrie shell magic is everywhere.

This fabulousness and realm of the fantastic is a statement of lived optimism. "It's not possible to constantly hone on the crisis," says Pulitzer Prize–winning author Toni Morrison. "You have to love to love and you have to have the magic. That's also life."[2]

Such juxtapositions are outgrowths of questions and persistent visions of how one perceives our world, albeit through a bombastic fish-eye lens. Within this lens is a seed for reimagining worlds. The fantasticness abounds in real spaces, some that inspire fictitious ones.

Dorothy in the film version of *The Wiz* traverses an otherworldly Harlem, one where inanimate subway columns can break away from their structures and chase you like zombies. Good witches are numbers runners disguised as glossy bag ladies, evil witches run fashion sweatshops, real lions hide in library statues, and babies are stars in the sky. The original *Wizard of Oz* was a theosophist text. The characters Dorothy, the Scarecrow, the Tinman, and the Cowardly Lion are steps along the journey of conquering those things which make us self-conscious: our intelligence, our desire to be loved, our fears. Dorothy was in a land very unlike Kansas. In fact, the line "you're not in Kansas anymore" is now a retort hurled at people as a reminder to level up. However, Dorothy in *The Wiz*, the film version at least, was in a hyper-animated version of a cityscape world she already knew. *The Wiz* was 1970s Manhattan times one hundred. The colors more colorful, the cityscape more bombastic, the subways creepier, the graffiti more alive, the con artists more comedic. This fantastic lens of looking at the familiar made Dorothy's realization that she already had everything she needed take a different resonance. There's deep insight that comes from finding the fantastic and wonderment in our day-to-day lives. We are reminded of the wonder of our very world.

Wonder and the fabulous beget wonder and the fabulous. The creatives among us look to the wonder of the in-betweens to spark more wonderous creations. Yaku Stapleton's debut in London's Fashion Week was inspired by role-playing online game characters. The Central Saint Martins student stretched the limits of fabric by shrinking and elongating synthetic materials, resulting in winterwear that was oversized functional fantasy. Culture critic Sienna Mayers says it was "somewhere between high fashion and costume design, the designer sent out a huge bubblegum-pink puffer jacket with an arm clawing at the chest, and fabric bursting from the sides."[3]

JOJO ABOT's film *Gods Among Men + Marching* is a play on the gods among us. The Ghanian artist is a blue-painted deity adorned in multi-patterned fabrics, layered to no end. But rather than be a demanding, chastising figure from on high, she skips across the urban streets of Johannesburg riding on carts without a care in the world, bestowing blessings and blending in coquettishly with humans. ABOT, who also directed the video, said the album title *Ngiwunkulunkulu* translates to "I am God" in Zulu. "May it inspire you to find strength in your daily work to eradicate injustice and blatant hatred in the corners of the world you occupy," she says. "May it expand your heart to have empathy that extends beyond your immediate borders."

Even works with heavier themes relish in the carefree fabulous vision of our world in brighter pixels: The sprinkled peppiness of Outkast's *ATLiens* in their color-coated music videos where strippers, gospel choirs, and schoolchildren dance in perfect spectacle as a testament to coming of age Atlanta. Lil Nas X as the Biblical Eve is kissed by an alien before sliding down a stripper pole to hell where he lap dances for the devil and steals his horns. Is he seduced by a bad boy lover? Is he claiming the beauty of queer love? There's a bombastic playfulness, a brash boldness, and a striking social commentary in all of it. But these works are also outgrowths of the familiar. Many artists play with the fantastic but see the wonder of our present, the beauty of irony, and the recovery of the discarded as gold fans the fabulous around us.

## The Black Fantastic

*In the Black Fantastic*, a sprawling art show and ode to the wonderment of the in-betweens, debuted at London's Hayward Gallery in 2022. Curated by Ekow Eshun, he states, "The Black fantastic finds productive tension in the to and fro between the everyday and the extraordinary."[4] Nick Cave's carnivalesque sound suits, a protest of police violence, and Lina Iris Viktor's regal self-portraits were among the pieces featured. *Ultra Wet—Recapitulation*, large-scale projections on three-dimensional pyramids by Tabita Rezaire, beckons viewers to think beyond exploitation. "Can you see, feel, and imagine what it's like?" she asks. Eshun described *Ultra Wet* as traveling between "scenes of South African traditional healers and the landscape of Egypt to discourses on African epistemologies drawn from the stars."

The pools of the brash fantastic assert that there is another way of seeing the world, one where the fabulous and its magical life is a norm. We walk hand in hand with the imagined life. To the extent to which we don't see it, we desire it to be. These fantastic leanings are a space of resolve.

Nisi Shawl's *Everfair* is an alternative history novel that reimagines the Congo's resistance—this time equipped with steampunk technology. Shawl says that they were frustrated with steampunk's colonial relishings. "I had been confronted with the idea that steampunk valorized colonization and empire, and I really wanted to spit in its face for doing that," they said. "Alternate history, you know, I guess I am really attracted to it just because I just dislike this privileged narrative of 'This is the way things are, this is the way things were supposed to be.' Just because something happened doesn't mean that that's the way it had to happen. And I think it helps us figure out where to go next if we figure out where we might have been coming from."[5]

Getting in touch with the wonder of our current spaces and the wonder of what could've been is a great launching pad for reimagining new ones. As we think about cocreating new worlds to come, what sprinkles of wonder do we want to take with us?

## Field of Dreams

We all have the ability to imagine. In fact, we are actually imagining something all the time. We imagine what we're going to do for the day. We replay incidents from the past, imagining alternate responses. We imagine the person we're talking to via email. We fantasize. Although our day-to-day imaginings may not always leap to the realm of the fantastic, we are constantly juggling images, feelings, or narratives that provide context in our day-to-day activity. Our emotions are often backed by images or sensations that form stories in our mind.

In some cases, we're recycling images we've seen before. We are flooded with images or sensations from the multitude of screens in the world (television, internet, social media, film), not to mention our own experiences, or descriptions we've read before. Many of us aren't trained to balance all this intake. Some of the info we are numb to. However, we are always taking this information in, storing it as memory. Think of yourself as life's little sponge. If I ask you to imagine a spaceship, one from the countless flying vehicles you've seen in films or comics may come to mind. If I ask you what it feels like to run from a zombie, you're referencing fictitious accounts, fables, and stories, not your own experience (unless you've made a mad dash from a zombie, of course).

The challenge with imagination is that we tend to drum up references that already exist, plucking them from our memory bank, much like the AI generative art programs that try to duplicate human creativity. I once spent days on an AI art generating program prompted by words and descriptions, attempting to generate an image of a Black woman on a snowy future planet where she was actually dressed in clothing that resembled winter wear. No combination of African woman, Black woman, African princess, Black cyberpunk winter princess, and fur coat could generate anything other than a really attractive brown-skinned woman in a fur, open-neck halter top with her six-pack midriff exposed. At best, she's decked in a short capelet covering her shoulders, one that matches her bustier. While these AI generated images were intriguing, it was clear that the AI was sourcing Black women from video games, comic books, or fashionable models in warmer climates. Despite the centuries of Black women who've lived in snowy climates (hello Detroit, London, and Chicagoland), this AI generator couldn't project any of these images into a future snow-topia that didn't resemble a frozen Dubai. The available reference points wouldn't allow them to go any further.

Sometimes when people have a tough time imagining something, it's not because they can't or that the imagined thing doesn't exist, but rather because they don't have any reference points in their memory. This lack of reference points can cause an emotional shutdown.

So, if a child is asked to imagine themselves as an astronaut, when they attempt to pull an image from the countless images they've seen and none reflect their ethnicity, gender, or sexual orientation, the child might have a tough time crafting a vision. Likely they've seen a spacesuit and they certainly know what they look like, but they can't merge the two cohesively. The concepts— their life and that of an astronaut—don't add up.

In other cases, the child could be baffled by how they would get to the point of becoming an astronaut, so much so that they can't imagine it. Perhaps the process feels faulty. Some teachers working with the child may not be able to imagine the kid as an astronaut either. Oddly, none of this comes into play if both parties are asked to image a flying panda or a purple people eater.

We can always take in another set of data and reference points to override bias, being intentional to do so. However, if we're not careful, we can allow the images and sensations we take in from media or our lives to dictate not just what we can imagine, but also what we deem possible. Such images, coupled with beliefs, can also become barriers to understanding our environment, the cultures we're in the midst of, or other ways of life. Sometimes, a lack of imagination can prevent us from knowing ourselves.

I was in a workshop once where a group of scientists and artists were led through a guiding meditation. Seated on the floor with our eyes closed, we listened to the facilitator as she walked us through our awakening on Mars. The exercise lasted for ten minutes. Afterward, as we discussed our feelings and what we visualized, I remarked that being on Mars felt familiar. "What do you mean it felt familiar?" she asked, her eyebrows raised. Had I walked the red sands of Mars? Not that I was aware of. But I'd seen enough images of spaceships on Mars, in both film and via the Mars rover, to have a tapestry to play with. What I hadn't absorbed from some media outlet, I was willing to fill in with ideas of my own. I was also open to the facilitator's descriptions as she led us through the Martian imagination.

Although my Mars looked much like Tatooine in *Star Wars*, and I was walking about the desert in a yoga pants and a tank top, others' had elaborate architecture, space bubbles, and aircraft. The creatives in the room had the more imaginative images, and some of the scientists were pragmatic, thinking about the sources of oxygen for backpacks or the nature of the head gear or protective clothing from radiation. Others, wrestling with the possibility of how humans could survive on Mars, couldn't envision anything at all.

Some people are stuck on plausibility. They can't imagine something, even if you're guiding them with words, sensations, and descriptions in the name of fun, because they simply don't think it's possible. In other cases, their imagining skills need a purpose. Why am I imagining a pink pony on Jupiter? Why am I imagining myself flying a space cruiser? This issue of what's probable for them is a block.

This way of thinking doesn't just infringe upon guided Martian meditations. Imagining resolutions to real-world issues is fraught with expectations around what's possible and what isn't. I hear this frequently with climate change. I can't tell you how many climate change experts I've heard who can explain the problem in high detail but conclude that it's too late to do anything. The work of convincing influential parties is too much work. Is it too late or are the imagined possibilities of what we'd need to do to make our planet healthier too great a shift to entertain? Is it a question of real-world blocks only or a lack of imagination? A lack of imagination or a lack of will? Although climate change is a complex issue, I find it interesting when experts say that nothing can be done. Nothing? Fortunately, there are people who feel otherwise.

Adults working with tough issues were once children, too, many of whom were socialized out of imagining things. I think about sharing my Mars description with the meditation facilitator and her judgmental response. Being imaginative and open is some-times viewed as a childlike quality or a sign of naïveté. While not sharing your imagination might keep you in the good graces of those preoccupied with status quo, I don't know if it helps the world very much. Nor does it contribute to resolving world issues, or further a society's valuing of humanity. Being imaginative is essential for artists, and it's a healthy aspect of adult life, too.

Rev. Johnnie Colemon, a metaphysics pioneer, described the imagination as a cookie cutter. The act of imagining forms invis-ible substance into a tangible idea ripe for expression. Many people popularly refer to this idea of envisioning goals and processes that appear in their life as manifesting. You imagine what you want, you align your feelings with this desire, and through your work or somehow through osmosis, this idea comes to pass. This method of goal setting is also coupled with release, a detachment from the outcome. You want something, you expect something, but you release your attachment to it, allowing it to come into your life in its own way. The imagination can be the gift that keeps on giving. Once unleashed, it's inexhaustible.

## Crafting a World

Visionaries speak of their visions for new worlds or creations as already in existence. Whether they are speaking prophetically of a future world, an imagined world, or one that presently exists, albeit unseen, is a matter of speculation. However, these spaces have a visceral reality for those who speak and engage with them. Our imagined worlds, in storyland, are places for problem-solving. But their creation reflects a real-world desire for new spaces. In the space and time chapters, we spoke of finding ourselves in multiple spaces, imagined ones, too. However, cultures also craft imaged idealized worlds that serve as beacons in the night. To dream of a world is to rethink, rework, and dream up new or improved systems in our existing one.

*Star Trek*, one of the most famous sci-fi franchises, is lauded for depicting a future world that's fairly utopian. The story's long-running history and reboots are comfortable for fans and audiences. Many of the -isms of the world don't exist. For much of the series' existence, there was no currency. There's no jail, but rather rehabilitation centers. "No one has a problem with *Star Trek*," Julian Chambliss, professor at Michigan State University, told me. "Many of us have seen some iteration of it. We just don't know how to get there," he says. However, not knowing how to get there doesn't have to be an impediment to imagining the societies we want, or reimagining how to reach that destination without leaning on the cataclysm trope that sci-fi frequently uses as a device for change.

In Marvel's *Black Panther*, Wakanda is a utopia wrestling with itself. A technologically advanced African nation that was never colonized, Wakanda is led by a young prince, T'Challa, who wrestles with its history of protectionism versus how, or if, Wakanda can use its technologies and methods to help the world. In Ta-Nehisi Coates's *A Nation Under Our Feet* and *Intergalactic Empire of Wakanda*, Coates explores how this leading world-respected monarchy has growing pains as it struggles to become a democracy. This struggle happens just as they discover a Wakandan sister empire in deep space. With characters named in homage to the Earth counterparts, this interstellar world has a class-based society with enslavement, colonization, and a dictator who must be eradicated. A spiritual pantheon of gods act as tricksters in T'Challa's evolution. In some ways, the story is a thought experiment that asks about the nature of power, responsibility, and culture in powerful societies.

Some visionaries imagine worlds as an escape, a refresh, and a reminder of hope. The use of the Biblical land Canaan for enslaved African Americans served this purpose. In one sense, Canaan was symbolic of heaven in the afterlife, but in another it served as a state of freedom, echoed in spirituals and poetry. Author Kevin Young, who now serves as Andrew W. Mellon Director of the

Smithsonian's National Museum of African American History and Culture, argues that Canaan's illustrious dimensions also served as a memory of a free life of those before in their African homelands. The dream of Canaan sustained life for the enslaved who harbored dreams of freedom. "For the Black slave, Canaan was both tomorrow and ever after; it was a place (Canada) they hoped to literally dwell in and also a release (crossing the river) into an afterlife they had more than earned. If some of this is Christian imagery, much of it is also in an African conception of Great Time in which one's ancestors are ever present," says Young.[6]

The idea asserted purpose, escape, and release. Canaan, as an idea, would continue to appear in other forms in Black Diasporic art forms. Ethiopia, an uncolonized African nation with rich traditions, would later serve as this existential state in twentieth-century art. Wakanda, in the collective imagination of the Black Diaspora, occupies this space today. Just as Coates used the lens of Wakanda as critique of today's power dynamics, the ethereal Canaan and uncolonized Ethiopia spoke to the need to escape the limitations for Black lives in their times.

Visionaries can also work to reimagine a disjointed past or dystopia. *The Book of Drexciya* takes a troubling historical reality and reimagines it as the basis of a new world. During the transatlantic slave trade, countless captive Africans were thrown overboard. In the story, a captured, pregnant African woman thrown overboard from a slave ship in the 1500s gives birth to a child beneath the sea. The child and others with his fate are rescued by water spirits and rise to become a new underwater nation that frees the enslaved among their many adventures. The graphic novel by Abdul Qadim Haqq and Dai Sato is based on the narrative of the iconic Detroit-based techno group Drexciya and their sonic water sagas. But it also reimagines a future past—the futures of those thrown overboard during the transatlantic slave trade, giving them new life and direction.

In other cases, these utopian worlds are real but feel imagined. Gayl Jones's novel *Palmares* centers the real century-old Maroon or quilombo society in Brazil. Quilombo dos Palmares was a community of mostly Africans who escaped from enslavement and formed a hidden community in the hills of Brazil. Some in the community were Indigenous or white and marginalized. The community existed from 1605 to 1694, one of the longest-running free settlements of its kind, fending off would-be attackers, most of whom could not locate them. The self-sustaining community was hidden. Palmares often raided plantations to rescue the enslaved. The residents were largely from Angola and were led by kings descended of royalty in their homelands.

Jones's novel follows a fictional woman, Almeydita, an enslaved girl in fifteenth-century Brazil. Readers follow her evolution into womanhood as Almeydita fantasizes and later strategizes to find Palmares, a land that sounds as fictive as it is real because of how distant freedom feels.

All the elder women in the story become her spiritual grandmother. Almeydita holds Palmares aspirations dear as she seeks to find a space of empowerment in the burgeoning Brazilian world. Jones reimagines real-world Brazilian culture and politics by following a bevy of figures in the story: impoverished European immigrants, frustrated European women scribes, colonial planters, dangerous priests, Native resistors, Black freedmen negotiating status, and an array of enslaved people find ways to survive under unusual circumstances.

Both Black freedmen and the enslaved are plotting, in their own ways, for new futures as they carve out a space of sanctity in their reality. Palmares is their bright, guiding star. This new Brazil in the making has competing interests in shaping new futures. Jones, a contemporary of Toni Morrison, wrote an ingenious work, her first in decades, and captured endless layers. At heart, the story is about navigating freedoms. However, the dynamic of Palmares as occupying both spaces of the real and unreal among its progeny and those who aspire to be there is ever present.

Julia Peres Guimaraes, a Brazilian student of Afrofuturism, argues that Brazil's thriving scene of Afrofuturist creatives and thinkers is informed by the quilombos. "I argue that Brazil is not just the country of the future, it is an Afrofuturist country par excellence, for at least two reasons. First, because at its root, popular culture and social movements were born from within articulations and tensions between diasporic knowledge and speculative traditions, marked by non-linear understandings of time. And second, because modes of Black resistance in Brazil draw concepts and practices from the quilombos, advanced social organizations (akin to Maroon communities), established over four centuries ago whose social egalitarianism and revolutionary character were lightyears ahead of their time."[7]

Etienne Toussaint, a law professor at the University of South Carolina, speaks on reimagining or critiquing just what we mean by equality as freedom. Speaking on a panel about Afrofuturism and the law of which I was a participant, he shared that we must rethink what equality and its achievement means. Is equality achieved when you have an equal number of people of all ethnicities above and below the poverty line? Is equality enough? These narratives of Wakanda, Drexciya, and Palmares explore the nature of equality and freedoms pulling from real-world spaces that bind liberatory and actualized imaginations.

## Mandorla Awakening II

Such contemplations also transformed Nicole Mitchell's compositions. "In 2009, while I lived in Chicago, a narrative centered around a utopian realm, which I called Mandorla Island, had emerged from my mind. It was based on the question: What does a technologically advanced, egalitarian society that's in tune with nature look like," she said.[8]

Mitchell's Mandorla Island narrative takes place in 2099. A society, designed by those who have "awakened their ability to communicate directly with Source," populates the island after a global war and virus. The residents are now immune to the virus. The narrative begins with a couple visiting from the decaying World Union. Inspired by the Earth-centric, egalitarian world of Ma-land, the couple must decide whether they will adopt the ways of the islanders or try to save their WU homeland.

Mitchell was moved to address her own frustrations with anti-Blackness in Orange County. She premiered *Mandorla Awakening I: Dorla Awakens* (*MA I*) as an experiment in diversity with people of varying backgrounds and artistic mediums. The wordless performance was an interplay of music lighting, choreography, and video performed in Chicago in 2011. Mitchell wanted to understand the cause of power ruptures in society, she says. She concluded that "base-hierarchical thinking was the root of human dystopia. . . . My intent was to inspire alternative realities for how we, as people, relate to one another by redefining difference. A core idea of that project is my belief that our imaginations can be keys to manifesting change."[9]

The work would be an ongoing one that defined her music, her practice as a musician and teacher, and how she cultivated community in her own world. She released the album *Mandorla Awakening II: Emerging Worlds* in 2017. The album won Jazz Album of the Year from the *Village Voice*.

Her book, *The Mandorla Letters*, is a statement of her utopian journey. The book intertwines her own personal narrative with the ongoing saga of the couple of Ma-land. This imaginative world informs Mitchell's practice and insights. She adopts hierarchy-free approaches in her music, a style she cultivated working with the legendary AACM jazz collective.

Much like the delicate state of Palmares for Almeydita or Canaan for the enslaved populace, this juxtaposition of imagined-world/real-world nature of Ma-Land (think Motherland) has dual meaning for the WU descended couple. "Perhaps it's a new planet, or perhaps it's another state of mind. Either way, transformation is inevitable."[10]

## Reflection Questions

Imagining futures is one of the best ways to alleviate blocks and strengthen your imaginative abilities. Imagining futures can also be a playground for problem-solving. Imagining refreshes how we can see the beauty of our world.

Imagine a world that values humanity and respects our earth, a society that you would like to live in. This vision should excite you. This space should make you feel elated. Let your imagination flow with inventions and social dynamics.

1.  What does this society look like? What does this society feel like? Describe it.
2.  What are the values in this society? List at least three.
3.  How do people create joy in this society?
4.  What are the cool innovations or inventions this society has?
5.  How do you contribute to the society in this world? Do you have a profession? What is it? How do you live life in this society?
6.  How do communities function? How do people gather and socialize?
7.  Does your society have currency? What is the means of exchange?
8.  Thinking on the idea of Sankofa, what are three lessons from history you feel should be bedrocks for this new society? Why?
9.  What does music sound like in this world? What does the art look like? Are there artists today whose work reflects your vision?

10. Select a song that is your world's theme song.
11. Where is this society located? How can interested parties get there?
12. Finally, what is your society's name?

Societal issues impact our lives. We can lose sight of wonder when we're immersed in them. But these occurrences don't have to be wonder blocks or prevent us from reconciling with a future that values humanity. Let's address a few. Think of a societal issue in our current time that you are concerned about.

1. What is the issue? Why does it bother you?
2. What does this world look like when the problem is resolved?
3. How will you live differently if this problem is resolved? What actions can you take that you don't currently take? What life decisions can you make that you aren't currently making or don't feel comfortable making?
4. How do you feel when this problem is resolved?
5. How would you feel if future generations in this society forgot the issue, its cause, and its resolve? Do you think it should be remembered? Why or why not?
6. Imagine one way the issue can be resolved. Think of one way that feels grounded for you. Maybe it's the creation of a chain of after-school programs or accessible mental health supports for all. Don't allow money or resources to be an issue. If it helps, think of yourself as having all the resources you need to resolve the issue.
7. Now think of a fantastic way this problem could be resolved. Something that feels outrageous to you. Perhaps a fairy godmother waves a wand or magical pixie dust fills the air and everyone loves one another. Feel free to explore your imagination or come up with something incredibly fantastic.

## Exercises: Symbols and Social Issues

1. Using pencil and paper or your computer, come up with a symbol for the society you've named. This symbol can be abstract, composed of basic shapes, or pulled from existing ones. The symbol should be imbued with all the happiness and the values you associate with your exciting future world. You can play with colors or keep it simple. What's most important is that the symbol makes you feel good and that you place it within view. Place this symbol on a wall in your home or as a screensaver in your phone. This symbol is giving your utopian world a space to live and breathe in your imagination. Note how you feel. If this symbol inspires you to write a poem or song, or any other endeavor, feel free to do so.

2. Think of one task you can do, habit you can make, or current skill you have that could help address the societal issue you're concerned about. Take the step and note the difference.

# 10

# THE VISION

## Creation, Invention, and Transformation from Visions

WE ARE IN AN EXPANSIVE UNIVERSE. We are always evolving, as are the people in the world around us. We adjust to our visions, and what we envision adjusts to us. But this process isn't always a conscious one. Rather than shapeshifting, taking on new forms to adapt to a changing environment, we are shapeshifted by the vision—morphing and growing to accommodate who we must be to bring it into the three-dimensional world.

Creatives have an intimate relationship with this evolution process. Creatives are constantly expanding mentally and emotionally (think of expanding space) to accommodate their dreams and visions. An image of an artwork comes to mind: The painter goes into a state of contemplation, note taking, research, testing new painting techniques or materials to bring it about. They dive into form, adjust sleeping patterns or diet, hang out at new places to be attuned to understanding both what the image is and how to bring it into form. While we aren't all professional artists, we can all have a relationship with a healthy creatorship in our sub-conscious. Our subconscious has many layers, sometimes filtering through our visions.

In the 1970s, Yaoundé Olu owned Osun, an art gallery in Chicago named after the Yoruba orisha, that was focused on Afro-futurist works. Today she works as a cartoonist and creates fine art. Olu was creating mash-ups of computer-generated images and traditional art styles that mirrored ancient futures in the 1980s. "With Afrofuturism we're all sharing the vibration in this cosmic soup," she shared with me. "We're transformers. The art is coming though us but not coming from us. The artist is the interpreter of the unseen. The artist is the arbiter of the unmanifested reality. It comes through artists. That's why artists are ahead of their times." It's our natural state to feel connected to visions, yet so much in our day-to-day lives doesn't have the language for what to do with them.

## Cosmic Soup

There are three kinds of visions we often deal with. The first is a series of unexplained images and/or sensations that come to mind. They have no known source and don't appear to be connected to anything incredibly familiar. Some feel like fragments, a snapshot from a larger story. Others are grand in nature, like natural phenomena, and overpowering. Both have a weighted significance that can't be explained. A journey ensues to understand the meaning of the image, one that takes us into unfamiliar spaces, mentally and physically. When we come into some form of understanding, we create or embark on a new path in community with others.

The second kind of vision is one where the directive is pretty clear. The vision is embedded with a form of action, one so resolute that the vision and the action seem as one. The vision isn't necessarily an action, but it spawns one. It comes in the form of a lightning-quick idea so complete that it feels as if it evolved out of contemplation or a life's work. The vision can feel as if your life's experiences conditioned you to be receptive and take action on the vision right away. In one sense, it's like the first vision with a speedier journey.

We also have visions that we craft, as we've done in earlier chapters. These are ones we're conscious of imagining; visions we are compelled to create. We shape these on our own or with a collective.

I don't consciously remember any story ideas born of a sleeping dream. However, I do recall visions when images became so intense that I had to write about them. These images and feelings were succinct and felt like daydreams (which we'll discuss later). However, they weren't daydreams, conscious narratives I enjoyed escaping to. They were simply compelling fragments. Literary critic Umberto Eco says that most stories begin with an unexplained, persistent image that comes to mind. The answer to what this image is becomes the story.

Where do the images come from? There are those who believe such images come from on high, descending from universal consciousness through our soul and mind as a funnel. Others say they're pulled from memories lost. Both very well could be one and the same.

There are some people who are able to take these visions, use them as a creative springboard, and rally people to help bring their inspired creations into existence. They can see the vision clearly. The vision serves as a guiding light and requires a healthy amount of personal transformation on the part of those who are helping to fulfill the mission or create the inspired work born of the vision. It's almost as if these visionaries are carriers of the vision, an idea or desire they have but don't feel is theirs exclusively. Sometimes they describe themselves as channels, open vessels to a universe with a message. When these visions uplift humanity, help the Earth, or make life easier, those who help craft and articulate the vision are called visionaries. This seismic shifting vision leads to other creations.

Usually, the implementation of the vision radically enhances the industry, community, or the world for the better. Sometimes these visions and their creations seem grandiose in largesse, like the visions of a Kwame Nkrumah in building an independent African nation, or a Dr. King and Ella Baker protesting for civil and human rights. Other times, these visions can seem modest but dire, personal but impactful. Perhaps the visionary is fueled by a desire to uplift themselves as much as they are others. But the results are profound. Sometimes the first step is modest, artistic, but heartfelt. The step fills the visionary with joy.

## Image in Space

Nathaniel Mary Quinn is a critically acclaimed artist whose work is often described as Neosurrealist or Afrosurrealist. Neosurrealism works are inspired by a dream state, whereas Afrosurrealism draws from the surrealness of life. Quinn thinks of his approach to the work as Afrofuturist. The Brooklyn-based artist told me in conversation that the images that come to him don't come from sleeping dreams. "I wouldn't say dreams, because people think it's something that occurs when you're asleep. It's not dreams, it's not to say my visions aren't influenced by dreams I've had," he says.

"I will say that every work of art that I make it does come from a vision, which is a mental picture in your head that just comes to me. What's important to note is it's not contrived. I'm not trying to force myself to have a certain mental picture. It just comes. When they do come, I never forget them," he says. In fact, he says he never writes them down because "I resonate with them so strongly that I remember them." Nor does he try to decipher their meaning. "I don't concern myself with trying to understand them. I just make them. As I make the work, then the work tries to tell me what it's about."

Sometimes the visions are clear and sometimes they aren't, he says. But he has to stay close to the detail he remembers or the process fizzles. "If the vision is a woman in a lace shirt, and I say I don't feel like painting a lace shirt, and paint something else, it doesn't work. I have to paint the lace shirt," he says. Although he'll inform the work by looking for comparable images for detail online or in magazines, he's completely married to the image that comes to him.

It's only through the creation of the piece that the meaning is revealed. This is a reminder of the value that comes from the process. "I don't say I'm going to make a piece about this and that. I say I have a vision, I don't know what it means. I'm not going to interpret it. I'm just going to make this piece."

But this evolution in embracing visions and not questioning them was a turning point in Quinn's career. "Those early works marked the beginning of my understanding of the importance of visions. Before I made those works, my earlier works were about things I felt I should make because I'm a Black artist, about being Black in America or race relations. But I never felt like it was an honest impression of my art practice."

The painting *Charles* was his first experience with the vision process. The vision was of a man in a racoon fur hat, similar to the ones worn in Chicago during his childhood in the 1980s. "The vision was about that fur hat really," he said. "When I finished making it, it looked like my brother, Charles."

Quinn hadn't seen his family in years. After Quinn's mother's death during his teen years, his family vanished. He worked very hard to put the trauma behind him, eventually crafting an art career. He learned to release his resentment through forgiveness and gratitude. He wouldn't see his brothers again for nearly two decades. Nor had he seen them at the time of the vision.

The vision was a spark. Subsequent images came to him— images he'd completely forgotten about. As he painted them, he realized they were people he remembered from his childhood in the

Robert Taylor Homes, a housing project now demolished. "Neighbors, drug addicts, random people on the street—all these visions started to come to me," he said. "All these people I knew—they all became subjects in my art."

*Charles* was the beginning of Quinn working with visions. Quinn thinks of his visions, which appear as a painted collage within a human image, as evolving out of connectivity with people. He doesn't resist the images that come his way. "You remove the judgements," he said. "You accept them as a human being."

## Transformations

When this vision process takes place outside the creative realm, it is sometimes called radical transformation. Radical transformation is a mix of radical thinking and radical action, or actions and thoughts that take one out of their day-to-day conventions. Some people have visions that transform their lives. This vision might come in the form of a dream or an altered state. The defining characteristic of the vision is that it is not consciously imagined, or self-generated, but seems to emerge from an inspired or spiritual source. When such visions take hold, they are hard to contain.

Alice Coltrane was a celebrated pianist working in partnership with her husband, revered trumpet player and composer John Coltrane. A trusted member of his band, Coltrane was devoted to her husband's beliefs about universal love, oneness, and music. With his encouragement, she began playing the harp, noting its Egyptian origins and embracing the instrument's ethereal nature. When her husband passed away, Coltrane says she spiraled. His death was a huge loss in the music world, but a very personal loss for her. A mother of four who leaned on collaborating with her husband, she was emotionally devastated when he left the Earth plane. Then an experience she calls "the awakening" occurred. Turiya, Coltrane's granddaughter, narrates the experience in a Luaka Bop documentary: "She experienced hallucinations in which trees spoke and various beings existed on astral planes and the sounds of a planetary ether spun through her brain knocking her unconscious."[1]

Coltrane would later describe this as part of the hapus, a period that prepared her to seek out Swami Satchidananda, a guru in India. Following her second trip she abandoned the secular life, becoming a spiritual leader, a swamini in the Hindu tradition, and founded Sai Anantam Ashram and Vedantic Center. She adopted the Sanskrit name Turiyasangitananda, which means "the transcendental Lord's highest song of bliss." Her evolved faith centered around music, a fusion of African American gospel, jazz in the spirit of her late husband, and Vedic songs, as healing. By the mid-1970s, Coltrane recorded some twenty albums, with Carlos Santana, Ornette Coleman, and Pharoah Sanders among her collaborators. She released several cassettes of music created with the members of her ashram.

"She believed she was playing spiritual music," writes Franya J. Berkman in *Monument Eternal: The Music of Alice Coltrane*. As Coltrane began to focus solely on her ashram community, she deepened her musical exploration. The cassettes were among the first Western-based Vedic-inspired songs produced. However, their uniqueness stands above the rest, in part because of her openness to fusing traditions.

"How do we make sense of these songs? They are at once African American and South Asian," writes Berkman. "Their histories can be traced to religious revivals spanning India's medieval period, as well to cultural formulations that coalesced in the New World among the descendants of African slaves."

Berkman continues, "Appreciating and understanding Alice Coltane's sacred music at the ashram—and, for that matter, the other music that she recorded and performed over the course of her prolific career—requires that we move beyond reedified categories of musical style and religious practice and honor the open-ended quality of cultural production, and the ways we pass on the life of cultures."[2]

Coltrane stressed the value of transcendence beyond limitation. She spoke of meditating for as long as twenty hours at a time. Her quest for transcendence and musical evolution gave her a new sense of self.

What was Coltrane transcending? She was seeking a perspective greater than the data streams of information around her, out of the systems and bias that defined. She yearned to crawl beyond the limited scope of knowledge valued and connect to the inspired knowledge from other spaces and times, ones that were presented to her as nonexistent or of no value. She wanted a perspective that took her beyond the route loop of existence. She wanted a resolve for the tremendous loss of a husband and creative partner. There has to be more—more meaning, more depth, more reason. Her vision was the impetus for a journey that brought her the perspective she longed for, one centered around oneness. Coltrane uncovered that she was one with the universe, connected to life in all its forms and yet not limited to form itself. She found a belonging in this connection that gave her life new meaning and purpose. Those who studied under her and listened to her music were transformed as well.

Sometimes we feel boxed in by algorithms of expectation, but we are part of a greater expanse. This connection to the bigness of the universe puts all else in perspective. "I think that it gave me freedom," she says in the documentary on her life. "It gave me my true independence. That no matter where I go in the world or whatever I do or whatever my involvement, I am free. The world cannot claim me anymore," she said. Coltrane's newfound understanding came at her lowest point. "I can act, I can be, I can live as I want to. There's no claim. No one can buy me. I have no karmas to pay. All of it has been given back to me and I'm free."[3]

I'm struck by Coltrane's openness. She became a willing vessel for music, following her own ear and not the conventional expectation of the time. She was willing to go to places, physically and creatively, that others weren't willing to go in. "Her music in the 80s and beyond represents a profound attitude of openness and ethereality in a fashion only attainable by an artist who turned the music into her life and her soul into the vessel," states the website for the John and Alice Coltrane Home. "This language of gospel, of Eastern thought and culture, of fiercely honed jazz, was manifested through a lifetime of unwavering dedication, even in times when it looked as if fate had turned its back."[4]

Although many of us have not had experiences in the vein of Coltrane's, it's important to note receptivity to evolution, commitment to mission, and dedication to community. Her full expression of self was as important as community enrichment. Meditation was a big part of her practice.

## Visionaries and Innovators

Although some start with the grand vision, others who become visionaries are meeting a present need: the unhoused need housing, a teacher needs classroom supplies, children need after-school activities, or the uninspired need hope. Their commitment and devotion to addressing this need makes the visionary resourceful. This resourcefulness may make them an innovator. They seek to meet an urgent need and use the materials that are available to them. They start with what they have.

Usually what they have, by conventional standards, is either not sufficient or simply not designed for addressing the need in question, but they make adjustments so that it does. In doing so, this unconventional measure that most would not have taken becomes uniquely perfect in meeting the need. Again, I think of artists. An artist needs to paint; they can't afford canvas; they use wood blocks or bricks found in the street. The form becomes malleable for the need and a new work is created, a new direction is revealed. We dub them creative and innovative as a result. The art they create touches hearts and minds.

Many innovators don't set out to be innovators. Their goal is to address a communal issue, one that they resonate with personally. However, the work and dedication elevates all who are around them. As their commitment intensifies, as they address issues in sustainable ways, they draw others to assist. Their capacity to address the need grows.

We each have the seedlings of being a visionary and an innovator within us. We are sometimes fueled by a dream, one that seems bigger than anything we could achieve, that prompts a grand desire for growth. It feels like a radical shift, one that makes us feel more cosmic than our life previously allowed for. The dream accelerates a path we didn't know we were on. This transformation may take us to new places with new people, but it requires change. We become a renewed person, whether that was our conscious aim or not.

It can feel as if all around us is changing, the familiar no longer familiar, our norms in question. We can feel as if we are on a seesaw. But as we take in the lessons, we realize that this experience was as much about changing us, bringing us to a new level of awareness, as it is about how our change can affect what we build with others. A new life mission is born. The change is essentially us becoming more of ourselves.

There are some who believe that the overview effect can cause such a transformation. Astronauts who've viewed the Earth from the far reaches of space speak of an overwhelming emotion that overtakes them, one we call the overview effect. As they look at the blue marble from beyond the stratosphere, they are suddenly hit with the recognition that there's a unity in life and they must dedicate themselves to it. Some organizations advocate for spaceflight so that we all can have this life-changing experience. I commend these efforts and know they can change lives. However, I don't think we need to go to space to have a grand transformation. (Although I think it would be very cool if we could.) It's not an experience we can wait on to create connections. Our dreams and visions can link us to the expanse of time along with our time in Earth's nature—our oceans, trees, or simply the energy of the people in our cities or the energy of the city itself.

Whereas the visionary is moved by the dream, the innovator within us is compelled to address a dire need. The two can work hand in hand. Both reveal a depth and a capacity we didn't know we had.

## A DJ Saved My Life

Derrick Jones, known as D-Nice, was first introduced to the music world as a member of the legendary rap collective Boogie Down Productions with KRS-One in the 1980s. Jones then had a successful solo career while intermittently working as a photographer and deejaying. As he focused more on deejaying, he experienced the highs and lows of a changing industry. His mix of R&B, classic hip-hop, and rock wasn't generating interest from larger EDM-friendly global venues. "I felt exhausted," he told the *Washington Post*.[5]

On the cusp of 2020, Jones was preparing to end his DJ career. Just as he was about to pivot to working in film, the pandemic hit. Coronavirus was taking lives and a wave of panic, fear, and sadness crashed over the world. Venues were shut down. Stay-at-home orders were in place. Performing artists could no longer work. The social scene came to a standstill as people sought to protect themselves and stay safe.

One Saturday in March 2020, as the world was gripped in fear, D-Nice hooked up his turntables and deejayed on Instagram Live. Jones says he was really just trying to find a way to stay connected with his audience and stay upbeat. But he also addressed a need. People were afraid. Millions were isolated, separated from loved ones, some of whom were hospitalized. Others were confined, suffering with the virus. Political tensions in the United States were at an all-time high. Everyone craved connection and comfort.

Word of the virtual set spread fast. Jones, in true DJ fashion, saved lives. Playing songs that invoked good times and family reunions, Jones wound up with over six hundred thousand people tuning in, including notables like former First Lady Michelle Obama and model Naomi Campbell. Both celebrities and fans were rubbing elbows online, giving live feedback about the music with one another.

I remember getting a text about the ongoing set and being thankful for D-Nice's generosity. I also remember listening for a few hours, moving onto something else, and tuning in an hour later, stunned that he was still spinning. Jones deejayed for an epic nine hours, unpaid, in a T-shirt and his trademark hat, nonstop, drenched in sweat, reminding us to keep our spirits up. The idea of a live DJ set where you could see the DJ on social media was unheard of. No one had used the platforms in this way. In fact, Instagram didn't have the capacity to stream for longer than an hour. The platform was not designed for longform concerts nor did it have the capacity for professional level audio. Jones made adjustments with his own audio system. He also had to log back in every hour as he was kicked off and continue the set. He touched hearts and minds worldwide. Everything about the moment was unconventional.

"Typically, DJs feed off the energy of the crowd, and that's part of what made D-Nice's performance exceptional: he stood, in all likelihood, in an otherwise empty room, and became the architect of a vibe washing over thousands of people around the world whom he could not see," writes Jelani Cobb, reporting on the epic set for the *New Yorker*.[6]

The set was dubbed Club Quarantine. Jones continued to spin on social media, sparking a wave of DJs, including Questlove, DJ Jazzy Jeff, and Hard Hittin Harry, to use social media to connect, inspire, and keep thriving. Erykah Badu produced a quarantine concert, Apocalypse One, featuring all women DJs including DJ Leydis and Natasha Diggs, along with a full band.

The event took place between her bedroom and an experimental room. Producers Timbaland and Swizz Beatz launched Verzuz, an IG competition, playing their music one by one as battle songs from the isolation of their studios. The series evolved into a love fest for recording artists to playfully battle, sing along with their records, talk smack, and generate joy.

What began as a few artists isolated in their homes singing along with their music quickly evolved into full concerts as the platforms adapted. What may have started as a nostalgia exercise for some fans in some cases refreshed careers, introducing established artists to new audiences. A performance arts industry that was brought to its knees received new life in stripped down, at-home performances and talks with fans. It all began with one man on a turntable, looking to lift his spirits, and others', too.

The purity of it all—a famous DJ spinning in his home in an attempt to connect with others doing the same—was emotional and astounding. "It's the magic of being authentic," said Marcellus Womack, who also wrote about the D-Nice experience in *Run It*. Marcellus is my brother and he's spellbound by people who are able to find "the zone." "He tapped into something like Serena Williams or Michael Jordan; he was in a flow," he said.

Marcellus received texts about the epic moment in the making, too. "I remember the first time listening, and it was just incredible music. I don't think I ever felt music like that in the DJ experience before," he said. "He was just doing it from the sincerity of his heart. It allowed him to make a dent in the universe, and led to a lot of opportunities, not just as a DJ but as a light." Jones was also able to magnify what DJs do, he said, "which is bring people together. He's very special to the culture. He played music. That was his service to the world and the culture during that time."

Jones continued to play virtually for a year. But his stamina during such long breaks was incredible. "The reason why I was able to play for 19 hours straight with five hours here, take a break and return again to play another five hours was because music has always been a form of therapy for me," D-Nice told For(bes) the Culture. "When things were going rough, George Floyd and Breonna Taylor, all I could do was play music that reflected what I was feeling. During that time, some of the music was very sad, but it was still healing. During the good times there's nothing like playing feel good music. You need your spirits uplifted and you play a Frankie Beverly record, or you put on an old Luther Vandross song, it just gives you a different vibe."

When the world reopened, Club Quarantine was in high demand, with Jones's upcoming gigs including one-of-a-kind dates at Carnegie Hall and the Oscars. ASCAP gave him a Voice of the Culture award. Moreover, Jones's use of social media platforms meant those platforms had to revolutionize their capacities to stream live performances to larger audiences.

Jones didn't go on IG with a vision of Club Quarantine going on tour. He was propelled by a need to elevate his own consciousness, connect with the audiences, and survive the moment in preparation for the next. He used what he had access to—a social media platform, his equipment, and his residence. He used his own talents, that of a DJ who could soothe and uplift with sound. His focus sustained him over the course of hours where his dedication and uplift helped everyone.

When I was chatting with Blacktronika creator and DJ/producer King Britt, naming artistic visionaries in recent years, D-Nice was the first to come to mind. "During the pandemic, he revolutionized how we use the technology. It's the same old tradition of using whatever is in front of us and using it for something great, like taking the turntable and turning it into an instrument. He was the first one to take the streaming game to the next level. While doing that he brought so much happiness. He brought the whole world together."

It's the intensity of the focus and the purity of intention that facilitated the uplift, his and those around him. "That's the zone Marcellus was talking about," Britt said of D-Nice's nine-plus-hour sets. "You're unaware of time. That's the God zone. All reality stops and you just are in it. Quincy Jones talks about it when they were working on Michael Jackson's *Off the Wall*, they were twenty hours in and falling asleep. That time between when you think you're falling asleep and still awake, that's when you're most creative."

We are in a time where we're encouraged to lead with what's marketable, what's sellable, as a form of connection. Such strategies have their place. However, if we don't watch it we can find ourselves functioning more as walking brands, calculating our every step to align with a market value rather than living as human beings operating from our best visions of ourselves and communities. We're told to be authentic more as a selling point than for the impact of authenticity itself. Although D-Nice is a professional artist who wants to be paid for his work, his selflessness in a time of need changed lives, his career, and the reach of the style of music he was playing. There are times when we want to address a need and there's nothing inherently marketable or conventional about the means to do so. If this is a stopping point for you, be wary.

When we do work, tapping into our inner visionary and innovator, the work should feel supernatural. We should feel in flow. There should be an experience of being in the zone, a sense of peace, a transcendence, a greater purpose. It doesn't mean that everything runs smoothly, or some problem-solving isn't involved, or their aren't some challenges, but there is a peace that comes from work that is aligned with your purpose even if the task is, by other people's standards, mundane. If you're not feeling this way at any point in the process, a shift may be required: a shift in mind, a physical shift, or an all-out adjustment. Maybe you need to go in a completely different direction. Move in the direction of inner peace.

If the creative aftermath of these visions uplift humanity and the Earth and are shaped in community, you're on the right track. If they don't, but rather they cause irreparable harm, and your personal success or that of only a few is more important than how this benefits humanity and the Earth, then you are not on the right track. There can be some debate about this. There are many a narcissist with delusions of grandeur who've led us astray with the promise of a false vision, one that doesn't enrich anyone's soul but may fatten a few pockets, namely the person hawking the vision. While I don't feel adept at describing the difference, I will proceed with an understanding that deep within you, you know the difference and will act accordingly.

## The Charge

One of the more difficult challenges in being a visionary and innovator is that this receptivity to radical transformation doesn't sit well with everyone. The vision or innovation may lead to lifestyle shifts that are deemed weird, unorthodox, or foster outright rejection.

Sun Ra attributes his vision of universal connection to an alien abduction. There is nothing conventional about discussing an alien encounter, even if it does double as a spiritual transformation. Nor is there anything conventional about naming oneself after a deity and dressing as one twenty-four seven. The experience radically shifted his direction in music. In turn, Sun Ra adopted variations of stoicism in his life to become more attuned to the vision. He abandoned smoking and alcohol and adjusted his diet. He meditated and required the same of his musicians. He lived communally with his musicians as they uncovered secrets in the music and vibrations that would heal and inspire. His Saturn/Ra mythology and alter-destiny helped him to reimagine himself and re-situate world occurrences. His new habits helped sustain his direction. However, they also helped the composer to deal with the challenges and rejections he often faced. From the strange looks from onlookers to the unwillingness of major radio stations to put him in rotation, Sun Ra's walk was not an easy one. Until fairly recently, he wasn't discussed as central to the Black Arts Movement, despite his contributions.

The *Cricket*, a music journal by Black writers and music theorists published from 1968 to 1969, frequently ran Sun Ra's poetry. The publication was created to provide a perspective on experimental jazz by Black creators who followed innovator John Coltrane's passing. Founded by Amiri Baraka, Larry Neal, and A. B. Spellman, the *Cricket* released four issues, and they would become pivotal in understanding the future-thinking consciousness of the experimental jazz artists who were eclipsed by a psychedelic rock scene. Such artists were trying to break away from the jazz standard, one they reasoned was hampered by co-opting. Artists such as Ornette Coleman and Sonny Sharrock were among those whose futurist music was analyzed. A collective statement of experimental jazz as a future world, Sun Ra's poetry and essays were an ample counterpart to the analysis.

In his essay "My Music Is Words," Sun Ra details his philosophy and speaks of the difficulties in presenting his music of peace and love. He speaks of the jazz greats he admired or worked with, including Fletcher Henderson. He's clear about the great obstacle he faces by playing music from the astral realms: "Freedom to me means the freedom to rise above a cruel planet," he writes. Yet, Sun Ra persists in sharing his musical message. Space music is his beingness.

"Space music is an introductory prelude to the sound of greater infinity," writes Sun Ra. "It is not a new thing project to me, as the kind of music is my natural being and presentation. It is a different order of sounds synchronized to the different order of Being."[7]

His commitment to expansion is asserted. "The alternative to limitation is INFINITY," he writes.[8] The journey our inner visionary and innovator takes us on can lead us to other communities where we find ourselves.

## Reflection Questions

1.  Have you had an experience with visions before? What was it? How did it come to you? Did it come as a vision or sensation? What did you do?
2.  Has anyone in your family or a friend had a visioning ability? How did it serve them or others?
3.  Have you had an experience that gave you greater awareness or a sense of connection to the universe? The experience doesn't have to be in the nature of the ones that Sun Ra or Coltrane had, but it can be transformative, nonetheless. What was it? How did it affect you?
4.  Do you feel you are here for a reason? Are there abilities you have that can help others? Are there abilities you would like to cultivate to help others? What are they? How could they apply?

## Exercise: Meditation, Mindfulness, and Being

Here I have exercises for meditation, mindfulness, and being in nature. Some of the artists we mentioned adopted some of these practices. These practices were part of what made them more receptive to visions. They build a relationship with what to do with a vision should one occur. Try one or all of them. These are individual experiences. The aim is that you will uncover a practice that helps you to still your mind and develop a conscious awareness that you are in a universe.

However, your mind can find stillness or peace in noisy environments and while you're moving. You don't have to be physically still to experience connection. The function of these exercises is to create balance in your day, make you less reactionary, and allow you to be more receptive to ideas, insights, and solutions. These practices are a reminder that you are, despite all that's going on in your life, part of an infinite universe. Try implementing at least one once a day for a week or two. Note how you feel afterward. Also note any adjustments you find in your week.

## The Silence

Meditation or being in the silence can help center you throughout your day. Regardless of your faith or background, a reminder that you are in a universe or a discipline of being receptive to new directions or ideas is a great practice. It also prevents you from being reactionary, reacting to the day's events rather than creating experiences. Spend two minutes of your day, in the morning if possible, and sit in silence. If you sit in a chair, keep your chest lifted and feet flat on the floor. You can also sit on the floor. Close your eyes. Although this is a nice practice to do to start your day, you can also do it in the midst of your activities. Take a few moments in your parked car, on the bus, or in the office.

If thoughts or a list of errands come to your mind, try to center on thinking nothing. Your goal is to still your mind. To think of nothing. To allow your body and mind to be an open vessel. The hope is that by stilling your mind, over time you will discipline yourself to hear or feel ideas more clearly. You can begin with one minute and build up to a longer time. Now, just because you're in the silence doesn't mean that you need silence around you. Claim a space of silence for yourself.

## Mindfulness

Mindfulness is the practice of paying attention. The objective is to stay present and to stay in a space of nonjudgment. This nonjudgment is as close as we can get to being objective, a tool that can help us be receptive. Veronica Womack writes and lectures on mindfulness for Northwestern University's Searle Center. "You're being aware of your present moment experience, your emotions, your thoughts, your sensations, and the external landscape," she says. This practice can be done in an array of tasks. Chances are that you've practiced mindfulness in some way before. Perhaps while listening to music, preparing a meal, taking a shower, or folding clothes, you found yourself being aware, present, or at ease.

"If you pay attention to your thoughts but judge yourself for having the thought, or have an evaluation call about what that thought means or what it means about that person, that's not an example of being mindful," she says. "You're putting value on the thought and the emotion. You're not being present because you're adding on to it through interpretation." Mindfulness can reduce anxiety symptoms and depressive symptoms because you approach your thoughts and emotions from a level of compassion and you're not ruminating on them. Nonjudgment is the key. Although there are times when you need to make judgment calls, your space for mindfulness is not that time.

Minds can wander. However, bringing yourself back to focus is also a mindful act. One quick way to get back to the present moment is through the breath or by focusing on the senses, Womack says. Ask yourself: What am I tasting? What am I feeling? Do I feel the jeans on my legs? What am I smelling? What am I seeing? "That's the come on back. That's the present moment experience," she says. Mindfulness can be a reminder that thoughts can change. Sensations can change. There's no need to hold onto them.

1. Can you think of a task that you do where you already practice mindfulness? Can you think of a task someone in your family does that's mindful? Your friends?
2. Select a task that you would like to do mindfully. In your practice, note the colors, sensations, sounds. Note feelings and thoughts, but allow them to pass. If you find yourself being self-critical or wandering, simply take a deep breath, recenter your breathing, and bring your attention back to the sensations of the activity.

## *Nature Moment*

We don't all have access to a wide expanse of nature. But at the least we have access to a tree or the sky. Take two minutes in your day (just two) and look into the sky and watch the clouds, observe a tree, or star gaze. Be mindful in your moment. I've found that taking a few minutes to watch the clouds is unusually refreshing. Something about this refrain forces you to think of nothing. If your night sky is awash in streetlight or smog, no worries, step outside and become aware of the air. Take note of the air. Is it sticky? Do you feel the breeze? Allow yourself to feel the weather, however briefly (even if it's raining). Take in the nuance. If you're in a city where noise is constant, see if you can find the silence in the noise.

# 11

# NOTES OF A DREAMER

## Creating Conscious Relationships with Your Dreams

OUR DREAMS ARE RIFE WITH MESSAGING. Nighttime dreams connect us with our subconscious. They can bring emotions that we ignore to the surface. They give form to concerns we didn't give conscious thought to. Some are premonitions, warnings, or connections to ancestral realms. They provide answers to questions we didn't realize we'd asked. Dreams are experienced as being very different from our world but cojoined or aligned. The logic is punch-drunk. Phrases that make total sense in the dream world make little to none when we awaken. Our best friend can be our mother, a television star can be a sibling, a witch can appear, those who've passed on are alive. We take on new abilities. We fly like a bird or we helm an aircraft. We run really fast or ridiculously slow. Some dreams are slow, easy glides and others resemble action adventure movies. In this stream of story lines, we are both a participant and an observer; in the movie and the theater patron shouting at the screen.

The funhouse mirror effect that defines our dreams, this feel of a wonky world both strange and familiar, is a universal experience that humans have sought to decipher for centuries. Books on dream symbols and numbers and dream interpreters abound. If you think back to our YOU ARE HERE map that indicates where and when we are in time and space, you'll see that the dreamscape is a map, too. I think of the dreamscape as a map to the secret underground, one that is tethered to the surface world, but not of it. It's similar to looking at the electrical wiring map at an amusement park. If you're not an electrician, the whole schemata looks like a mess of wires, colors, and codes. Even if you are an electrician, you have to figure the map out, looking for key markers to understand the layout. Regardless, the electrical map is essential to the whole place working. But this "figuring out the map" process is a waking experience. In the dream, we're in the center of a rush of moving action, trying to keep up with the circus pace. In the dream, we are in a physical space of slumber.

The messages in dreams are unique to our own makeup. Although there are symbols that can have a broader cultural significance and there are varying ancient ways to cast dream experiences, this universal experience has a unique temper that is crafted for us. Whether we remember our dreams or not, scientists have established that we do, in fact, all dream. On average, we dream three to seven dreams a night. This dream experience is essential to our existence as humans. We need to eat, drink water, sleep, breathe oxygen, and dream for survival. This necessity of human survival is the one we know the least about. Having a conscious relationship with our nighttime dreams (and our daytime ones), much like building one with our visions and imagination, helps us gain a working understanding of our subconscious. Our subconscious is part of a larger collective conscious. We connect deeper with ourselves and with others as we come to understand how our dreams work for us.

Shaman Malidoma Patrice Somé says that dreamers should invite ancestors to share messages in dreams. Somé was trained in Western medicine and the Dagara indigenous traditions of Burkina Faso. He says that ancestors like to help their progeny. "The ancestor must have clear instructions and should be invited to come in a dream," says Somé. "Ancestors usually love directions like this. The line between this side and the other side is not such that things coming to us from there are always clear and understandable. We must help our needy ancestors learn to communicate with us. Otherwise, they think we understand and have simply chosen not to reply to comply."[1] He adds, "A person with a body is an ideal vehicle for Spirit to manifest things in this world."

I was once part of a collective in which I had a dream partner. Periodically we would meet and talk about our dreams, with each partner taking turns asking one another about our nighttime dreams, making comparisons and spotting themes. Although neither of us was an expert, the questions helped us to verbalize our thoughts about the dreams. Our discussions helped me to make connections between related ideas that were obvious to my dream partner but not to me until they were verbalized. Dreams are odd birds, and talking about them can feel like serving up our vulnerability on a silver platter. Dreaming and dreamers are revered in some spaces and vilified in others. These societal message impact how or if we interact with our own dreams in waking spaces. Discussing dreams aloud with a trusted partner made both the dream and my relationship to it more tangible. I couldn't dismiss it as easily if I shared it with someone. As a tangible discussion point, I was acknowledging the experience. This acknowledgment is a step in renewing our relationship with our subconscious.

## Lay It Down

Tricia Hersey, founder of the Nap Ministry, is an advocate of naps. "Lay your ass down," is one of her mantras.[2] She reasons that our bodies are overworked, we are laboring for capitalist systems, and that the grind is designed to make us think of ourselves as machines. "You are not a machine. Stop grinding," she says.[3] The recommendation is easier said than done. Some misconstrue her messages of rest as one of perennial leisure. "People still think the rest message I'm sharing means don't ever work a job, have a career and just sleep all day. It's amazing how an exhausted and traumatized body and mind refuses to see and hear what is actually being said," she says.[4]

Success is associated with working around the clock, not with resting. But rest is a source of rejuvenation and sustained success. Naps are a means of reclaiming time, self, and personhood. However, naps are also a way of normalizing the value of dreams and the dream state. "We believe our bodies are portals. They are sites of liberation, knowledge, and invention that are waiting to be reclaimed and awakened by the beautiful interruptions of brutal systems that sleep and dreaming provide," writes Hersey, author of *Rest Is Resistance*.[5]

## The Dream Journal

There were periods in my life when I would place a notebook beside my bed. As soon as I awakened, I grabbed my trusty book and wrote down every part of my dream I could remember. Some days all I remembered was a fragment.

Initially, my dreams just seemed like a bunch of chaotic half stories with no rhyme or reason. People I forgot I knew, random figures on TV, and others were characters in *Alice in Wonderland*-like stories. Dreams would jump cut from one half-cocked adventure to the next. Over time, the process of writing my dreams disciplined me to remembering more and I found myself writing pages upon pages of dreams from a single night. At points I felt I was writing a fluid stream of consciousness, a tome of related symbology.

Eventually, I did begin to see patterns. I noticed reoccurring dreams, premonitions, threads of worry from conversations the night before, answers to questions I posed, moments with people who passed on, urgent reminders, and release through adventure. These dreams were coded in metaphor. At some point, all the dreams seemed to take place in a loosely threaded world. I noticed reoccurring locations of ballrooms and islands. My dreams had a visual and emotional language of their own. This language only became apparent after looking at dreams over a period of time.

Among the surprises were the reoccurring dreams and how they weaved into my waking life. I was completely unaware that I was having the same dream several times a week. The dream began with me walking into a dance rehearsal. (As you may have noticed, all things for me circle back to dance.) I'm surrounded by friends I performed with in high school. We're all adults. We have ten minutes before we're supposed to perform and I'm stressed out trying to remember a routine I haven't done in years. I'm given a costume from high school that does not fit; I have no time to stretch. I remember the song and some of the steps but not the entire routine. The dance studio has a mirror and I can see my own frazzle. There's this overwhelming feeling of trying to recall something familiar and the pending worry of going on stage completely unprepared. The dream always cuts off before I make it on stage.

The dream would switch up—a different combination of friends, a different studio, another costume that wouldn't fit—but the core theme remained. Somedays I'd make it backstage clad in a too small ensemble, other times I was holding the costume in hand staring in the mirror. Subconsciously, I always kept dance attire in the trunk or wore something that in a pinch was suitable for a quick spin or kick. One day, in waking life, I was at a club, surrounded by friends I hadn't seen in awhile, some of whom appeared in the dream, and a song came on that we'd done a routine to some years back. I was mildly petrified that my dream was coming to life. Was this the moment? Are we all supposed to get in formation, Beyoncé style? I laughed it off as anxiousness.

I noted this dream and assumed it was a message to stay ready. Stay prepared for the opportunities to come. That was my resolve for years. Finally, I had a dream where I did make it onto the stage. My outfit fit. I remembered the choreography, and the whole stage turned to champagne rose gold (I can't explain that part). Yaaaay for resolution. I noted this in my journal. My reoccurring dream had come to an apex. A subconscious issue resolved!

After noting this resolution I threw myself into the day's work, not thinking much of it. In the evening, I was at an event space, the Soho House actually, and bumped into Peter Gaona. Gaona, who is most known for his Reformed School fashion creations and accessories, also worked with a renowned professional dance company. We were in the same dance classes in high school. Peter was in a bit of a rush. He ran up to me, hurriedly sharing that a dance workshop he was co-teaching with another professional was in progress. It began in ten minutes, and he thought I should be in the class. The class was more advanced than I thought I was prepared for—a full-on contemporary/modern class based in technique.

I didn't have any dance attire, I told him. No problem, he had some for me. The clothes fit exactly. I had no excuse. There was no time to stretch. The dance room had a mirror. There was another friend in the class. The whole time I'm thinking, *You've got to be kidding me.* In the class, we were doing steps I hadn't done in years. But I did just fine. I was pretty flabbergasted about it all. When I got home, I received an email for a work opportunity that would greatly impact my career. The opportunity required that I travel overseas by the end of the week. This was an affirmation that this dream was both metaphor and premonition. If I hadn't written these dreams down, I would've missed the significance.

Every dream isn't a premonition, but most are some kind of metaphor. This metaphor does have a direct relationship to our experience. Maybe it's all a wink and nod from the universe. The irony of the dream and its relationship to my waking life did not escape me. It was a reminder to pay attention to my dreams, be aware of them, and uncover the language. This uncovering doesn't have to be an intense form of study. Insights from dreams will be revealed in life experiences when we stay aware. This experience is a reminder of our universal connection and an inner modality beyond our conscious mind that is a form of intelligence. What does it all mean? Beyond the lesson we are to stay aware. Be present. When I told Peter about the experience and the dream later, he shared that he'd had the same reoccurring dream, too.

## Daydreams

Daydreams are often spaces of escape, a visioning of where we'd like to be or a re-creation of an experience we'd like to have. Sometimes we rework past situations in our favor, imagine saying things we couldn't or shouldn't say. We imagine things we might like to do but may not for the sake of convention. We imagine people we'd like to share with. Usually, a daydream has some conscious impetus. It's an expression of desire or an imagined experience that releases emotion. When daydreams are an expression of desire, they are indicators of experiences we feel will create a more fulfilling life. As we become conscious of our daydreams we bring them to our attention as well. Why am I daydreaming about being a trapeze artist in a circus day after day? Is there a joy or experience that I need to replicate more of in my life? The daydream may not have much to do with the circus at all but rather what being a trapeze artist means for us. Does it symbolize freedom, a need to go out, a fashion shift, a bit of excitement? Yes, yes, yes, and yes.

On the other hand, daydreams are very healthy ways of taking our mind off things, like a mini vacation that lasts all of two minutes. For some, daydreams are a refresh. Although daydreaming is rich with insights, it's OK to daydream for a daydream's sake, too.

Some daydreams are purely a release of a difficult emotion. In this case, it's best to let the emotion pass without judging ourselves. Daydreams are default ways of working through an unresolved emotion. If you're daydreaming about telling your boss where he can stuff it in the most egregious way possible, or, as in a scene from Issa Rae's *Insecure*, throwing your cheating boyfriend's newborn like a football, you're resolving an emotion through the daydream. If this emotion isn't resolved through short-lived escapism, then it's OK to talk to a professional to gain new tools to work through the unresolved emotion.

## Nightmare Insights

Janelle Monáe is celebrated for her music and compelling portrayals in film. She gleefully pushes past gender binaries and respectability politics. For most of her career, she took on the persona of an android, a narrative that's shared in her albums. The story for her album *Dirty Computer*, and the accompanying emotion picture, as well as the book *The Memory Librarian* that followed, first came to her in a dream.

The dream was a nightmare: A woman is kidnapped in a movie theater. Her kidnappers aim to erase the woman's memories—memories of her identity and past loves. When Monáe awakened she was frightened. What did it mean? What was happening? The story became the impetus for Monáe's creations. The unknown woman soon evolved into android Jane 57821, Monáe's android persona. *Dirty Computer* follows the android outlier through her romp of love and romance, one that doesn't fit. Culture critic Mary Retta says the album is "both cautionary tale and Afro-futurist prophecy; a testament to Black queer survival in unbearable conditions."[6]

Fans can't help but notice the real-life metaphor of Monáe's urgent need to push past the restrictions of pop star norms and family expectations of how a person who wants respect should conduct themselves around matters of sex, intimacy, and liberation. This turn in Monáe's work was born of a dream. All of our dreaming variations are like gifts. The insights we pull can fast-track us in moving with the desires or purpose we may have surfacing in our life.

## Reflection Questions

Having a conscious relationship with our dreams can unravel deep meanings. Bringing these dreams to our conscious attention through journaling and chatting with others helps us to make connections we can build upon for healthy lives.

1. Can you recall a compelling dream? What happened? Why did this dream stand out?
2. Can you recall a recurring dream? What was it? What meaning did you find in the dream? Did the meaning change over time?
3. Can you recall a dream from an ancestor? What occurred? How did you interpret the dream?
4. Have you noticed any patterns in your dreams? Perhaps there are reoccurring locations, familiar people, or repeated themes.
5. Have you ever had a dream that inspired a creative work, decision, or action?
6. What do you daydream about? Why?

## Exercise: Dream Book

1. Keep a dream book, one allocated to the recording of your dreams, at the side of your bed. As soon as you wake up, before you check your phone or hop out the bed, record what you remember. Make a commitment to do this as often as possible. Periodically throughout the month, reread your dreams. Note any relationships you find. Feel

free to share your dreams with a friend who can provide their insight, too. You are looking for patterns, emotions, narratives. Dreams aren't usually literal. You may notice connections right away. You may not notice any for some time. At the very least, in your periodic rereads, note how you feel about what you're dreaming.

2. Try asking a question before you fall asleep. Note if you have any refreshed insights the following day.

3. Ideas often come to us all the time. Rather than let them fly, make a habit of writing them down or noting them in a recorder. Some of these ideas may be great to build on, others not so much. But your goal is to become aware of those ideas that come to you. By noting your ideas and desires, you may see a theme emerging that could lead to new creative solutions, projects, or hobbies.

4. Note your daydreams. How do these dreams make you feel? What emotions or feelings do you experience in the daydream that you would like more of in your life? What can you create more of in your life?

# III

# RHYTHM
# AND DANCE

# 12

# ENERGY

## The History and Future of Dance

SIMPLY STATED, rhythm is a series of repetitive patterns. Variations in rhythm reflect differing approaches to space/time philosophy as an embodied experience. Dance is embodied rhythm. An embodied experience is both grounding, in that we are connected to our Earth, and astral, in our connection to the broader universe. As a reminder, being in the body is not just about the body itself but rather the wisdom that comes from our physical form, that which makes us of Earth but is not relegated solely to the Earth plane or, for that matter, matter itself. Being in the body gets us out of our heads and is a recognition that our mental machinations are one source of many in understanding ourselves and the world around us.

Dance is a space/time technology, one that connects humans to the patterns or rhythms that unify our universe, our societies, our collective states of elation. Every culture has its own core rhythms—ones reflected in its music, dance, and language—that speak to how people gather and operate in harmony with the universe and one another. Cultures have preserved rhythms that have uniquely sustained life or were sources of vitality for the culture.

Dance is its own energy generator. When we dance we are always communing with ourselves, those around us, nature, and the universe. Dance is an acknowledgment of the sharing of energy. It's also a wellspring of joy, a display of gratitude, an assertion of connection. Dance is an acknowledgment of a continuous flow of energy. Rhythm speaks to a flow. We learn how to be in flow with the universe and those around us while maintaining the highest state of elation.

Through dance, we learn how to be in community, to share space, to connect to universal rhythms while acknowledging individual expression. Much like the jazz artists who were obliterating boundaries, dance is a process of pushing past physical and sometimes social limitations to express harmony. We forge connection to the rhythm, becoming one with the flow, the shared pattern. The joy this creates is incomparable. The emotional release is healing work. The synchronicity of bodies in motion, finding shared space and timing with strangers or loved ones, moving between one another's time, is an unspoken unifier and mirror of our communal heights as a society.

Dance is not a mind-centered activity. Sure, people may think through motions beforehand or move in ways that are familiar to them, but it is a statement of being in a flow. It is a form of intelligence, another way of knowing. This flow, while dynamic, requires being present. This state of being present transcends the moment. We are as connected to those sharing the rhythm in the moment as we are to those who've found life in motion before and those who will find life in these movements later.

We dance because it makes us happy. I dance because it makes me happy. A friend of mine likes to say that we can't dance and keep our worries present simultaneously. The tribulations of the moment dissipate while dancing. Layers of worry and doubt slip away like the shedding of old skin. Dancing reminds us that we are bigger than the problems we face, part of a universe more dynamic than our present challenges. Dance forges the state of being that optimism aims to establish. The uptick in energy from dancing is enough of a refresh to face our problems differently, with a renewed perspective, one not born of conscious contemplation and fretting, but one pouring from universe-sourced elation. Dance is a reminder that making time for our earthbound cosmic relationship will always garnish a reward, a generation of joy, a carousing of energy.

André Zachery is a choreographer and artistic director with the Renegade Performance Group in New York. He crafts Afrofuturist dances. His work *Respiration* is an homage to N. K. Jemisin's sci-fi novel *The City We Became*. "You can't really understand Black cultures if you don't have a relationship with dance in the culture," he told me. Understanding dance is an avenue in understanding Afrofuturism at work and how it can apply in our lives. As much as some of us dance, we rarely talk about dance and the energy work at play. It's often understood but not articulated. As I reached out to dance-loving colleagues and friends to discuss the energy work in movement, we found ourselves grasping for language to root it all.

I often reference the Hindu chakras, codified for thousands of years in India, in discussing moving meditations. Moving meditations require breathing and body motion. The motions are deliberate; specific stances may be held. The chakras point to seven key energy centers in the body, through which life force energy or kundalini rises through our grounding with the Earth, through our chakras, and out through our head, connecting us with the universe. The grounding occurs in a crouched position, one that is closer to the ground. In this sense we are a tree, connected to the Earth and the sky above.

This energy vantage point is one way of describing energy flow, and it is the first way I framed energy in my Afrofuturism dance experience work. We do specific moving meditations with breath and motion aligned with chakra points as part of the yoga tradition. But these movements, ones I was taught with conscious breathing and motions, are not dances. Yoga, as I was reminded by performance artist Amrita Dhaliwal, stretches our bodies to prepare for long periods of meditation in stillness.

## BODY CHAKRAS

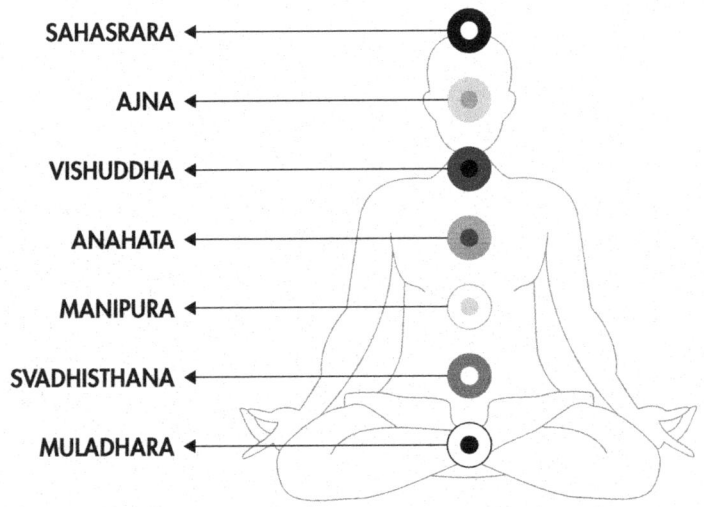

SAHASRARA

AJNA

VISHUDDHA

ANAHATA

MANIPURA

SVADHISTHANA

MULADHARA

These meditations were a step in helping me explain dance as cosmic experience. However, dance is a moving meditation of another order. Learning moving meditations aligned with chakras was a step in helping me find the language in framing the energy work in the African-based dances I grew up with. The chakras are the most commonly referenced energy system for movement in the West. However, the chakra system itself was not a focal point in the creation of African/African Diasporic dances. When I asked a Havana-based professional dancer about the contained motions in Cuban rumba some time back that differed from, say, the broader spaces that accompanied the wider dance stances in African America or Jamaican dancehall, he shared that the dance was designed to electrify energy centers throughout the body. This conversation sparked a realization that varying dances and rhythms reflected different ways of embodying energy. The African/African Diasporic systems broadly have other reference points, some that align with the Hindu chakras but tread other cosmic waters.

Dance, as a space/time technology, is inherently spiritual or cosmic. I say cosmic because I believe one can have an experience of being interconnected with a universe and humanity without having a specific spiritual belief. Some forms of African traditional dance are performed in a context where the body becomes a vessel or is mounted by a powerful spirit. This is the case in Ifá, a spiritual path that originated among the Yoruba people and is practiced in the Americas as Candomblé and Santería, where each orisha or spirit has a dance and is channeled by a dancer who takes on their persona. This also occurs in vodun where a loa, or ancestor spirit, communes in the body of a dancing person. In fact, it's a tradition in most African forms of spirituality. Even dance and rhythm in Black Christian churches in the Americas invoke a catching of the holy spirit or spirit possession dances. It's within these styles that dance innovator Katherine Dunham became an initiate in spiritual practices to learn. In these instances, people are moving in specific ways and undergoing practices so that their bodies become temporary temples for ancestors or deities to express.

However, most social or celebratory dancing in the African/African Diasporic world is not about the mounting of the spirit. Yet both traditional and contemporary dances cherish universal connection as an instant pipeline to the cosmic. The contemporary dances draw from traditional ones. We are often dancing to sacred rhythms, doing movements or assembling from the ancient, all in a contemporary landscape that is conscious of the joys but not the source, cognizant of the celebration but not the reason.

Sometimes our freestyle movements, when we go with the flow encapsulated by rhythm and excitement, lead to this awareness. We're at a party spinning around and are struck by an overwhelming happiness, an intense release of frustrations, a perception of connection that goes beyond our immediate space. Other times we perform traditional steps with specific meanings, or partner forms such as salsa or Chicago stepping, which allow for individual expression. Regardless, the feeling is one of intense freedom. The experience is freedom as awareness. Just as our emotions bubbling from imagined and virtual spaces pour into our physical one, we take the awareness of connection through dancing into our day-to-day activities, too. This experience keeps us lifted.

Dance is embodied liberation. The purpose is remembering our oneness, our shared existence with one another, and the shared path we have as humans on this Earth plane. The purpose is to experience sheer joy, liberation, and deep connectivity as one. The connection is deemed as liberating, and the liberation is a reminder of connection. The experience is awareness. We become aware of our cosmic identity, that which connects us biologically and experientially to all around us.

I talked to various dancing colleagues about energy for this section. The people I spoke to are dancers, dance scholars, and performers Erica Olivares Bowen, Kenneth "Djedi" Russell, André Zachery, Meklit Hadero, Sylviane Greensword, and Joshua "Stretch" Ishmon. I'm sharing their names because although the framing of energy in African and African Diasporic dances is something I understood from countless experiences dancing, the epiphanies on how to talk about energy came while communing with others who also dance. As we conversed, thinking of ways to frame energy in African/African Diasporic dancing, we agreed upon three ways. We agreed on the mounting of the spirit, we agreed on the joy generator of individual expression, and we all mentioned the ever-present circle. In fact, there wasn't anything we didn't agree upon, as each had a view that informed the other. The focus on the circle, this wheel of the world, unlocked connections that were literally hiding in plain sight.

## The Circle of Life

Most African/African Diasporic dances center around collective dancing in a circle. Break-dancing ciphers, freestyle dance circles, traditional dances, sabars in Senegal, the dinki mini in Jamaica. A drum beat or DJ kicks off the moment, maybe libations are poured, and a dancer spins or takes their place dancing, and everyone forms a circle around them. The dancer at the center is the focal point. When they're finished, they return to the circle and another person heads to the center to show their best. I think of it as the original *Soul Train* line, a moment where we showcase our best and are cheered on for doing so.

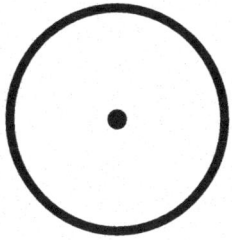

You at the center of the dance circle.

The rhythm is accented by clapping or other percussive instruments. The people forming the circle hold the space, cheering the person on. And this circle of energy continues, with one person heading to the center followed by the next, as long as it needs, too.

## The Kongo Cosmogram

Circles speak to life. Circles are continuous patterns of energy. Circles are unifying. Andre Fu-kiau, a Congolese researcher, dedicated much of his work to documenting the Bantu-Kongo philosophy to counter the impact of Belgian colonialism. He focused on the Kongo cosmogram, a spiritual symbol he described as the simplified "wheel of the world."[1] The cosmogram symbol was created by the Bakongo people who stretch across modern day Angola, the Democratic Republic of the Congo, and the Republic of the Congo. The cosmogram is a circle with an embedded cross. The cross is the dikenga or yowa. This circle is a bridge of the seen and unseen worlds, the spiritual and the physical, as a statement of life in all forms. It is divided by the kalunga line, a river that separates the worlds but keeps us connected. Millions of people from the Kongo kingdoms were captured in the transatlantic slave trade, and their philosophies are ever-present in African Diasporic cultures today.

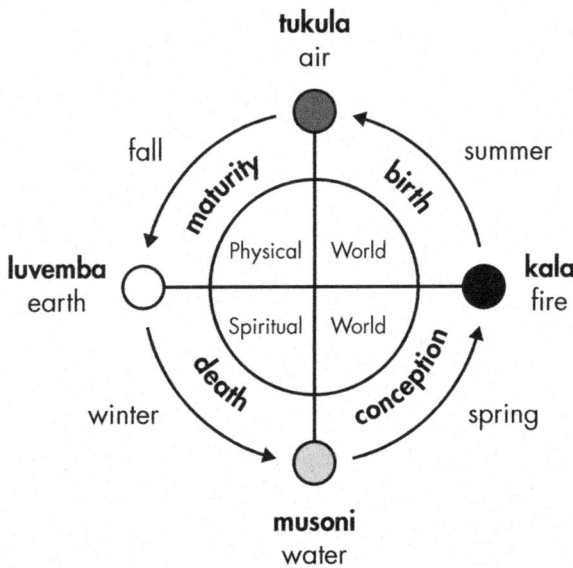

The Kongo story of origin says that the universe began as a void. This void existed in the form of a circle. Nzambi Mpungu, the creator god, called for a spark of fire, the kalunga, that expanded to fill the circle, becoming a force that birthed the elements that comprise our universe, our stars, and planets. Kalunga is the force.

Mpungo, who is sometimes called Kalunga, is also a god of change (remember Octavia Butler's oft repeated phrase "God is change" in *Parable of the Sower*). Change and perpetual motion are constants in the Bakongo philosophy. The circle is the primordial shape of life's essence. Everything comes forth through the circle. This circle isn't one that marks off territory or forges a separation, but rather is one that encompasses the whole.

The kalunga line in the cosmogram forms a river, a threshold between dimensions, implying that we can float between. Just as the circle connects spirit with the physical, it encapsulates the big bang or how the spiritual or nonvisible gave birth to the physical. The Bakongo philosophy is based in fours. The cosmogram mirrors the maturing faces of life and reincarnation: conception, birth, adulthood, and transitioning into the ancestor realm. Then one is born again, the pattern repeating. These four stages of life are reflected in the four movements in the rising and setting of the sun. In the philosophy of the cosmogram, we too are these suns, one of many providing light in our world and human affairs. This rising and setting symbolizes not just an arc of life's maturation, but also an arc of our creative evolutions as we take on new actions and move on to new phases, ideally elevating in awareness with each progression. From the vantage point of Earth, the sun feels like it's moving. But the eternal light that we are is a constant that only appears to change. We, the sun, are always shining. The occurrences in our life, our opportunities, and affairs are rotating around us.

The cosmogram is a way of thinking about creative power, the kind of power that created the universe and all else. It's also a way of thinking about how life force energy flows. One highly charged energetic point is the circle's center, where the axes cross and the dikenga is formed. This crossing of energy is potent. It is the inception of the known world's birth; it is the shaping of the invisible into form. This intersection is the point where visible and invisible worlds meet. References to the crossroads in blues and hip-hop speak of this magical moment literally.

Author Sterling Stuckey credits the ring shout as the source of all African American music. Elements of blues, jazz scatting, work songs, and hip-hop can trace their roots to this religious ritual performed during enslavement. Enslaved people had no legal control of their body, and they couldn't dance or display public joy. They couldn't use drums, a favored communication technology, either. The rings shout is a collective rhythm formed by people who must be contained in their movement or risk death. In the absence of instruments, music is created with body percussion and a stick. The people form a circle, barely lifting their feet but creating a sifting sound as they move across the ground, following one another in a circle. Participants were careful never to cross their feet, otherwise the motion would be mistaken for a dance. No one stands at the center, but the center is understood as the wellspring of energy. The tempo quickens, the circle moves faster, and a connection with ancestors and spirit is reinforced. The energy of the circle is continuous, flowing, meditative, rejuvenating, and life sustaining. Energy is contained, due to duress, but focused.

When circle dancing of all kinds begin, the dancer who kicks the cycle off works in concert with a musician, DJ, or drummer to anchor the energy, an unspoken homage. They stand at the circle's center, at the axis of the crossroads, the most powerful point of the dikenga. The circle of people forms to hold the space, becoming the physical representations of an invisible universal circle of primordial life. The interplay between the dancer at the center and the cheers and rhythm of the circle forges the expansion of the kalunga, or life force energy. When the dancer at the center is finished displaying their finest moves of the moment, they shift into the collective and allow someone else to do the same. Everyone who chooses gets to be the focal point of the energy. Shy ones are encouraged. All who take center circle are supported. No one is jeered. The person at the center of the circle rarely overstays their welcome, and they nearly always return to the circle. They rarely leave the circle once they realign. The space one holds for us, we have to hold for another. We are sharing a circle, we are sharing the Earth, we are sharing a human experience. The pattern repeats. This celebration is an embodied moment, in which we are collectively aware of the mutual support we crave and provide.

When standing in the circle's perimeter, we are not an audience. We are not passive watchers or voyeurs in a magical exchange. This is not a showcase where we can tune out or tune in. We are participants in the flow of life, as active in our hand clapping in the circle's rim sustaining good vibes with head nods as we are when we eventually move to the center to flex our best. This experience of energy exchange and the cosmogram at play is pretty ubiquitous in African and African Diasporic dances.

When I attended my first sabar in Dakar, I was told that we were going to see a dance performance. We were outdoors in a neighborhood community space. The moon was high, a light breeze ascended, and over a hundred people, mostly women, were seated in chairs in a circle. The circle was enormous. The drummers numbered in the dozens, stoking the sounds of rhythmic thunder at the circle's perimeter. A group of men rushed in with the energy of a comet and poured libations on the ground before exiting. I looked around, waiting to see where the performers would enter from. Then one woman in the audience came to the center of the circle and performed the mbalax. The dance is best described as an explosion of energy, with arms that form circles and kicks that suspend. Then another and another did the same. As the pattern continued, I realized that we, the people in the circle neatly seated in our wooden chairs, were the performers. I was thrown by the chairs, but this was nonetheless a cipher, the kind of circle formed for freestyle rap or break dance.

The mbalax is Senegal's national dance. The sabar is a monthly event in various Senegalese communities where people, mostly women, can have a moment of sheer freedom. There's something to be said about a culture that, knowing the stresses women endure, makes time for collective joy and relishing of freedom for women on a regular basis in a communal space where all can participate freely. This event is free. There's no contest, although everyone aims to be their flyest. The collective is supporting the collective.

Once I made the circle dance and cosmogram connection, I saw it everywhere in the cultures. I have to thank André for talking this through with me. Even dances that form lines in the African Diaspora are in fact circles. The promenade effect of the second line in New Orleans or the prized moments of coming down the *Soul Train* line are actually circles. *Soul Train* aired for over thirty-five years and helped codify Black dance styles in pop culture lexicon when it popped off in the 1970s. On the show, the dance entailed two lines of people facing one another, and two people come down the line together, freestyling or doing a prepared dance as they flex and primp. When they're done, they go back into their respective lines, cheering the next duo on, prepping to do it all again. This dance pops up at parties and gatherings today.

African American line dances, from the electric slide to the cupid shuffle and countless others, are essentially a unit of people turning in a circle. The dancers are standing in lines, dancing in unison, but they rotate as a collective, turning in all four directions, much like the cosmogram, forming a circle that repeats in the arc of incarnation. Black fraternities and sororities known for stepping, a mix of chants and rhythmic stomps, often circle the dance floors, moving around the crowd's celebrations. There are other cultures with dances that take place in a circle, but the circle dance as cosmogram produced in three-dimensional body movement as an expression of a cultural philosophy is significant.

Many African philosophies point to a similar way of viewing the circle as energy. However, the Kongo cosmogram, also called the Bakongo cosmogram, isn't simply a circle. Kiatezua Lubanzadio Luyaluka, of the Institut des Science Animiques in Kinshasa, writes of the circle's other dimensions. Luyaluka says that the cosmogram is a simplified version of a spiral. Although the intersecting dikenga speaks of the invisible giving birth to the physical, the circle itself is a collapsed spiral. Viewing the cosmogram as a spiral explains both the collective energy of the circle and the energy of the individual dancer as dance generator.

• *You are here*

In Congolese philosophy, a person has a life force in the form of a spiral or zingu, and when they transition to the spirit world they form another life force or spiral. The two spirals, in the physical world and in the beyond, form two joined spirals.[2]

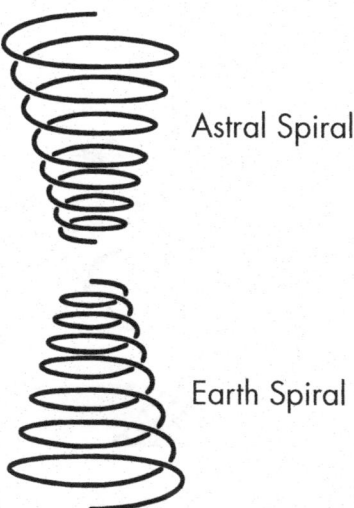

Astral Spiral

Earth Spiral

Sometimes this spiral is thought of as a double rainbow or two snakes, male and female (symbolic of life creation, not gender), who give birth to life in all its dimensions. This joining of the two spirals, or life forces or zingu, is the energy flow that the circle dances capture. In those dances where someone is at the circle's center, the crossroads, they are bridging life in this world and the next. When they dance as a unit, as in one of the many African American line dancing styles, they are one spiral. In the case of the *Soul Train* line, the two lines are two spirals, male and female symbolically (although not in makeup), creating two impromptu bursts of dance bravado as they connect one world of energy to the next. This idea of a snake's coiling as a spiral of life is also invoked in Haitian voodoo.

Damballah Wedo is one of the most powerful loa in Haitian voodoo. As father of the sky, he takes the form of a wise, primordial snake. He sustains life as being life force itself, circling the world with his coils. He is wed to Ayida Wedo, also known as the rainbow serpent of fire, wind, fertility, and water. As a couple, they are two spirals joined, a double rainbow. Their relationship is the source of creation. It can't go without mentioning that our DNA, that which holds the codes of our biological makeup, is a double helix, two spirals.

Damballah Wedo and Ayida Wedo

DNA double helix

This spiral theme appears when we dance in groups but also as we dance individually. The spiral describes the motion of the energy, a whirling synergy of joy. Joshua Ishmon reminded me that our bodies can be thought of as rotating off of a core. The dances that define African and African Diasporic dancing—isolated hip or chest rotations, reggae style twining, Puerto Rico's bomba, break dancing, Brazilian samba, belly dancing, body rolls—are dances that often reflect circular motions or spirals, and I would add to that, vibrating spirals.

In this snake metaphor we see more alignment with Tantric chakras and energy. I was reminded that African American shake dancers in the 1950s and '60s often painted colored circles where their chakras were on their bodies. These performers were asserting space on the margins, creating their own center of gravity. They were some of the earliest American adopters of yoga and Tantric teaching in the United States, but they applied it to enhance not just their life, but also their dancing.

The cosmogram and its spiraling energy doesn't work from the premise that our root chakras need more activating. Traditional African dances and their derivatives broadly have deep leg postures, a form of rooting. There's an assumption that we are rooted but not always aware. Whether we are conscious of our relationship to the Earth and the larger cosmos or not, we do in fact have a bond. Dancing brings this awareness to the forefront.

Partner dancing, the interchange of two people, is much like the two snakes joining, a cojoining of energy but also a cojoining of moving as a unit. Sometimes these dances are sensuous, but most times sexuality, despite the creation metaphor, is a byproduct of a perspective, an outsider gaze. When we operate from the mental space only, never communing with the intelligence that emerges from presence in the body, energy sharing and spiraling movements are misconstrued and judged as sexual. This celebration of life in its many forms is about liberation and communing.

The spiral is a reminder of community and communing. Performance artist Pap Souleye Fall portrays his character, Dead Pixel, in a neon green ensemble that resembles a motion capture suit, as an homage to the pixels that blot our computer screens. "It's this weird bridge between the physical, digital, and analog, all happening at the same time," he says.[3] He's reminded in his performance of the tradition of African ritual and dance that asserts "how we're supposed to act with each other, around each other." Dead Pixel poses the questions: What are we socializing? How are we socializing? How are we together with people? Communing as the spiral is where the answers unfold.

## Be Present

Dance is an embodied experience of being present. Khari B., who is known as the Discopoet for his house music affairs and spoken word poetry, leans on dance for its ability to shake off worry. "You're open. The nowness takes over," he told me. "You forget the past, you're not worried about the future, it's about just being in the moment. Depending on where you are in your own consciousness, you lose sight of things around you. You're dancing in your space and just connecting to the music and all of that coalesces into one thing. You, the vibration, the sound, and the time. Then some jerk bumps you and knocks you out of it," he joked.

Dance is a reminder of being present, but it's also a technology for compelling us to do so. Issues we have with our body, judgments about appearance, or criticisms we hold onto fall away while we're dancing. The act of dancing negates it, rendering our self-conscious preoccupations irrelevant. This happens because we are instantly connecting to primordial design, moving in ways that charge our existing connection to the shape of our DNA, our universal essence, the circle we spiraled from.

Are there specific traditional dances that anchor specific feelings of transcendence? Yes. However, we don't have to know any of these to feel a connection through dance and rhythm. Khari B. came of age in the house music scene. "The way we are with house music, there's no set of formal moves, you're really in your own creativity anyway. It leads to that moment where you're really able to let go," he said.

"Dance has never been a conscious thing. I'm moving and the music has me moving my legs like this. Because it lacks conscious thought, you are able to release yourself into the moment, and that's what leads to this ascension." It's our awareness that dance evokes a universal connection that can deepen our dance experiences.

## The Dance Commitment

There was a period in my life when dance was naturally occurring. My family liked dancing. I was in dance classes, so most of my friends were dancers or at least enjoyed dancing. College was filled with parties where the people I was with were all-out committed to dancing to the night's end. I performed regularly. When I adopted the Lois Lane life, writing for publications during the day, I continued to frequent parties, doing the most, and was also taking classes. As time moved on, I found that I had to be more committed to dancing. I attached myself to house music and Afrobeat scenes, descending upon one of my friends' annual house music parties. The party became an oasis. In a time when friendships were changing and going out became less routine, I found myself around people who weren't enthusiastic about dance. They inferred, in so many ways, that dance was something you did as a kid, or at a wedding or a chance gathering. Suggestions to do so in any other context were met with disdain.

It became clear that a commitment to dance would be a solo sojourn. As schedules became packed and the upward mobility climb became intense, I found my free time taken up by stomping out fires for a volunteer organization, and dance, this ever-present experience that was always a party away, became less frequent. While I might've been speaking as a latter-day dance evangelist, convincing nondancing friends of the art form's value to their resistant chagrin, the truth was I was talking about dancing more than I was doing it. I was wholly unaware of this shift until a friend, listening to me talk about dance as if it was an evaporating pot of gold, stopped me and asked, "Why aren't you dancing?"

The question, much like when Sun Ra posed Why you aren't in space? gave me pause. I had a litany of excuses to explain things away but no real reason. So, he called me on it again. "Why don't you go teach kids?" This was followed up by another suitcase of neatly folded reasons ranging from having never danced with Alvin Ailey to not getting to pointe level in ballet. "You've been dancing your entire life. What are you talking about?" he asked. Something in my dance life had given me the impression that I needed to be an ensemble dancer on Broadway or be crowned Miss Samba to call myself a dancer.

This resistance to embracing these claims can be shaped by a host of factors. Sometimes we feel we have to achieve a level of success before we can claim a pastime. We feel we must have some high level of mastery, a formal title. We might be beset by a sense of failure, of not taking our talents to another level.

We can feel uncomfortable with our bodies. We can feel intimi-
dated, self-conscious, out of touch. Guess what? We don't have
to be professionals or have a home teeming with trophies to
enjoy dance. We can proudly say we're dancers if we are in fact
dancing and like to do so. We can love dance without having
any formal recognition of being an expert. This claim frees us
to dance when we want, as we want, where we please. It frees
us to be in the flow and experience the conscious awareness of
liberation. Calling ourselves a dancer, claiming what we enjoy,
makes us receptive to dance's transformational properties. We
become consciously connected to dance energy at play in our
lives. This connection clears a path for more joy and freedom
in the spaces we traverse.

## Joyful, Joyful

Embracing the dancer life, even if we're excited about dance, can
feel like we're pushing against inertia. Much of Western society,
outside of appreciation for professional dance, in my opinion, is
uncomfortable being in the body. The body is sometimes dismissed
as something that needs to be fixed and fine-tuned, hidden or
ignored. We can be made to feel ashamed about our bodies, how
we're born to look, its changing shape. Something is too big or too
small, too sexual or not sexual enough. We're told that some looks
are healthy and desired and some not so much. Those beliefs we're
fed throughout our life seep in. We can internalize messages we
know are wrong, and they affect how we show up in the world.
Confusing messages have an impact on how we treat our bodies,
whether we claim joy or not.

Being comfortable in our body is liberating. This liberation
inspires as many people as it irks. How dare you be comfortable
in your body? How dare you assert a healthy relationship with the
universe and the space around you? How dare you be joyous of
your own volition? How dare you carve a space of joy?

I think about the dancer and choreographer O'Shae Sibley, who was stabbed after voguing at a Brooklyn gas station in 2023. The joy he felt creating beauty with his own body, a self-asserting queer man, doing a feat-defying dance born in ballroom culture as a testament of pride, was publicly challenged. He was confronted by angry men and killed by a teen. His life was taken for experiencing liberation in his body and being wholly comfortable in doing so in a space that was not "designated" for dancing. Claiming this liberation in his body and in a public space was perceived as threatening to "the way of things."

Dance is a form of self-expression and a release. Germaine Acogny is cofounder and artistic director of the Ecole des Sables in Senegal. Acogny created a contemporary African technique that draws students from around the world. "Dance is a specific weapon, it can bring people together. By dancing, regardless of whether it is a professional or amateur, it enables us to respond to all the bad things that are happening around us and in the world—whether that is the environment or war, it gives you a weapon you can use, a voice to speak with," she says.[4]

There's a stigma around dance. Moreover, there's a stigma around African and African Diasporic dances. Dances evolving from Black cultures can engage hip rotations, chest undulations, and frenetic footwork. Historically, these motions are deemed as sexual, too high energy, too complicated, or too big under the conventional white gaze. Such dances can make one visible in a world that is often pushing us to be smaller. Although I wasn't raised with this limited perception of dance, I did contend with it in various spaces when I continued to dance as an adult. I can't tell you the number of people who mistook me saying I was a dancer or liked dance as code for being an exotic dancer or a stone's toss away from being a sex worker. Exotic dancing has its place, but anyone having a joy for dance isn't a qualifier.

I recall being at a conference of philosophers, many of whom thought of themselves as being culturally astute. A dancer in academia with a contemporary Caribbean aesthetic performed. The dance was rich in elegant body undulations, with small hip and bust rotations, her movements tight and arms often outstretched and reaching toward the sky. She reminded me of a coquettish peacock. The theater was small, no more than forty people in the audience, so there was no way to escape her gaze or switch the channel. Nor was there a need to.

Her performance was amazing. She was building a specifically contemporary Caribbean dance language. After her performance, one male in the mostly male academic audience asked how was he supposed to watch this performance and not sexualize her. In his eyes, and likely many in the room, they didn't know how to enjoy or even observe her dance without resorting to unbridled desire or a power-based sexualization of the performer. I don't know if the performer gave much of an answer. I think she was as stunned as I was. But I would never forget the question.

I noticed the same sexualization in a salsa dance class I took. Women were paired with professional male dancers. Partner dancing requires being in sync with a partner, a feeling that some of the women, who weren't used to partnering, mistook for attraction or desire on the part of the instructors. Others misread critique or direction from the male dancers as sexual rejection or mansplaining. Although these men were attractive guys, they were dance teachers, not lovers or seducers. But it was difficult for many of the women to think of their male dance partners in any other way. They'd been socialized to think of partner dancing as an indicator of romance or lust. They saw partner dance as a negotiation of power, not the ease and flow being one that prevents you from tripping all over each other.

Many in Western society and beyond are socialized to reduce a dancer's enthusiasm for dances rich in Black aesthetics to the dancer's need for attention or sex. In turn, many who like dance are encouraged to think of it in this limiting box. Dance as sexuality morphs into a means of validation, short-circuiting the larger cosmic connection. Although some dances are sensual and some can attract admirers, African/African Diasporic dances are so much more. On the other hand, because dance is highly valued generally in Black and Brown spaces, there's also a fear of being in social spaces and not being good enough. Not being amazing can feel as if you're somehow disappointing the culture.

This fear of being sexualized or being rejected around desirability, or simply not being good enough, keeps some people from dance altogether. But for the sake of connecting with your own body and the space/time continuum through music, and to become the joy generator and experience the connection that is you, you'll have to toss these fears aside by dancing.

Dance workouts are encouraged because they are done under the guise of being a pragmatic use of the body whereas dancing for the sake of dancing is not. Dance is really about joy, expression, and connection. But there's something about making time for dance as joyous expression, with no end goal beyond that, that is perplexing for some.

Dance brings me joy. At various points, I would get so caught up in work and the demands of life that I wasn't making time for an art form I enjoyed. Among the blocks I used to prevent me from dancing more was this idea that I needed to go out in order to enjoy myself. Yes, delights of life can be born from dance floors, parties, and classes, but you don't need to drive across town every time you want to move to the beat. We don't have to be at the event of the year to move or be in a space with lights dim enough and a crowd big enough that we disappear. As we now know, we can actually dance where we are, in our home, in our living room. Eddaviel (Edison Montero), an Afrofuturist artist, says his love for dance began when watching his parents dancing in the morning while drinking their coffee. "My father says the key to life is to do five merengues a day," he says.

We don't need to wait for the right DJ to enjoy ourselves. Get that playlist going, find a mirror, and go. Sylviane Greensword grew up studying dance in Algeria and France before attending college in Louisiana. Her father loved to dance and would push the furniture aside for the family to dance in the living room. She learned modern and later created dance troupes that merged African dance styles and break dancing. Today she teaches wedding choreography when she's not teaching Afrofuturism.

"I dance all the time," she says. "I dance when I drive. My kids have the TV on, they're dancing, and I join it. My daughter is teaching me the TikTok dances. I have health issues, but I still do my dance workouts every week because of the energy it gives me."

I'm all for dancing in community. Yes, RSVP for the must-attend event of your heart's desire and dance. However, you don't need to rely on the right conditions to do so. You don't have to be amazing. You don't have to be the best—but you have to be committed. Make a playlist with some of your favorite songs or find a set online by your favorite DJ and dance to it. Give yourself permission to be joyous or to uncover the joy in dance. Why are you stopping yourself from feeling the cosmic, unifying connection?

## Mirror Moment 2

In Dakar I went to what I'll call a mirror club. There are a number of red-hued dance venues lined with mirrors from floor to ceiling where people are dancing with their reflections. Many dance venues around the world have mirrors where crowds can catch glimpses of themselves. But I'd never been to one designed specifically around the joy of self-admiration. When I told my Senegalese friends, they were surprised that I'd been denied what was a pretty normal experience for them. At the club, we were assembled in a line, spaced enough to see ourselves, and we danced. Dancing in the mirror with yourself is rich with joy and humor. When you're dancing with your reflection, you can really hype yourself up, course correcting as needed. I was laughing at myself, I was making faces. I was all in and doing the most. Although I could see others in the mirror, too, it wasn't about them. We had each come to dance with ourselves. When I found out how common these spaces were, I thought it was the coolest, most self-affirming experience. It was like dancing at home but in a way cooler venue with better lighting and pulsating speakers. You're not waiting for a partner or a connection with a stranger, nor do you have to overcome awkwardness in doing your own thing.

When I began getting back into dance, I made time to dance for me. There was nothing formal about this experience. In some cases, I was still in my pajamas or workout clothes. I'd put on some Fela Kuti or house music and just dance. I wasn't doing anything choreographed. I just wanted to see what motions gave me joy. Although there was a mirror around, how I looked wasn't the point. It was all about how I felt.

## Reflection Questions

1. Think about dance as a universal connector or joy generator. How does this make you feel? How do you relate to this idea?

2. Have you ever experienced dancing in the types of circles mentioned in the chapter? What was the context? Did you have multiple experiences? List and describe them.

3. What is your experience with dance? Did you dance as a kid? Does your family dance? What kind of dancing did you do growing up? What kind of dancing do you do now?

4. Think of moments when you enjoyed dancing. What did you like about it?

5. What do you like about watching people dance? How does watching others dance make you feel?

6. Are there specific dances or movements that you like to do? What are they? What do you like about them?

Dancing can bring up an array of body issues and memories. Criticisms, discomfort, and unresolved emotion can surface. We can work through these by acknowledging them and freeing ourselves to dance for ourselves.

1. Do you like dancing? Do you find joy in dancing? Why or why not?
2. If you like dancing, do you currently make time for it? Why or why not? How do you make time?
3. Do you ever feel sexualized when you're dancing? Can you recall a moment? How did you feel? Did it impact the way you dance? How?
4. Were you ever teased for how you dance? For how you look dancing? How did this impact you? How does it impact your relationship to dance?
5. Can you recall a moment when you were uncomfortable dancing or uncomfortable watching someone dance? What was occurring? Why did you feel this way? What feeling or thoughts came up for you?
6. Have you ever experienced dance as a form of releasing tough emotions? Anger, sorrow, frustration? How did dancing help?

## Exercises: Dance

Let's take a moment to get in touch with our body. Play the song "Maggot Brain" by Funkadelic. "Maggot Brain" is slow, intense wonderment. This song is one of my favorites; it's also ethereal and slow moving.

1. Find some space in your place and move with the rhythm. Think of your body as being connected to a larger universe, harmoniously aligning with people and nature. Take a moment to allow the feeling of this connection to

wash over you. You don't have to do anything specific. Move as you wish. Think of movements you can do that engage your feet, legs, hips, chest, arms, and head. Experiment moving various parts of your body in isolation or all together. Think of movements that make you feel like you're moving in a spiral, such as hip rotations or spins. If thoughts of feeling silly pop up, push them away. You are open and receptive to acknowledging your connection to the universe and humanity. Utilize the space around you. Make small movements and large ones, adapting as you need to around the furniture in your place! Try dancing on the floor or along the wall. House culture adores dancing on the speaker!

2.  When you're finished, jot down how you feel. How do you feel doing each movement? Which areas did you enjoy moving and which were difficult for you? Are any thoughts, memories, emotions, or ideas coming to mind? Is there a move you wanted to do but didn't? Why not?

3.  Try dancing to "Maggot Brain" again, and this time do whatever you like including those moves you didn't want to do initially. Be aware of the spiral that connects you with the universe and freestyle. Be playful and give yourself to the song. Laugh at yourself. You are under no pressure to please anyone. Don't allow the day's worries or being self-conscious rob you of the joy from the connection. Get out of your head and just move. Allow the joy of the connection to sweep over you. Repeat with one of your favorite songs. Take a break if you need to.

4.  Gather a group of friends and pick your favorite high vibration song from the playlist on my website: https://www.ytashawomack.com/playlists. Form a circle and one by one dance in the circle, freestyling as you like. Enjoy yourself. Cheer on those at the center. This space of joy should feel natural. Do this as long as you like.

Let's do some mirror dancing. Our aim is to enjoy ourselves. We are our own best partners.

1.  Find a mirror in your place, play your favorite songs or ones from the playlist, and enjoy. Feel free to dim the lights if you wish. Try different movements. This isn't so much about how you look but about appreciating yourself, how far you've come, and the great experiences you have in store. Be as playful as you want. Love yourself and allow the joy that sweeps over you to be your daily armor.

2.  Think of dance as your yoga. Try dancing in the morning as a morning routine. You can also try dance breaks midday. Whatever the case, make time to dance for you. I suggest doing some light stretching first and keeping some water close at hand. The purpose of this is to enjoy yourself. Explore different moves. Take up all the space in your room. Experiment with dancing on the floor, dancing on the wall, and note how you feel. If there's a move you stumble upon that you really like, keep doing it. Although this experience will have some fitness benefits if done consistently, the aim is to incorporate dance in your week as moments of joy to kick off or extend your day. Commit to making time to dance several times a week. You can dance for as little as five minutes in your own home. Note how you feel each time. Note how you feel over time. How do you feel in a week? In a month?

3.  Dance to a Future: Write a paragraph about what an idealized future would look like. Take note of what this future feels like. Pick a song from the playlist and devote a few minutes to dancing, with the intention of affirming a heathy, happy future. Allow yourself to feel the joy of the joyous future you envision. Note how you feel afterward.

# 13

# NATURE'S MEDICINE

## Movement Outdoors

In 1986, Tommy Sutton, renowned tap dancer, wrote a book to articulate the core tap dance exercises and aesthetic he used as the foundation for his long-running dance school, Mayfair Academy. Sutton performed with the likes of Duke Ellington, Cab Calloway, and tap dancer Bill "Bojangles" Robinson during his career. In his book, rather than detail his exciting life or dive straight into the dance combinations he's most famous for, Sutton wrote an homage to dance and its roots in nature:

> From the beginning of time, mankind has marveled, delighted and been mystified by the natural rhythmic sounds of nature: the raindrop filtering through the trees in musical meter; the rush of the winds through the elements in a cadenza of muted melody; the pulsation of his own heartbeat in perfect rhythm. . . .
>
> Mankind's natural, inherent need to excel could only be expressed in his emulation of the image of God, experiencing the wonderment of the beatitudes of life's sound

from nature's own symphony, and birthing the beat which permeates the whole of existence. Man sought to capture and explore all things to the glory of God—the beautiful movements of all God's creatures, as in: the grace of the swan; the elegance of the elk; the litheness of the panther; the stretch of the cat; the syncopation of the bird on the wing.[1]

Although, many of us think of dance more as a social or celebratory activity, it does evolve from the wonder of mimicking motions in nature. Earlier, we spoke of the spiral energy at play, but many dance movements originated as replications of natural forces and animals around us. Germaine Acogny incorporates dance and nature in her instruction in Senegal. Known as the "Mother of Contemporary African Dance," students from around the world come to learn her rigorous dance aesthetic. During their residency at her Ecole des Sables, students both practice and perform intense routines in sands off the Atlantic Ocean. Supported by Senegal's first president and Negritude writer, Léopold Sédar Senghor, Acogney's work would codify traditional dances into a core aesthetic. "Now, I think contemporary African dance can come from anywhere. In the United States, it's taught at many universities. You can teach it or get your master's in it. That took a long time, but finally, it's becoming recognized just as European dance is."[2]

However, Acogny says that nature is her inspiration. "I am mainly inspired by nature, the dance of life!" she says. "I am more connected to my traditions, my roots of dance, to nature and responding to certain events—they are what inspire me the most."

When Acogny was preparing to lead a workshop in Yorkshire for the Ageless Festival in July 2022, a journalist asked her what students should expect. "You can expect to transform your body to be part of nature," she says.

Nature has so many beautiful movements, for example, you might dance as the buffalo or the deer. We explore beasts in Senegal specifically, and the trees, I have developed beautiful movements for both of these trees. This will help dancers to grow with their body language. Through this technique I have discovered, each movement has its own rhythm, performed by percussion.[3]

Although dancing outdoors in the sand is intense, there's a beauty in dancing on natural terrain, barefoot with an ocean nearby. Dancing in nature, with the breeze, the sound of the ocean, and soft terrain beneath us is an active engagement with our environment. I think about the dances we do today as originating with this holistic understanding.

In the Ifá religion and its diasporic counterparts, powerful orishas have a call-and-response dance. These orishas, male and female, symbolize aspects of life and personalities that are tied to nature elements. Yemoja, the orisha of the oceans, embodies maternal energy. Her waters nurture and are powerful protectors. Oshun has the flirtatious flow of the river, a reminder of beauty and the sweetness of life. Shango, the fierce protector, embodies the liveliness of thunder and lightning, with those dancing in response swinging a metaphorical ax across their body.

Music, too, reflects the sounds of its environment. The swing and metallic dings in reggae mimic the swings of workers in hills and mines. The techno of Detroit was a soundscape that mimicked the factory life and a city population in decline. The space age in the 1970s and '80s, post–moon landing, led to dances like the moonwalk and the robot. This tendency to re-create our urbanized environments in music and dance may necessitate thinking more consciously about dance and nature elements.

When I work with teens and adults creating Afrofuturism dance experiences, I sometimes divide the class into elements. Each element has a goddess, and participants can decide whether they feel aligned with a goddess of fire, water, air, or earth. As a collective, they discuss why they align with this element and how it speaks to their personality. They list the traits of the element as reflected in their personalities. Within their groups they come up with movements and create a quick dance that reflects the element. Sometimes, rather than work with an element, the groups will select a star or a space phenomenon. As you can imagine, water dances evoke liquid movements while air inspires lightness and openness. The fire dances are erratic and sweeping, while the earth ones are grounding and rotate on an axis. In a world where we're not always conscious of the nature around us—our night skies dimmed by artificial light, cell phone towers adding extra charge in the air, walking on concrete rather than soil terrains—these groupings help us to connect. We connect with natural phenomena and how it speaks to us personally. In doing so, we engage subtly with those in other times who created such dances as an homage to the elements that give our world life. What is it like to dance with an element? As an element? What sides of ourselves do we connect with as a result? The outpouring of love and this hug from our natural world awaits us.

I've been a part of collectives or events where we dance outside, the moon lighting our way or the sun blazing at our backs. The whisper of the wind under the pulsating base, or the mist from the lake cooling us off. Dancing outdoors adds more sensory experiences to our dance moments. Group dancing outdoors at festivals and picnics in tree-filled parks adds another sensation to our connection. Even if we're dancing at block parties and street festivals, twisting away on concrete, there is a beaming sun above, humidity in our air, and a breeze we crave. Again, we don't have to wait for an outdoor festival to move with the wind. We don't need music either. The sounds of the rhythms of our streets, our very heartbeats setting the tempo, an engine humming, a lightning bug, and a small space under the sky are all we need to move.

## Reflection Questions

Dancing with and in nature brings a touch of magic in our life and enhances connection.

1. Have you ever danced outdoors or in nature? What did it feel like? Is there a preferred nature space or outdoor area where you would like to dance?
2. Do you have apprehensions about dancing outdoors? What are they?
3. If you were an element in nature, what element would you be? Which element do you have an affinity for?
4. Jot down the qualities for your chosen element.

## Exercises: Elemental Dance

1. Do you have the personality of fire, water, air, wood, or earth? Think of yourself as a goddess of a nature element. You are a walking myth come to life. Jot down the qualities of your chosen element.
2. Once you've chosen your element, write a poem or flash fiction about this element. The story can be fantastic with fantasy elements if you like. It doesn't have to be very long. If you're not comfortable writing, you can record a story out loud. If you're doing this exercise in a group, you can come up with a collaborative story.
3. Think about movements that best embody your chosen element. Maybe moving your arms in a wave speaks to you as water or a spin reminds you of air. There are no right or wrong answers here.
4. Pick a song that speaks to this element.
5. Take a few minutes and dance, freestyle, centering this element. Play the song you picked. Think of yourself as being in harmony with your chosen element. Feel free to

include the motions you noted. Also feel free to add any elements around you that symbolize the element. If you choose water, perhaps you can have a cup of water nearby. If you choose fire and decide to use a candle, be careful!

6. Find a spot in nature, sans music, where you can freestyle dance as your element as well. You can find a spot near the element of your choice, your own yard, near a tree, or in a park. If none of these spaces feels accessible for you, just go outdoors, anywhere. Be aware of those around, but don't be attuned to judgement. Be aware of the sounds, sights, or feelings around you and see if they inspire. Alternately, you can tune them out and focus on your oneness. Try this using the environment as your musical tapestry and also try doing so with music on your headphones or speaker. Allocate a few minutes to dance, recognizing your spiraling oneness with the universe. You can also try this exercise and choreograph a short dance in homage to your element. This is really fun to do in a group.

8. Repeat your goddess exercise at another point and imagine you are a magical being of the future. Write a short story or poem. Select a song that represents your idealized future and dance in homage to the people of today's time. Note how you feel.

# 14

# FLOW IS AS FLOW DOES

## The Life Force of Rhythm

My first trip to Paris was one for the books. This one specifically. I was with a group of women, with Josephine Baker on my mind and an Afrofuturism book in the making. My first night in town, we went to a jazz club. The featured performer, an artist we weren't familiar with, was featured prominently on the club's poster as the drummer and bandleader of a neo soul band. No more than thirty people were in the audience, with about half as many people in the band. The drummer-bandleader was doing a freestyle improvisation session, one where musicians and singers could riff and join in.

I experienced something that night that I'd never experienced before or since, an experience that would stick with me forever. The drummer, a well-dressed man with an Afro, black suit, and open-collar white shirt, could not keep time. I implore you to think hard about your live music experiences. You've probably seen some good bands. You've likely witnessed bands that weren't so good. You've seen little kids perform at an assembly for school, in the early stages of music education. But you likely have never paid for a ticket to an act promoted on a marquee to see a band whose drummer-bandleader could not keep time. If you have, I send you my blessings.

Because the drummer couldn't keep time, all the well-intentioned jamming of the horn players, the singers, and the other string instruments trying to jump in sounded like chaos. It was one of the most disorienting moments of my life, like hearing nails scratch across an old school chalkboard as you're whirling like Dorothy in a tornado to nowhere. My friend, intent on enjoying the twenty euros we'd spent and not wanting our first night in Paris to fade into a night of regret, sauntered on stage. Dressed in a black, floor-length dress of slinkiness, her dark tresses falling toward her waist, she stood before the drummer, pointed to her hips, and instructed the beleaguered lost man of music to follow her hips as she moved them like a swinging pendulum, dictating the rhythm he should follow. Slowly, he caught the rhythm of her motion. And this friend literally saved the show. She sat on the drummer's lap the entire night, helping him keep time. Because the drummer found the base rhythm, all the other musicians were able to join in and this musical catastrophe turned into one of wonder. I wound up being the closing act, living out my dance dreams, but that's another story.

Earlier we spoke of dance as a reminder of our relationship with the universe and those around us. Rhythm, as we mentioned, also speaks to a relationship in community and seeing the world beyond its cosmic and Earthly implications. Rhythm is a way to think about culture, the rhythms of the people around us. Many of us are accustomed to a rhythm in life, one underscored by our environment and values. As we shift from one cultural space to another, that collective rhythm can change. There are lessons in all forms of rhythm, many which overlap. Sometimes we are locked in one rhythm, one universal pattern, and not others, missing the insights and the relationship to culture and space that each rhythm reveals.

## Negritude in Paris

In 1928, Léopold Sédar Senghor sailed to Paris from his home in Senegal to attend school. He was one of many students from the French-speaking Caribbean and Africa who would seek higher education in the French capital. As he aligned with a cadre of like-minded students in the francophone world, they were all contending with colonialism's impact on their ability to express themselves. French-speaking nations including Senegal, Ivory Coast, Martinique, and others were still under the colonial rule of France. But no amount of study would make these students French enough to be accepted in French society. Moreover, valuing their African and Caribbean cultures put them at odds with their education. To be successful in the francophone world, one was forced to divorce themselves from the fabric of their home culture. In the late spring of 1935, Senghor, along with Martinique-born poet Aimé Césaire and others, released the journal *L'etudiant noir* and introduced the term *negritude.*

Negritude was a play on the word *nègre.* To be called *nègre* were fighting words in the same way that calling someone Black in the Americas was before the "Black is beautiful" era of the 1960s. This inversion of *nègre* in the form of *negritude* became the Black francophone exploration of cultural pride, producing creative works spawned from anticolonialism and new political and cultural theories.

Senghor also wanted to capture a unifying aesthetic of Black arts. African art at the time was widely dismissed as primitive fetish culture. However, Senghor sought to articulate the binding philosophy behind African works. He identified the core aesthetic as rhythm.

Usually when people think of rhythm, they think of music or dance. However, Senghor, while mindful of this context, was referring to the plastic arts. Plastic arts are works with a three-dimensional effect, art such as traditional African masks that must be sculpted or molded. He reasoned that such art had a rhythm. Art, like music, is a relationship to space and the illusion of time. There are breaks in lines, brush strokes, colors, and patterns that imply tempo. Art can form a language. Traditional mask works are artifacts often designed to bridge dimensions with an intention and a theme of unifying times and spaces.

"This ordering force that constitutes Negro Style is rhythm," writes Senghor in his essay "What the Black Man Contributes" in the collection *African Art as Philosophy.*

> It is the most sensible and the least material thing. It is the vital element par excellence. It is the primary condition for, and sign of, art as respiration is of life—respiration that rushes or slows down, becomes regular or spasmodic depending on the being's tension, the degree and quality of the emotion. Such is rhythm, originally, in its purity, such is it in the masterpieces of Negro art, particularly in sculpture.

However, rhythm, rather than being a field of constants, always introduces a new element, a new pattern in its continuity. He continues,

> It is not a symmetry that engenders monotony, rhythm is alive, it is free. For reprise is not redundancy or repetition. The theme is reprised at another place, on another level, in another combination, in a variation. And it produces something like another tone, another timbre, another accent. . . . This is how rhythm acts, despotically, on what is least intellectual in us, to make us enter into the spirituality of the object; and this attitude of abandon that we have is itself rhythmic.[1]

Emotion would change the timbre of the rhythm. Emotion had value.

Souleymane Bachir Diagne writes of African philosophy being embedded in art. Dagne is a philosopher and professor of French and philosophy at Columbia University as well as the director of the Institute of African Studies there. "This metaphysics, to present it in a word, is a metaphysics of rhythm which, according to Senghor, is at the core of African thought and experience." In fact, plastic works are a visual music. Senghor's artist life would be defined by informing rhythm as aesthetic. Even as he became Senegal's first president, he continued to prioritize art and African aesthetics.

"What is rhythm?" Senghor asks in the essay "*L'esthétique négro-africaine.*" "It is the architecture of being, the internal dynamism that gives it form, the system of waves it gives off toward Others, the pure expression of vital force. Rhythm is the vibrating shock, the power which, through the senses, seizes us at the roots of our Being."[2]

And when he speaks once again of repetition, it is to clarify that there is almost always the introduction of a new element, variation in the repetition, unity in diversity. Senghor aligned this perspective on rhythm with all African art forms, a perspective infused with passion. "When the poet writes a poem, he does not calculate, he does not measure, he does not count. He does not look either for ideas or for images. He is, in front of his vision, like the black Great Priestess of Tanit, in Carthage. He speaks his vision, in a rhythmical movement, because his is impassioned with a sacred passion."[3]

In essence, the nature of life force is rhythm. A rhythmic attitude requires receptivity to wavelengths or being aligned with the wavelength of the art created. Sometimes described as spiritual, this process of assessing combinations of rhythms depends on a force/rhythm "which orders the whole into an indivisible organic unity."[4]

Sylviane Greensword deep-dived into break dancing with New Jack Attack as a teen in France. She shared that the experience made her hyperaware of rhythm as patterns that translate visually. It's geometry, she says. In break dancing, uprocking, the traditional breaker prep move "before you get to do your acrobatics forms a triangle before going on the ground. You go diagonal to the front, to the back, then you go to the floor it's a complete square. You create a five-pointed star, then you can actually spin on your back, and depending on how many people do it, it forms a picture. If you snapped a camera, you can take a picture. If we were wearing clothes soaked in ink, it would create a pattern on the stage."

## Rhythmism

Turtel Onli is a Chicago visual artist who named his own art process *rhythmism*. Onli spent formulative years in Paris at the Sorbonne and Centre Georges Pompidou. While he was unaware of Senghor's work, he told me that he was motivated by the same observations. "I was totally responding to my own work and my own practices, coming out of the Black Cultural revolution. I just felt that just calling it Black art was pretty limiting and low brow," he says. He was looking to fill voids in how art by Black artists is framed. He defined his work as a combination of the sounds of the brush and the field of patterns he created.

"If you use a brush and a pencil in a certain way, you get feedback and sound, you get tactile and sound," he says. "If you tap dance, you get feedback from the floor. You get feedback from a paintbrush. It was the feedback in the process as much as it was the rhythm in the composition." In fact, visual patterns have rhythm breaks just as they do in music. Think of denoting a break beat on canvas.

"People almost refuse to think of visual art in composition. When it comes to visual arts, rhythm is a principle of design. There's repetition and movement that happens in a work of art," he says. As for the label of African art as primitive, a description still taught in some art schools, Onli prefers to think of it as foundational to form. He emphasizes this fact in his art classes at Harold Washington College. "When you get control of rhythm, it gets less spontaneous and gets more ordered and you can project it. It follows your expressive paradigms."

Rhythmism was the basis for his fine art and for the futuristic comics he created. *NOG: The Protector of the Pyramides* took place on Planet Nuba, an all-Black planet. He introduced it as a comic in Paris, later running it as a comic strip in the *Chicago Defender*.

But Onli received a great deal of pushback to the art style and the futuristic Black subject matter. He launched the comic independently, distributing it himself. By 1998, fed up with the resistance to Black futurist comics, he launched Black Age of Comics. Onli thought of his style as a futuristic one based on traditional African styles. "A lot of work I did looked like Yoruba work. I didn't know who the Yoruba were when I was a kid. I did my DNA and saw that I was 60 percent Yoruba from the Kingdom of Benin." To that end, he views his rhythmistic style not just as visual, but as a DNA-informed process, one reflecting a lineage based in rhythm of continuity. Nevertheless, as aesthetic, rhythm springs from a beingness. "I don't see rhythm as resistance," he says. But he does see rhythm as a gateway connecting times and spaces.

It's part of our charge to be aware of the rhythms that may guide our spaces, the ones that come naturally to us and the ones we experience as we move about our day. Being in rhythm with those around us or sensing when someone is not can be fine-tuned by thinking about our evolving or childhood relationships to rhythm. Rhythm as a cultural experience—ethnic, regional, or otherwise—is all around us. As we observe, we can interrogate what these rhythms mean for us or the comfort we may find in them.

Coco Elysses, a percussionist, composer, and former president of the AACM, the long-running experimental jazz collective, shared with me that she grew up seeing relationships between rhythms. "It's a vibe," says Elysses. "It's a pulse that can be marked through the subdivision of time. But there's all kinds of different things that come into play with rhythm. The feel makes it different. It's the architecture of time and space. That's what rhythm is to me—architecting time and space," she says.

A child who grew up acting, dancing, cheerleading, running track, and jumping double Dutch, she saw the world in rhythm patterns. A percussionist/composer who plays and creates Afro-Latin, African, jazz, and experimental styles, she feels that "rhythm has a very central role in my life. It's philosophy, a vibe, a theory. It's also being in the moment." She's aware of Sankofa as a rhythm of life and perception. She juxtaposes this with a dream she had, where she was her mother and her daughter all in one. Much like Onli, she sees rhythm as a continuum. When she shifts from one music style to the next, learning new rhythms, she views it as all immersive.

Earlier we spoke of being a synergy of dynamics that predate our birth and speak to our futures. We can also think of some of these streams of time, the ones that lift us, as another way of thinking about rhythm. We can operate on or fall in rhythms from other times with gifts of wisdom that can appear as a rhythm in our social spaces.

"Understanding the rhythm is understanding the rhythm of the people, how they converse at dinner, how they say a thing, how they be a thing," Elysses says. "If I can understand that, then I can understand the music, and then I can understand the rhythm. It doesn't happen without understanding the culture." The same approach applies in group improvisation, a feature that the AACM is known for. In this case, Elysses says she looks at what each band member is bringing and how this forms a culture of its own.

Our relationship to rhythm can help us harmonize with others and enter spaces we're less familiar with. We spoke of dance as a technology that facilitates instant oneness. However, our exploration of how rhythm shows up in our lives, our engagements, our culture, our speech, also reflects what we view as norms. Our ability to shift to spaces familiar and unfamiliar is often linked to our relationship with rhythm.

## Reflection Questions

We are surrounded by a world of rhythm. Music aside, there is rhythm in the world around us.

1. What is your relationship to rhythm? When you think of rhythm, what comes to mind?

2. Can you identify any rhythms in your environment, beyond the world of music? Perhaps it's the tapping of your keyboard, a leaky faucet, your pacing when you jog, the rustling of the trees, a friend's metaphors, or a pattern in flowers. List as many as you can.

3. Can you recall any examples of rhythm that you grew up with? What activities do you hear a rhythm in?

4. Are there any rhythms in your environment that are comforting for you?

5. How would you describe the rhythm of your home? Your job? Your neighborhood? Your culture? Your favorite music?

6. When you think of rhythms in the future evolving from the sounds, life, and machinery around us, what comes to mind? What activities, invention, sounds could generate a rhythm of the future?

## Exercise: Find Your Rhythm

1. Over the next few days, be conscious of rhythms you notice. The rhythms can come from anywhere. Note them and jot them down.

2. Find a few items in your place that are great music makers. Pick objects that aren't formal instruments—pots, spoons, buckets, glasses, bells, bricks, party horns. Take a few moments to play around with sounds. Make this a moment of joy. Find sounds that you like and make

time to create them. If you're doing this in a group, play until you find some space of harmony. Be joyous. The goal isn't to create amazing music, but to note how sounds and sequences make you feel.

3. Make a list or a playlist with songs that have sounds or rhythms you like. A friend of mine once said that our favorite songs usually have similar sounds and rhythms. See if you note any similarity in the rhythm patterns. What do you like about these patterns? What do they remind you of? How do they make you feel?

# 15

# A STORY OF EIGHT COUNTS

## Polyrhythms and Defying Expectations

THERE ARE RHYTHMS WE GROW UP WITH—ones piped into our radios and streaming services and community spaces that shape our view of the world. These rhythms become a default comfort space. We assume they are norms, ubiquitous, universally loved, or present everywhere. Some of us think one range of rhythms is superior to another. We've found ways to move or function with these patterns. We are married to these patterns of sound, and if we're not careful they can box us in. (Yes, the box again.)

Arriving in ballet and tap class at age six, baby-pink leotard and bustling tutu, you take your position and are guided through a routine that's broken down into nice counts of eight. In prep, the teacher begins by counting off to the beginning with a "five, six, seven, eight . . . and one." One marks the first step. One is where everything begins.

1

Many dance schools across the country work off the eight-count foundation, with the obvious number one as the beginning of the sequence.

1 2 3 4 5 6 7 8

If you're taking music lessons, the timing of the notes are broken down into four/four measure, a total count which adds to eight. Any dancer worth their salt can choreograph a phrase to this count. It's all a neat, largely Western approach to counting time in music, an approach that is so ingrained, so ubiquitous, so pervasive on our airwaves, that anytime I'm listening to music, my body becomes a human metronome. I can pretty much tell you what count the music is on generally. But I'm not solely projecting this framework of counting onto music. A great deal of music born out of the West can be spliced into eight equally measured beats because 4/4 measure is a popular foundation.

Most traditional African music and its rhythms cannot be neatly situated in an evenly distributed count of eight. Traditional music from India and parts of Asia doesn't fall on an eight count. There's an abundance of music around the world that does not fall on this assumed paradigm. You can literally limit your perception of the world if you're married to the almighty eight.

You, dear reader, are very likely living in an eight-count bubble. I was that person, pushing past an eight-count universe, not knowing there was a world beyond. I craved complex rhythm and a source explanation. I had a very happy life dancing in an eight-count world, discovering rhythms between quarter notes when I wasn't cramming micrometered motions between them. Seeing the world through orange-speckled glasses in crazy eights isn't all bad. But that world was about to implode.

Hprizm, also known as Kyle Austin of the Antipop Consortium, once told me dancing was body math. In this sense we are thinking about music as a measure of time. When you're dancing to music, you are interpreting the beats, finding life between them with motion. These beats, if you will, are also spaces. You dance on the counts and on the multitude of time frames between them. Much of the joy in dance is uncovering motions to make within these rhythms. As we move, we are in time, around time, finding all manner of ways to splice time and space. I remember times dancing to house music at parties and an unlikely combination of motions between rhythms felt as if I'd unlocked a world gushing with euphoria. Finding time in space, with your body or otherwise, is akin to opening a portal.

Khari B., a house dancer and poet, knows this well. "What really sends me to the moon is doing something I know my body has never done before. I'm not trying to do it. I say, ooh, this has never happened. I can go home after that. I got somewhere I've never been physically. It still happens to this day. As many parties as I've been to or as many times as I dance, it can be really small, imperceptible to anyone else. I know that it can happen at any time."

The truth is, there are any number of rhythmic motions one can make between counts. If you want to think about it mathematically, which no one wants to do when they're dancing, the simplest breakdown is just to divide counts in half.

### 1 *and* 2 *and* 3 *and* 4

You hit the beat, you accent midway between the beat. You can also break each count into three. This can read as triplets.

### 1 *and a* 2 *and a* 3 *and a* 4

This is all semiformal dancer speak for explaining what rhythmic count you're on.

Growing up in a bevy of dance schools and classes in the
United States, this isn't really a process I questioned. All of the
world can seemingly be whittled down into counts of eight. I grew
up in a soul, hip-hop, house, jazz, funk, and Latin jazz world, so
rhythm (and blues) was a world order. However, every now and
then, our instructors, in their efforts to align counts, had to throw
the eight-count metronome in the dancetopia waste basket. Actually, it happened a lot.

I think about the time my tap teacher, Jackie Record, taught us
fifteen-year-olds to perform to a Max Roach–esque jazz drum solo.
Breaking this rapid-fire rhythm into counts was like metering out
the beats for rainfall. "Forget the counts and follow the music," she
said in her own frustration. Or the time she had us tap dance to the
Salsoul Orchestra's "Magic Bird of Fire," a Broadway disco, funk,
Latin fusion that was epic in every sense of the disco world. There's
nothing about this song that screams "tap dancing for teenagers,"
and yet our instructor had a vision from the gods and an outpouring
of one of the more complex routines of our lives. We were going to
push ourselves to perform in rhythms that this song was not designed
to contain. We were literally stretching the boundaries of beats you
could squeeze into a single measure by shifting speed, the musical-
ity of our rapid motion taps creating an audible rhythm within a
shapeshifting existing one—our dancing feet were drum solos within
the song's ever evolved dramatic horns and drum pattern. I will
forever thank her for naturalizing a complex relationship to rhythm
that punctuated a desire to hear and move in harmony with them.

This idea of counts as measure would be a tangled one that
would become an unexplained time quagmire for the formulative
years of my life. This lording of the eight count had me subconsciously counting everything rhythmic in that manner. It was a
framework, like a framed window through which I saw the world.
My body understood the world like this. I remember friends of

mine and myself trying to squeeze in some local multi-tick hip-shaking motion into a pom routine we were creating and we couldn't figure out the best way to count out the rhythm to explain what we were doing. We'd made the troubling mistake of choreographing moves that weren't easy to explain in fractions without our heads exploding. Without the counts as parameter, the team was lost. Sometimes, if you couldn't explain the move in fractions, it was best to punt the idea back to the dance gods.

Some of you may be thinking that you *never* think about counts when you're dancing. When you're freestyling, dancing at a party or festival, counts are a nonissue. You're going along with music. But you are, ideally, moving to a beat. There's some order in the universe that can find a way to count. I shared my experience with Afrofuturist singer Gira Dahnee, and she says count breakdowns weren't top of mind when she danced, although she admitted that she had memorized her childhood choir director's frenzied hand direction motions and has never forgotten them. "I used to mimic her as a kid but the way she kept time stuck with me." So, while she wasn't thinking about them, she was subconsciously aware of them. Over time, as you listen or move to music, you can form an expectation around how music is supposed to flow and how you flow with it because you're trained or socialized into doing so. You can place judgments on music that doesn't "fit" into your count expectation, deeming it as bad, noncommercial, difficult, unappealing, dangerous, too free.

Unfortunately, the human metronome of eight counts can become a filter for processing movements. The eight count becomes a defaulted convention, one you can be wholly unaware of. I remember Afrofuturist violinist and composer Renee Baker saying that she didn't want her music to be predictable. She didn't want the first phrase to dictate the rhythm of the next. Conventional, as in Western, music structures are boxy.

Now, the challenge with the human metronome approach isn't that you can't move to complex rhythms, but rather that you can't explain them, for teaching purposes, wholly by using counts to describe the rhythm. This became a big issue when hip-hop and break dancing popped onto pop music consciousness. How do you teach the windmill or a backspin in a world of eight counts? But if you're trying to teach a step, or learn one, conventional Western dance teaching aesthetic says you need to funnel it into counts—eight counts specifically.

This approach, one which is supposed to be a common denominator for all to understand, much like a music chart, can also become a block. Sometimes, if you're squeezing motions into the order of the eight count, the count can feel like yielding fence. How far can I stretch this eight-count wire fence without busting it?

Kéwé Lô, artistic coordinator for Black Rock Senegal, and I bonded over dance. A dancer herself, she much like me sometimes felt trapped by some music frameworks. The DJs were ordering her movement, she said. "Sometimes I dance to music I don't want to dance to and I just flow over the beat," she said. I could relate. Flowing over the beat was a means of dancing where one isn't trapped by the predictability of the beat, and yet, were still on it.

## Salsa Revelations

I'd taken salsa dancing after college. I grew up in a family of Chicago steppers and boppers, so the language of partner dancing was familiar to me. I could follow well and I was a decent salsa dancer. Salsa emerged in the 1970s from the Latine scene of NYC, fueled by the exciting music of primarily Puerto Rican and Cuban communities. Salsa is based on Cuban *son*, a style that came of age in the 1950s. Cuban *son* is based in rumba. Rumba, a partner dance that hails from Matanzas, Cuba, was essentially a spiritual dance evolving from the Yoruba-influenced religion known as Santeria that, pre–Cuban revolution, was hidden in party music to preserve African rhythms and spiritual practices.

I knew none of this when I began taking salsa dance classes at a performance venue in Chicago. I knew that I was drawn to the rhythms. I knew that I loved the music as if it were calling me. In my tap dance life, we'd danced to an array of Latin jazz over the years—again a music form not exactly designed for tap dance, but one that made me way more astute rhythmically than I realized.

The venue in downtown Chicago was a place where you could take lessons and then join the salsa party that followed—learn the basics and get tossed into the fire of people who've done this dance their whole lives. The salsa party was an opportunity to practice. Looking back on it, I don't think the instructor grew up in Latine dance culture but found her way through the competitive dance scene. If you saw the 1990s salsa film *Dance with Me* starring Vanessa Williams and Chayanne that centered the tension between competitive dance and dancing for the people, you see where this is going. The film, dashing romance between the two main characters aside, was about a clash in approach to thinking, explaining, teaching, and understanding dance. One approach was exacting, regimented, while the other had a core aesthetic that was equally as exacting but came from a completely different space of dance as holistic, dance as community.

One year, my family reunion took place in Las Vegas (a great locale for a family reunion, by the way). The reunion was in the same hotel as a national salsa convention. After the family festivities, a few of us wandered over to the convention afterparty. The music was amazing. The dancers were whirling with style and finesse. An unassuming gentleman in a white T-shirt, dark slacks, and a white baseball cap approached me. In gentleman conjecture, he asked me to dance. Then he asked was I a one or a two. I had no idea what he was talking about.

I don't even know how we began. I was waiting for the musical "and one," a prep he seemed completely oblivious to. He didn't wait for me to get into position. Nor did he do some dramatic step forward to ensure I stepped back as assurance that we were in sync. All I know is I was suddenly spinning, trying to keep up, but I was a wiggling larvae in outer space. I was lost. His fluid moves were all elegance and funk, finding ebbs and flows within base counts I couldn't even identify. He was dancing salsa. I was dancing salsa. But it's like we were moving on two different planetary levels. I don't think we were even dancing to the same music. *What count is he on?* was the question flashing like a neon sign in my mind. Seeking stability in a comet of dance motions, I dove for the eight-count ground floor in his moves and there was none. How is that possible?

At some point, I looked on at my dance partner in wonder, not able to move with or around him, nor understand what rhythms he was moving to. I had never in my dance life been so discombobulated. When our time together ended, and I acknowledged that he was gracious in letting me share the same tile squares with him, he remarked that I was a two like he was. With that, a mystery unfolded. A two is professional salsero speak for dancing in the Afro-Cuban style. Clearly, it was a style he thought I had a propensity for. I was dumbfounded and intrigued as to why my modest salsa life played no role in being able to follow him.

Most important, where was his one? Where is the beginning? Where is the recovery point in the repetition? Where is the one count in this 4/4 measure, eight-count world I'd been brought up in?

## The One

James Brown's entire music catalog is based off the magic of the one. "In short, Brown wanted music that was as indefatigable as he was," writes Tyler Golsen in *Far Out* magazine. "What he stumbled on was the importance of 'The One,' the first downbeat of every measure of music. If the band constantly hit 'The One,' then everything else could flow easily after that. It was a basic concept that could lead to unlimited sonic possibilities, and Brown milked those possibilities."[1] Milk them he did. Brown's innovation of "the one" birthed funk, contemporary R&B, and hip-hop, and rewired the DNA of American music into the future. "The one" was practically ubiquitous. It was everywhere. It's a universe. Even a healthy dose of lighter pop music from the West is wired off an accented one for cool measure. The Chicago stepping I grew up with is on the one. In fact, nearly all the music I grew up with was on the one. There's many a funk paradise portal that's opened with the universal synchronicity of this approach. George Clinton's Parliament has a song in honor of the one. "Everything Is on the One" on *The Clones of Dr. Funkenstein* album is a laid-back groove in which the song's lyrics repeat the title. Everything is on the one, an esoteric statement of universal harmony.

Music lovers who aren't aware of counts but are accustomed to the almighty one will feel the shift in the force when it's gone. You hear it in the J.B.'s "Funky Good Time," 50 Cent's "In da Club," Beyoncé's "Crazy in Love," or P-Funk's "Star Child (Mothership Connection)." Even when there isn't a force of nature James Brown accent, there is at least an obvious first count in much of the Western pop world. But the dancer I was spinning like a wobbling planet with wasn't on the James Brown one. He didn't seem to be on any one at all.

There's nothing more disorienting than a rhythmic person dancing or listening to music and realizing that they don't know where the first count in a phrase begins. Where's the beginning of the repeated phrase in the music? It's an expectation. Otherwise, your whole world is asunder and your sonic ethos is flipped. I'm not the only one who has had this moment of musical backflips.

Many musicians trained in African American or other Western styles, when learning traditional African or Afro-Latin music with rumba origins and entrenched in African rhythms, have found themselves in search of the one to no avail. Even if you find a one, just clapping along will have you off beat. I'd argue that the James Brown one is an African Diasporic innovation on a European form.

A fusion, which I'll explain later. African traditional music doesn't lean on the one.

The one, as we'd been trained, doesn't always have a bass, snare, or bombastic entry that repeats with special emphasis every four counts. In fact, it may not repeat every four counts at all. But when it comes to African polyrhythms, just hurl that eight-count football into the next solar system where it's more applicable.

For some of you, this may not sound like the cataclysmic ordeal it can become. Shawn Wallace, a teaching artist and composer, agrees. But when the one is virtually invisible, it can send you in a tailspin, he says. "It'll have you questioning the universe," says Wallace. He remembers the first time he heard a drum line of batas, a West African drum, and was in search of the elusive one. "It's like you're playing double Dutch and trying to figure out when to jump in."

Jazz saxophone player David Boykin, who once hosted a one-hundred-year anniversary to Sun Ra, once told me that when he first learned African traditional music he was also asking his instructor about the one. "I couldn't find it," he says. A student of Brown's methods, Boykin was fascinated by the versatility and rhythmic freedom that Brown's one revolutionized. In search of understanding the one's magic, Boykin later read that Brown said that the one wasn't always on the one count itself. "Then I was really messed up," says Boykin.

This quest for the one is so ingrained, Ahmed Best, an Afro-futurist who starred in the *Star Wars* franchise, shared in a workshop that while taking his djembe lessons, his African instructor in frustration asked, "What is this one you guys keep looking for?" When people are in search of the one, they're looking for the beginning of the repeated sequence. They're looking for the pattern, or the beginning of the pattern. But what if the pattern is entirely different? What if your assumed norm doesn't apply? Rhythm aside, we often bring our frameworks into life scenarios to order the world around us—frameworks we are completely unaware of.

The almighty eight is one of them. My trained template of ordering the music dance world was not making sense of my Vegas dance partner, just as our frameworks for life may be the equivalent of looking at world affairs through a lens of eight counts.

Quincy "Leon Q" Allen, my usual salsa dance partner, cousin, and trumpet player, plays a range of African American, Afro-Latin, Caribbean, and African dance styles and loves noting the relationships. It's not that African or Latin music rooted in African polyrhythms don't have a one count. The one simply isn't the strongest beat. "Most people are listening for the slap on one, but the slap is on beat two," says Allen. There's a one, they just can't hear it, he says. Thus, why my white ballcapped dance god in Vegas said we, or rather he, was dancing "on the two." As for polyrhythms, some of us are expecting to hear a drum set to order our world. But there is no drum set. "The drums mark the four in a polyrhythm if you're playing a drum set. If you're not working with drum sets then you have to feel. And if you can't feel, you're lost," says Allen.

This lost feeling is a good thing. It opens a door to uncover another rhythm, another way of understanding the world, another means to connect with culture and ourselves. This lost point of trying to find the rhythm is a gateway, another portal to springboard evolution and elation in our life. We have found ourselves, metaphorically in a new space. Rather than retreat in fear or be dismissive, this lost point is our opportunity to dive in a new way of understanding our body and the world.

## Reflection Questions

Many of us have paradigms for viewing the world that we are unaware of. Musical rhythms evoke worlds. Some of our assumptions about how we perceive the world could mirror how we see music we're familiar with and unfamiliar with. How do we move past our musical assumptions, ones that can be social parameters?

1. Do you have any general assumptions about how music should sound? Where did these assumptions come from?

2. Can you recall a moment when you were listening to music or dancing to music and felt disoriented or uncomfortable? Why did you feel this way? What elements in the music prompted this feeling? Did you choose to overcome it? Why or why not?

3. Do you have expectations about what makes music comfortable for you? What are your expectations? What elements should the music have?

4. As you think about these rhythm shifts, do you note any relationships between how you shift space when you move into unfamiliar environments or spaces with other norms that you aren't accustomed to?

## Exercise: Find the Count

1. Select a James Brown song, any James Brown song. Can you hear the one count he's known for? It's on every four count. How does this music make you feel? What comes to mind as you listen to it?

2. Watch the documentary *Free to Dance* from PBS. This video will give you insights and history into the aesthetics of Black Dance. It's available on YouTube. Our goal is not to have you dancing like an Alvin Ailey dancer. However, I do want you to note how you feel watching the dances. What thoughts and feelings come up for you? Do you see any consistent themes in the dances? What are your biggest takeaways from the documentary?

# 16

# PORTALS IN CLAVE

## The Musicology of the Diaspora

BEING AN AFROFUTURIST DOESN'T REQUIRE that you be a musicologist. Nor are all who profess to be Afrofuturist also mistresses of the dance realms. However, a relationship to music of the African Diaspora can only enhance one's understandings about cultural space/time relationships that are perceived, experienced, and shaped. Many musicians and dancers pulling from African/ African Diasporic pantheons or those innovating in those spaces were actively manipulating time through their chosen frameworks. In some cases, they are reframing or reclaiming time, consciously or unconsciously, from modern linear perceptions of time, much of which is rooted in colonial thinking. By so doing, they are claiming a space/time relationship to how they navigate time in a broader universe. Dance can be a way to assert oneself as being in harmony with a universe where time and space aren't limitations but rather opportunities for expression.

All of us have genres of music or artists that we tend to listen to a little more than others. However, a great deal of ideas about space, time, and rhythm in Black cultures are evident in the music. Sometimes we can limit our experience or insights gained from Black music and its Afrofuturist leanings around the world if we keep our music playlist narrow. Although you don't have to love every genre, there are insights to be gained, not to mention great experiences to be had, by listening to and engaging with music beyond your usual shuffle. Having a relationship with complex rhythms is a good thing. At the very least, it's nice to have a working knowledge of the genres themselves and perhaps uncover relationships between the music.

The clave count and salsa dance were my door into breaking through the eight-count dimension. I bought a Cuban music anthology CD before the days of streaming and found myself leaning to the full range of jazz, salsa, and timba. Listening to it and dancing to it in the styles designated for the music are two different things. But I was determined to find my anchor in my (new to me) portal of musicopia. I listened to Celia Cruz. I listened to Pachito Alonso y sus Kini Kini. I dove headfirst into playing catchup with Fania Records. I listened for the joy and I listened for the clave sound.

So, what *is* the ordered world of counts in Afro-Latin music worlds and African polyrhythms? Much of it is on a count called the clave count. Salsa emphasizes the clave. In the clinical sense, the clave count goes as follows, *one, two, one (pause), two, three,* or *one, two, three (pause), one, two.* The count is usually played by two wooden sticks called the clave, and their beat lays the foundation for this musical universe. The clave is your gateway to understanding the Afro-Latin/African polyrhythmic universe.

The story goes that the clave sticks themselves were originally wooden bolts used on Spanish cargo ships that came to Cuba. Enslaved Africans and their new generation of freedmen used boxes, tables, pots, spoons, and any number of elements to duplicate the percussive sounds of their African homelands. The wooden sticks from the Spanish ships became the percussive tool of choice to keep time and build the new sonic world. The boxes became cajons, and by the early twentieth century, modern drums in the spirit of their African drum origins were created.

However, clave is deeper than its timekeeping ability. Arturo O'Farrill, Grammy winner and founder of the Afro Latin Jazz Alliance, says he once asked Machito, the godfather of Afro-Cuban jazz, to explain clave. Rather than describe counts as I just did, and as O'Farrill expected, Machito provided context.

"He said 'clave is about respect,'" says O'Farrill, who shared his insights in an interview with me for Carnegie Hall's Afrofuturism Festival. "I understood immediately what he meant. It was about respecting a tradition, a different way to count." He adds that jazz and European music is "about a pulse orientation or whatever the speed is. Clave is a way of keeping time. It's not rhythm, it's a particular way of keeping time. It's a much more African based thing because it's a larger entity of phrasing." He compares the approach to breathing. I think back to KRS-One and his description of hip-hop as breath.

Clave "is African across the pattern base, a larger phrase-based way of looking at timekeeping. It's a larger entity than the beat. The beat is important, but what really matters is community." Earlier, we spoke of music as forming space and building a relationship with oneness in the universe and conscious links to those around us.

African polyrhythms are two or more rhythms played simultaneously at the same tempo. In musician language, one rhythm is on the 6/4 count and the other is on a 4/4. African rhythms may have a series of talking drums and rhythm drums. Clave, he reasons, is a way of keeping large ensembles of musicians in community without having a distinct leader. The community is the music. "When you see music-making by larger groups of people, it becomes an undulated largesse," he says.

"The most freaky experience I ever had in my life: I went to Trinidad and came upon this parking lot and there were 150 drummers, 150 steel pan drummers," he said. They decided to sit in the bass section. "So here I am in a group of twenty-five steel pan bass section . . . At first you just see the individual beats. Then you realize, this 150 steel pan drummers became this big, undulated steel pan creature." It was as if everything slowed down, he said. "I understand that [music] is a community service, that's what music is. It was one of the most emotionally powerful things in my life. To see that move slowly, time stops, and human beings [as] a community."

So, when I was standing in wonderment trying to keep up with my Las Vegas dance god, we were in two different universes. He was finding worlds of body rhythms between a clave count. I was on the other side of the stratosphere of eight. Or was I?

In the case of my dance partner, I wasn't moving with him. I was trying to fit an ordered form and wasn't in flow. How many times had I been out of flow because I was asserting a paradigm? Throughout my life I was dancing on all kinds of counts that fractions weren't designed to measure. But I didn't know how to articulate it because I was married to the grid. I couldn't see my own movements because of how I ordered the universe. At various points I was likely dancing on clave but didn't know what it was.

Much of our work in our Afrofuturism is finding language for philosophies that are embedded, sometimes hidden, not always at the surface. As I thought about African ancestors coveting ideas about community and space/time in dance and sonics, it became imperative to bring these ideas lingering in the structure to the forefront. We are collectively in a space where the principle of Sankofa, the retrieval of the best of the past and moving it forward, becomes a perception tool to see ourselves. When we are locked in paradigms, we aren't just in a box that prevents us from broader connections with people and culture, we are in a box where we can't see ourselves. We can't see our potential. We can't see who we can be or what can make us joyous. Our inherited frameworks are one way of understanding ourselves, but they aren't the only way. Identity is ever evolving. Beyond the sound dimension, our rhythm foray expands our sense of self.

## Dance Evolution

My quest for these new, or not-so-new, rhythms sent me through a swirl of dance worlds, like a detective mining for beats. Newness in music was exhilarating. I grew up taking ballet, tap, modern contemporary, and general African dance classes, and immersed in the glories of hip-hop, pompom, and house music dancing. But after my whirl in Las Vegas, I started taking an array of new classes—tango, flamenco, samba. I took classes with Erica Bowen in Havana. I would seek out house music clubs and crunch all these moves together. All of this was a personal quest for sustained dance utopia that somehow wound up with me teaching kindergarten kids. This rhythm quest had me shifting from spaces that some saw as differing but where I found commonality, complements. Moving from one rhythm to the next conditioned me to be open to shifts in the force. Shifting space and finding grounding helped me to be more immersed in environments that had fluctuating differences but could be integrated into my norm. Our experience with rhythm helps us to shift space, go deeper, and cherish the complements in being that enrich our souls. Perceived difference becomes just that, a perception that is not a barrier. This experience shifts how fluid we can be as we sail and engage in more spaces.

## Deep Space

I taught kindergarten kids dance five days a week while I was writing my book *Afrofuturism: The World of Black Sci-Fi and Fantasy Culture*. Again, I felt that I was in two different universes, one requiring a heady gymnastics on Black futures, and another requiring the physical demand of guiding squirming kids to the path of a performance-ready holiday dance. At the onset, I didn't feel that either informed the other, as if I was leading a double life.

However, I reasoned that dance kept me in the body and writing was in the head.

Teaching kindergarteners was not my first choice. I had assumed that because they were younger, some styles would be more difficult to grasp. I was wrong about that, too. My approach with the students was simple—never stop moving. Because I never stopped and their attention spans aren't the longest, I was forced to introduce multiple styles. They learned yoga, salsa, hip-hop. We danced in ciphers; we did *Soul Train* lines. I was amazed at how easily they could pick up fairly complicated moves. But the demand of it all kept me squarely present. They were the longest, most exhilarating two hours a day I've ever spent. I was almost hyperpresent, every minute elongated with time. I was hyperaware, hyper in tune. The hyperreality of kindergarten energy compelled me to tap into another sensory perception. I was with over two dozen whirling spirals, every nuance shifting direction.

Sometimes when we have an intense purpose and a dynamic environment, our ability to harness rhythm leads to expanded, almost granular awareness. Time seemingly stretches. This space is an invaluable one. As we become conscious of it, we also have to become conscious of when we're in it and how to get out.

At the time, I reasoned that writing and teaching dance were two different art forms, one very heady and the other physical and intuitive. Then Kevin Kitrell Ross, a minister at Unity Sacramento, posed a question that would create another shift. "Where do you imagine yourself to be when you're dancing?" Ross asked. I was sharing that my at-home dance sessions, where I'd freestyle to the music of my choice, were hard to shift out of when I wanted to go into writing mode. In my mind, as I danced I was anywhere but my living room. "Then that's where you are," he said. "It's the creative space."

But the creative space, as he described it, requires another shift, one that ironically may require us to do a bit of reorienting. In one sense, we are moving from one portal to the next. This very embodied experience may require that we hop into our bodies again. Attuning to one rhythmic space and shifting to another demands some relief or a conscious break. The rhythms of life make us shapeshifters, but in the in-betweens we need to come up for air. My break was usually coffee, a phone call, a meetup with a friend. Other days I learned to step away and look at the clouds, watching them sail along the horizon.

## Dance Is a Language

Dance was the language that bonded me with Nadia Beugré, a celebrated African contemporary dancer, during my first trip to Paris—the same trip with the drummer rescue. I couldn't speak a great deal of French; she knew no English. But a friend translated for us, and we had a robust conversation on none other than the magic of the counts in between. The conversation was prompted after a night of dancing, and she saw my new artwork for my space-tastic *Rayla 2212* character—a Black woman living in a former Earth colony two centuries into the future.

The Ivory Coast–reared dancer couldn't stop looking at Rayla. After studying the digital image, she asked why I wanted to write a story about an African woman in space. The question unfolded into a timeless dialogue. How we got from discussing a Black woman in space to stories of African queens and a dance counts breakdown would mark my first creative conversation about Afrofuturism and dance. In time, I would recognize that our winding conversation was a fluid one. Speculation about Black women in space is evidenced by women on Earth asserting leadership and finding space in the in-betweens. Talking about Black women in dance is talking about Black women in space.

As I began to see the relationship between dance, writing, and my work in Afrofuturism, I devised an Afrofuturism dance therapy program, one I now title an Afrofuturism Experience. Depending on where we grow up or how we learn dance, we likely learned one style at the expense of another. Maybe it was the popular dances of the day, a partner dance, a fad, a TikTok routine, or a style that requires training. However, there are lessons in time, space, and wisdom in all dance forms that evolve through actually doing them and immersing ourselves in these arrays of rhythms.

My hope, with so many African dance styles challenging the way we're "supposed to move," is that engaging in a range of dances in the diaspora could help people better connect with themselves—with sides of themselves they've denied, looked over, or are yet to uncover. Moving to the rhythms can unlock relationships to space and time, reveal patterns, remove blocks, and reorient ourselves and our relationship to the universe. Journaling about our experiences doing various dances can make us comfortable in our bodies in all spaces.

The aim of the program is to introduce students to an array of African/African Diasporic dance styles, encourage them to write about their experiences with these styles as they choreographed, and to think about what insights they gained from these explorations. I found that students, through storytelling and dancing, were suddenly asking questions about space, time travel, ancestors, futures, all completely unprompted. We did freestyle dances in honor of our futures, and several students felt as if the people of the future and the ancestors were the audience. Others, after a museum visit and an impromptu dance with the bucket boys on the street, asked if there were other universes or multiverses where they existed, too. The teens were thinking of themselves as being in community with a larger universe, because that's what African/African Diasporic music and dance can facilitate.

Kenneth Russell's dance expertise is in both traditional African dance and tap. He frequently comes into my workshops as a guest teacher. "In African traditional dance you become the beat," he said. "Tap finds the rhythms in between. In African dance, you become one with the rhythm." There's no "and one" count to prep the beginning, he says, referencing Wallace's double Dutch example. "It's more like a *go*." When Russell went to Nairobi, Kenya, performing on stages and dancing at parties, he had to reorder his sphere of possibility in dancing, too.

This being one with the beat, one with the rhythm, is an expansion of the oneness we experience as we dance. When we lean into this perspective, we aren't in flow, we are the flow. We are rhythm ourselves.

## Pattern Masters

Kéwé Lô, an accomplished dancer and Dakar-based director at Black Rock Senegal, took me to my first sabar. She affirmed something I'd learned in African dance classes before but hadn't clicked with until I was watching this communal dance celebration. Those of us stuck on finding the one can't find it because the drum follows the dancer, she said. As I listened to more mbalax music and asked questions, another revelation was shared. A colleague in Dakar, a big James Brown fan, noted that mbalax music isn't easy for everyone to perform or move to. However, much of James Brown's music actually shared the mbalax rhythm. I thought about Brown himself saying that the one wasn't always on the one. Perhaps he was giving language to the feel of polyrhythms and clave.

O'Farrill says that many of the rhythms in hip-hop, reggae, and beyond are sacred rhythms, and some who are playing them just aren't aware of their origins. "You listen to these rhythms and you say you don't know what they are," said O'Farrill. "Nonsense. That stuff is in your soul."

O'Farrill educates on jazz and Latin music's Africanisms. He adds, "Learning is remembering. Teaching is remembering. It is in our soul. We are connected to Mother Africa. Even physiologically, DNA wise. These rhythms, they come into our bodies. The ancestors are understanding," he says. "I'm a pretty horrible dancer. I have no shame," he jokes. Nevertheless, the rhythm runs deep.

He, too, urges people to go to the countries where various rhythms originate or are cultivated. "You must go there physically. Go to New Orleans. Go to Vera Cruz. Go to a second line parade. You have to be in the midst of a jazz funeral to understand New Orleans." Until you go and see these things, it can be hard to get the context, he says.

Mwata Bowden, former president of the AACM, loves the variation in clave and polyrhythms. "Once you go on a rhythm quest, you're in for a life long journey."

## Reflection Questions

1. Which of the following music genres did you grow up listening to?
   Soul, amapiano, R&B, blues, Afrobeat, funk, ragtime, jazz, rock, kizomba, hip-hop, house, techno, reggae, dub, disco, high life, Latin jazz, kompa, salsa, cumbia, samba, soca, neo soul, mbalax, rumba, son, calypso, Congolese rumba, Ethiopiques, African rock, Black rock, soukous, bebop, gospel, bossa nova, trip hop, spirituals, dance hall, reggaeton

2. What genres of music created or shaped by artists of African/African Diaspora do you listen to the most?

3. What genres of music within the African/African Diasporic pantheon do you listen to the least? Which ones are tougher for you to connect with?

4. Which of the genres listed are you unfamiliar with?

5. Think of yourself as a rhythm, a spiral connected to a greater universe. What song reflects your rhythm? What song reflects your ideal self? How does it speak to you? Jot down the qualities that the song has that are your own.

## Exercises: Genre Reflection

1. Listen to the songs listed here. Feel free to dance to them as well.
   "I'm Satisfied" James Brown
   "Dawal (Version Mbalax)," Youssou N'Dour
   "Traigo, Te Traigo" Pachito Alonso y sus Kini Kini
   "Yemaya" Okonkolo
   "Expensive Shit" Fela Kuti
   "Bemba y Tablao" Arturo O'Farrill

2. Select music from the genres you listen to the least or are less familiar with. You can add other genres that aren't listed. Make time throughout your week to listen to songs from these genres. Note or jot down how you feel. What insights have you gained?

3. Earlier you selected a song as your ideal rhythm. Let's make this song our personal space of celebration. Freestyle dance to this song in your space. Let this song be a reminder of you at your energetic best.

4. Take a dance class, any dance class, in a genre whose music you love but don't know how to move to. The rewards are endless. Dancing through our spaces and connecting to our rhythm poises us for the world of story. Through rhythm we can find the flow of our narrative, unearthing it and sailing on the worlds it takes us to.

# IV

# THE
# STORYVERSE

# 17

# MY MULTIVERSE

## The Multiplicity of
## Telling Our Own Stories

OUR WORLD IS A STORY. We find ourselves in story through the tales of others. We are the star of the story of our lives. Our perception of the world around us is through the lens of story. These narratives collide, overlap, and reassemble. This realm of threaded tales is nearly as old as the wind. As we project them into the future we become carriers of culture and engines of the next. The tales that will guide us through the new millennia are in the making.

Chanda Prescod-Weinstein is a particle cosmologist and theoretical physicist. She compares her work of studying dark matter and quantum fields in the early universe to being the "keeper of a deeply human impulse. . . . I am a griot of the universe—a storyteller. And although I am the first Black woman to hold a tenure-track faculty position in theoretical cosmology, I am certainly not the first Black woman to be a griot of the universe."[1]

## Multiverse

Once upon a time there was a story. This story was really a theory. This theory was conceived by theoretical physicists who came up with ideas to explain the universe. This story was one of several, backed with math and an ample bit of evidence to explain just why our universe was expanding. The beginning: About fourteen billion years ago, a massive explosion, called the Big Bang, birthed matter and the laws of physics. The facts: Our sun is one of hundreds of billions of stars and counting in a galaxy called the Milky Way. It appears that every trillionth of a second, some part of the universe doubles in size. It also appears that the smallest units of life don't function like the larger ones and you can't quite call where one of these small units of life will be. You can only say the probability of where it would likely be. Thus, a new story was born: The theories that we may live in a multiverse.

These theories are pretty bonkers if you don't know science and the quantum realm. There's the shadow theory, which says the quantum particles or ourselves have shadows and we, or rather our particles, are bound to matter reassembled in another universe—matter that isn't a duplicate of ourselves, but some other formation. Our shadow could be a nebula, an invisible unicorn, a cloud over a humanless world. There's the bubble universe theory, which says other universes are still forming, bubbling off from our own as an extension of the Big Bang. These bubble universes have their own as yet to be determined law of gravity. There's the many-worlds theory, which states that every possibility of everything that can happen exists in its own universe. As these probabilities increase, so do the number of universes. Somewhere, in the midst of these expansions, there's us. We are on Earth.

Writer Taylor Witten and I had to make sense of this ever-expanding universe just enough to tell another story: one about a girl named Niyah. Niyah, a preteen who dreams of being a scientist, meets her future self. Niyah's adult self is a theoretical physicist who guides her through key aspects of multiverse theory. Along the way, Niyah thinks about ideas of space and time that she learned from her grandparents, who adored African art and blues music. *Niyah and the Multiverse* is a sky show that runs at the Adler Planetarium in Chicago. The first of its kind animated project debuted in February 2024. Of the three theories explored, the many-worlds theory has the most science to support it.

The many-worlds theory is also the multiverse theory most explored in pop culture storytelling. Much of the Marvel Universe is built around the idea of alternate universes where characters made other life choices with different outcomes. In this theory, the belief is that the probability of things likely to happen to us, some by choice and others by circumstance, split into different realities. In other words, there's a you that decided to read this book, and another you that opted to take a nap. There's a you that decided to go to college and a you that dove into a working life. These two seemingly inconsequential options become realities that split; two realities, two time lines, that don't engage with one another. With each option or choice, more realities split.

However, in our imaginations, the options or choices we take and don't take interact with one another. Our story can become a series of what-ifs, some interpreted as lucky saves, some riddled with regret, some surfacing as curiosity. Gratitude is often the healer and harmonizer between two probability time lines that changed our trajectory, our story. This notion of a multiverse does make our story closer to those Choose Your Own Adventure books from our childhood. Our story, our sense of self, is ever expansive.

Lucian Walkowicz is an astronomer and artist who consulted on *Niyah and the Multiverse*. Walkowicz, in the midst of explaining these mind-racing theories to Taylor and I, stated it plainly. "The universe is weird," they said.

We are always, I think, trying to figure out our story. It is the human quest. Sometimes we are given our story, a societal narrative that explains the world from which we spring. There's a story within that story about how we should order our steps. We're told which decisions will bring rewards, which ones will lead to peril. Some stories are laid out like red carpets before us, a prescriptive checklist to follow. School, marriage, the good job are the floorboards to our existence, the story plot to follow. Sometimes we're told, for one reason or another, we will do none of these things, that our story is not one that falls within the story bought and sold. When neither story aligns, we seek new heroes, new stories. Perhaps we hop the time lines in the multiverse.

"Storytelling is a multiplicity—a cacophony, to borrow Jodi Byrd's word—of stories that intersect, contradict, and overlap," writes astrologer Alice Sparkly Kat in *Postcolonial Astrology*.[2] "New stories emerge from the intersections of this cacophony of stories." The gaps between these tales of tortoises racing with hares, heroic Maroons, and women who follow stars out of despair to new futures—we take these gaps and create other stories.

We have stories born of cosmology, a metaphysical way to order our universe, the realms of the visible and invisible. A realm where ancestors, spirit deities, and nature spirits take form. We form stories to explain what the Bantu call vital force or the East Asian sphere calls chi, the life force behind all things. These stories can help us see beyond the terrestrial ones sold and auctioned. The things we fear morph into monster tales. The things we love become heroic stories. Some metaphysicians say that all of it, the past, the future, are happening at the same time. We look to our stars and see the storied travel of light reverberating for another world's past. We wish upon stars thinking of futures cast in the light of its otherworldly history. We step in oceans that carry memory but feel brand-new.

Stanford Carpenter, cultural anthropologist and comics scholar, reminded me that our brains are absorbing input and reinterpreting data. "Look around the room," he said. "Our eyes don't take in the picture of the room. Our brains are reinterpreting the data. We see what we think is there. From that perspective, looking at your face is a speculative endeavor. It might not look that way at all to a person with a different kind of perception." Is the world we see merely collectively agreed upon light waves?

But we don't just see light waves. We see texture and shapes. On top of this sensory perception, we see indicators of emotion. We look into what appears to be a face of brown eyes and contoured cheeks and we see smiles, laughter, furrowed brows, sneers, a glare of disappointment.

Story is how we find meaning. We organize our lives in story, because it's through story that the wonders around us make sense. We ascribe meaning on top of meaning on top of meaning then regurgitate it as a story. "We live in a storytelling ecosystem. That doesn't mean stories are mist. Even mist is water and it can make you feel wet. It runs the gamut from the imagined to the physical and visceral," says Carpenter.

We organize story on a sensory level to perceive our world. We ascribe meaning to the physical gestures we see, hear, perceive. These foundational stories are cognitive tools. We can't so much as touch a keyboard without the feeling evoking story.

This perception is nonstop. Even in our sleep our subconscious speaks to us in story. A state where we are processing streams from our subconscious unfolds as a lucid story. These stories, the ones born in the night, are whole universes of their own.

"We use story to organize," says Carpenter. "Our putting time and meaning on something informing stories can literally have physical impact on us. You see someone who you like and you have a good feeling. Your body feels calm. You see someone who is scary and your heart races, your hair stands on end. You see someone you care for and fall in love. You see someone who you used to care for, and then you have the feeling of a broken heart. It's not just stories out there floating around amorphous."

The meaning we find in story informs the decisions we make, the roads we follow, the rivers we sail and those we don't. The

Afrofuturist stories we weave assemble another tapestry of stories, another waterway of meaning that makes another set of decisions possible, probable, and real. Again, I think of Nina Woodruff-Walker, executive director of the Museum of Children's Art, a museum that centers Afrofuturist programming: "We haven't lost as much as we thought." Futures past that were lost are uncovered and redirected in story. Story is our guide to inner and outer dimension.

We look back to the stories of early and not-so-early humans around the campfire as they listened to griots and enlightened others who weaved tales to order a world. Today, our campfires are often screens with descrambled pixels, stories sailing on digital soundwaves, etched on dead trees. A man grips a plastic object with a silver tip and his jokes are amplified.

Algorithms are stories. Algorithms read our data plucked from internet scrolls, likes, and ride-share purchases. Where we place our index finger on a screen becomes fodder for a story to some marketers about who we are. They assess our data to figure out our story—a story we didn't tell, a story we don't know we're telling. This story is interpreted and assessed with hundreds, thousands, millions of others, popping up as an advertisement in the form of a suggestion that it's the red car that you want or it's the latest emo rap that you'd like to listen to. But you don't want a red car. And you don't listen to emo rap.

Other algorithms read our blood sugar levels, our heart rates, revealing another story of DNA and stress and the food we ate last week. These stories of how many steps we take and the food we ordered are fed back to us as mirrors, telling us our story. These stories aren't captured by someone you met on the street or through a conversation with a friend on the bus. It's a story contained in a system created by a human as a predictor of what you are likely to do, what you should do. What you can do in the future. Am I my data? Am I my consumer profile?

The story in the human genome is that we are all, regardless of where we originate from in the world, related. There are stories we live by. There are the stories we tell. We all have stories about who we are, where we come from, how we got here, and where we expect to be. When we don't have one, we weave one from what's left behind, memories, an overheard tale, a dream, a left behind artifact, an album cover, a piece of jewelry, an unresolved emotion.

We swap stories to bond with others. We look to the stories of others, those from other times and the new ones created, to commune, to find meaning, to understand life. We are swimming in story: commercials, TikTok, films, music, dialogue, news, psychic readings, mission statements, weather reports, collages, public art, jokes, smack talk, tall tales, lies, conspiracy theories, excuses. We pass the time with friends by sharing stories about our day, our dreams and wishes. We post stories on social media about how fly we are when we're sad. We rewrite the story with a selfie to the world: *I look cute today.* I am, despite it all, using this post hoping the next like will kick off enough endorphins to make me feel better about the day.

Immersing ourselves in stories from varying lenses pushes us beyond our story frameworks. In this ecosystem, Afrofuturist stories about new futures, alternate worlds, and futures challenge conventions we didn't know we had. They can bring us closer to ourselves. They can help us recognize that our story is one of many in a multiverse.

"The fundamental thing that comes to Afrofuturist stories is that it creates an opportunity to break from patterns that we never question," says Julian Chambliss, professor at Michigan State University. "That act of creating a different path is fundamental in how to get there. The guy who invented the cell phone got that idea from *Star Trek*. He was inspired by a prop toy on this sixties TV show to come up with a cell phone. Science fiction is really important because it gives people space to imagine these things that are departures to see something different and better."

Stories also impart values: wisdom systems, morals, aspirations, possibilities. We discover both who we are and who we can be in story. Our sphere of what is important and what isn't is dictated by the river of stories we swim through. The realm of speculative fiction is rich with worldviews that help us to reexperience ourselves. We are challenged, we connect, and often we see ourselves and our world a little differently. The risk that speculative fiction writers take sends us on journeys as gleeful as they are daunting. Yet, the lens of life is as much a mirror of ourselves as it is of the writers who pen the stories. Samuel Delany's epic writing is not designed to make our lives easier. But his tomes of wonder, while challenging conventions, do make us more humane. We see ourselves, who we can be, who we don't want to be, who we used to be, through the convictions that writers like Delany, Octavia Butler, or Toni Morrison craft. We see friends, we see strangers, and we sometimes experience lives we could never live, or fantasies that feel all too real because of their fresh audacity to tell the story. Story is a truth. Not the truth, but a truth for a life lived and a dream remembered. I remember rapper Tupac Shakur's aunt telling his life story and that of his mother in the documentary miniseries *Dear Mama*. Gloria Cox was a sister and aunt and by proxy a witness to their story. In wonderment at two dear lives of deep souls cut short, she wondered why she was still alive. She, too, had challenges and triumphs. She asserted that it must be so that she could tell the story. She jolted the audience by warning them her dear sister and Black Panther, Afeni Shakur, wanted the story told "with warts and all."

## The Glitter Ball

Who are we if not the stories we tell ourselves? Whether these stories are true, fictive, or speculative, we lean on stories to order our world, just as some lean on drum sets for sonic world orders or visions to advance our cause. Michael Gonzales, an arts and speculative fiction writer, shares that he wrote a story once about an incident in his life and a fellow colleague said he didn't have the same recollection. Gonzales was resolute in his response:"Then write your own story," he said. Whether we are sworn scribes or not, we, in some form or fashion, communicate who we are through story. What do we learn from our future stories?

We write our futures with our actions. We surge through time powered by intention, fueled by desire. We are not floating. We are, as our YOU ARE HERE map reminds us, somewhere in space and time, connecting with a vision of ourselves and what our world can be, who we can be. Our dreams, that which inspires us, and our nighttime sleep world adventures are springboards for stories. We are walking stories. Some of us share the details with others or record in our phones. Some of us carry our values and virtues in oral tales while some of us turn to pen, paper, laptop. If you have a story you want to share, you can play with an array of forms to do so. You are important. We are important. Our life is a walking proverb of lessons. But our stories aren't about us alone. Our stories are connectors, but they are also records for us to assess what's important to us.

People often tell me that they want to tell their story. Sometimes they're thinking about finding fame and fortune. Usually, people simply have something to say. They want to shout to the world that their life matters. We want to get our tales out, if not to the world, simply out of our head. I encourage all of us to simply record your voice telling one. If you prefer to write, you can do that as well. Don't be concerned with an audience. Don't be concerned with perfection, simply share your tale. Maybe it's real, maybe it's fiction. In this case, expressing is the goal. Reflecting is the goal. Sharing is secondary and optional. We have stories, we have dreams, we have futures, and we have a human right to express them.

## A Modern Griot

Perhaps you are a griot, sharing the tales of others, reminding the world of other times, future times, now times. Being the modern griot is the reason that Mama Edie Armstrong became a professional storyteller. Armstrong, who also works with Urban Gateways, runs a program called Finding the Light. Originally a speech pathologist working with English and Spanish speakers, Armstrong was encouraged to become a storyteller because she saw the dire need for them. Stories are healing, she says. Our society underestimates how oral storytelling helps with literacy. She shared with me that she was troubled when meeting young children across the world who did not know stories, cultural stories, about themselves.

"I inspire a sense of identity, and sense of worth, a sense of understanding of a past, a sense that they have something to contribute. It's great to give them wisdom lessons from different cultures. It's also been valuable," she says.

Once, she was asked to alleviate ethnic, racial, and immigrant tensions at a laboratory. Armstrong wanted to get the mostly male company to share their stories. "The status quo were having a difficult time with that [demographic] change. The personnel director wondered if I could do anything through storytelling. This was a mandatory meeting. They come in and you see this attitude. It's clear they didn't think that coming to see a storyteller was anything they needed to do for the day," she says.

As Armstrong told a story, she noticed that the audience began to relax. "They spoke their own truths and told their own personal stories," she says. They talked about the kinds of things they were afraid of and what made them upset. "If they had a bias, this space gave them an opportunity to hear one another's real stories instead of ruminating in the assumptions that they had. Before that moment, Armstrong says that the employees didn't really care about one another's stories.

The stories we tell ourselves and others can ring for a lifetime. "We must recognize that our words can contribute to the health of our relationships or their demise. We can say something to someone that can hurt for a lifetime. Saying something cruel to someone or making them feel unnecessarily guilty about something," she says, pondering, "you can't unsay it. By the same token there are things that people can say to people that will inspire them for a lifetime. The choice is always ours."

How often do we find ourselves telling the stories of others as a window to our own? We compare and contrast, sharing what we would do or wouldn't do. We learn from sharing, from listening. Stories can create empathy. But you don't need to know someone's story to respect them as a person in the universe, as a person sharing our world. Nevertheless, our stories remind us that we are part of a vast interdependent ecosystem of stories known, unknown, and projected.

It's OK to share tales of wonders and future, of reality and aspiration. These stories are gateways, ones to build futures upon, ones that paint the picture of the next, ones that sketch the overabundant now.

## Reflection Questions

We may be the stories that we tell ourselves. However, stories change. Let's think upon the stories that bind and define us.

1.  What is your story? When you tell people who you are and where you come from, what do you say?
2.  What is your family story? In short, is there a family narrative that defines the family? Perhaps it's a migration, a story about found or lost wealth, or an achievement?
3.  Identify a community you are a part of. It can be an ethnic group, your neighborhood, a found community, a digital

community. What is the story that binds you? What is the community's narrative?

4.   Can you recall an oral story that you're fond of? What is it?

5.   What stories resonate with you? Name five stories in any format (film, novel, songs, oral history, folktales, current event, jokes, plays, poems, spiritual stories, performances, etc.) that speak to who you are. Why do they speak to you?

6.   Thinking upon the stories you've listed, think about how these narratives speak to your views on the future, your views of the present.

7.   What stories about the future do you have an affinity for? List at least five. Again, you can pick from stories of any medium. What do you like about these stories? How do they relate to your ideas about the future?

## Exercises: Find Your Story

1.   Connect with a loved one, a group of friends, or family, and ask if you can share a story with them. The story can be personal, fictional, a family story, or of any nature. You can also do this in a group.

2.   Try the same exercise from number one and tell a story that takes place in the future.

3.   Select a work of Afrofuturist or Black science fiction and fantasy writers to read or listen to on audio book. You have an array of authors to choose from: Samuel Delany, Nalo Hopkinson, Sheree Renée Thomas, Jordan Ifueko, Tananarive Due, Stephen Barnes, Octavia Butler, Oghenechovwe Donald Ekpeki, Nisi Shawl, N. K. Jemisin, Deji Bryce Olukotun, and so many more.

# 18

# A NATURE STORY

## Climate Change and Our Stories of the Land

EACH FALL, ILLINOIS'S SINNISSIPPI PARK transforms into a forest of the future. *Somnium: The Book of the Forest Lament* is an immersive multimedia art experience cultivated by artist Eddaviel (Edison Montero). He works with some thirty community members to bring the spectacle of the living forest of a future to life. A sea-green portal stands as an interdimensional arc bearing images of newborn life. Humans are no more, and the environment has evolved beyond the realm of imagination. Giant glow-in-the-dark jellyfish are now earthbound and abide in the trees. The tully monster is reborn as the beauty it once was. A towering masked spirit twirls much like a zangbeto, the night spirits of the Ogu of Benin, Togo, or Nigeria. A hulking snake of many colors lines walking trails as audiences follow the spirit of the forest, one who speaks through the Inriri bird, deeper into the world of wonder. The story draws from Taino myths and an Afrofuturist lens of Eddaviel's home in the Dominican Republic all commingled with the prehistoric reimaginings of his colleagues in Illinois, USA. "I wanted to tell a story from the perspective of the forest," says Eddaviel. The forest speaks. This lush wonder only compels the countless patrons to go deeper with the land's magic. Is the forest speaking to us? Do we hear the message?

Filmmaker Chelsea Odufu was enchanted by the baobab trees of Senegal. Learning of storytelling griots whose spirits lived among the epic trees, she thought about the layered wisdom in the foliage—divine, human, and nature based, all intertwined. In her experimental film *Beloved Baobab* she aimed to "personify the elements," she says. "I wanted to personify the jinn or the spirits that lived in the baobab." The film, a juxtaposition of the awe of the natural world and the sting of seaside pollution, is a reminder of the calamities of progress and the abandonment of the stories of the land. The ever-watching baobab knows the story.

Artist Grace Lynne Haynes explored the explosion of nature emerging in her Afrofuturist series *The Sea Is the Only Highway*. Women and children are reborn in full-bloom flower-scapes abiding as the celestial in seatopias on land. They flaunt '90s-inspired hairdos and appear as spectrum-colored marvels. Haynes reinvisioned the biblical Rapture of new beginnings, where nature and human life reemerge intertwined.

Both Odufu and Haynes were featured in the Harvey B. Gantt Center in Charlotte's *Becoming the Sea* exhibit, a selection of works from Black Rock Senegal residents. My zine *Fluid* was showcased as well, and featured poetry and prose in which water spirits speak through ancient rivers of Ghana and Senegal and follow their progeny through freshwater lakes and water faucets. Nature was reaching out to us and as channels we sought to relay the message.

## Temperature Shifts

When Aliyah Collins decided to create the Afrofuturism and Climate Change conference in Chicago in 2024, she wanted to

encourage people to think more deeply about community practices that restore the Earth—practices that many are likely already
doing. "There are so many people growing food with their neighbors and educating one another on environmental justice issues,"
she says. She yearned to bring these practices to light and encourage all to think on building futures. The event included tours of
Black and Brown urban farms across Chicago and talks with artists addressing climate change issues. Most of the audience were
students from Bennett College looking to reimagine their communities. I was among the mix of attendees, talking about culture
and relationships to land as we ate a mix of locally grown food
at a farm-to-table dinner at Cedillo's farm. An elegant experience
where trees whispered amidst the soothing roar of freight trains,
the sensation of eating from the land was indescribable. I realized
I'd never eaten a full dinner outdoors in my hometown's urban
oasis amidst the garden where our dining treasures sprang from.
I marveled at how special and rare this moment was. I marveled
at the fact that it shouldn't be rare at all. Attendees were discussing how they could incorporate urban farming in their lives. They
swapped stories about travel and queerness, safety and dreams,
parenting, gentrification, and community. They wanted to learn
more about the region. They left inspired, empowered, knowledge-
able, and open to learn.

Although the solutions to climate change are vast and intricate,
the issue that kept surfacing for me was our societal disconnect
from the ancient stories of the land. Land stories center community. Could our modern severance from nature be rooted in the
fact that generally we don't know, value, share, or understand the
stories of the land, the whispering of nature, or the tales of its
ardent caretakers across the regions? Some don't know where we
fit into such ancient tales. Is our future closely bound to reestab-
lishing our role as conscious caretakers of the lands we live upon?
Does our advocacy work best when we know the natural ecosystem
around us and what it used to be? Do we need a refreshed story

binding us to our evolving environment, one that helps us reconnect to our natural world?

"Pretty much," says Rob Callahan, an Indigenous futures writer
based in Minnesota. He believes everyone should know what grows
naturally in a region and what can grow harmoniously that isn't
native to the region, along with the stories that inform. He's dedicated much of his life to learning the stories and practices he
applies. "Our ecosystems are so delicate," he told me. "The slightest
adjustment can shift everything." How we reintegrate those stories
and values will shape our collective future.

Afrofuturism's relationship to planetary health is a central
focus for Cosmic Northside, a Canadian-based conference created by Quentin VerCetty. VerCetty speaks of early commingling
between African and Indigenous histories in Canada and the desire
to recover and build upon their environmental practices. "We think
of Octavia Butler and think of ourselves as Earthseeds," he says.
"Renewable energy has been a big focus on Indigenous futurist
and Afrofuturist here. We want to protect the resources and the
innovation that we are putting forth."

## Dreams of Nature

As a child, I could gaze upon half-moons or be bewitched by leaf
patterns. However, nature was this amorphous thing out "there"
somewhere with scary animals, a heap of inconveniences, and
unknown factors. Nature was hard-labor work like farming. Farming was the past—a messy history of coercion, long hours doing
something other than your life's purpose.

The forest, the realm of campers and spooky folktales, was a
soiree of shadows. People of ill intent hid in the forest. Unknown
animals and sounds from nowhere echoed from the tree-filled
abyss. There were no streetlights in the forest, only flashlights and
moonlight. The nefarious and their ilk snatched life from people
deep within the forest. Goblins and scary people looked to tackle

you in these places. Kidnappers hid in the forest. The forest was not for children or strangers to the forest and to those who didn't want them there.

The coastlines of lakes were safer. You could play in the sand or swim in the shallow end. Rarely if ever did I see fish, only seagulls who mimicked pigeons flocking across city beaches. The sand we played on was strewn atop landfills from the rubble of the Great Chicago Fire. But the lakeshore was safe for daytime. Rivers were the lake's dirtier counterpart, with one branch dyed green for Saint Patrick's Day. These rivers connected to other rivers that took one into the lands with other unheralded stories.

The sky was more interesting. The moon shining brightest among the faintest of stars—that is, if you could see them past the towering skyscrapers and rooftops. The sky spoke more to the future, but it was hard to see. It was easiest to survey while in motion, looking out the passenger window on an expressway via car or train. I remember aiming for a sky view with my first childhood telescope in my home and being forever blocked by garages, power lines, and buildings. However, as theoretical physicist Chanda Prescod-Weinstein would later remind me, we don't see the stars of our ancestors. Our cities of lights create light pollution. Smog can be the thin layer that blankets the sky. Only few among us can see the stars in their full brilliance.

Yet, the city of my birth was still awash in nature's presence. I could see the celestial sun rise and set, green grass growing, and maples and oaks casting shade on sunny days. Dandelions and sunflowers were everywhere, shooting through blocks of asphalt that formed the sidewalk. Grass could grow thigh high if uncut over as little as two weeks, resembling the heather described in nineteenth-century novels. A walk through a cluster of trees on a city college campus would reveal an owl, cardinals, blue jays, sparrows. Then there was the lake, thousands of years older than the oldest tree, that stood as the anchor for nature's vastness.

For Tim Fielder, a graphic novelist, connecting with the land is a future story. The city of his birth in the Deep South "has blood in the land," he says. Currently living in New York City, he feels artists and Black and Brown people are shuffled about at the whims of gentrification. He doesn't feel connected to that land either, although he's been there for decades. He aspires to build on shared land with his brother outside of Atlanta. For him, it wasn't a question of connecting with nature but of creating a sense of home. Today is the rat race, tomorrow we'll find home.

## Finding Home

Sakena Young-Scaggs says she doesn't remember a time when she wasn't aware of environmental justice. Growing up in the shadows of the factories of Newark, she had asthma as a child. Her barometer for environmental health is a simple one: "What does it take for me to breathe?" she asks. Currently, Young-Scaggs is the senior associate dean for religious and spiritual life at Stanford and pastor of Stanford Memorial Church. She and her son have acquired land in various states that they aim to cultivate into oases of refreshment and connection. Knowing the stories of the land is key. "While they are colonial lands and Indigenous lands, they also become Black lands, because we have put our sweat and blood into the land, too."

As I grew into adulthood, I learned the stories of land struggles, migrations, gentrification, sundown towns, and the shifting access to space or the fights for fresh air and water. Access to nature is presented as a privilege for those with summer homes, wilderness expertise, or getaway expense accounts. Even these nature quests are treks through synthetic nature: a space where trees aren't so old; soybean fields stretch like seas; cash crops never meant to grow in abundance take up land the size of football fields; and stocked ponds lure fishing lovers. The stories of the land can feel like whispers of the bygone era.

Phil Cohran, one of the founders of the AACM and a musician who studied with Sun Ra, would take students to areas in Chicago and identify plants that were native to the area—plants one could live off of. When a colleague told me he was on those walks, it dawned on me that I didn't know what grew here naturally, what was edible and what wasn't. Dandelions, my only edible connection to the region, I later learned, aren't from North America at all. Cohran would teach star constellations, the stories of those who came before, identifying who came from which ones. He'd wait for these stars to provide answers and reveal futures. When he saw the cover of my *Afrofuturism* book some years ago, he noted that if the work had been created in ancient times, the geometric shapes forming the blue face and the mass of hair would be aligned with a celestial marker of time.

Some of my friends have vivid memories of neighbors with robust city gardens, plucking from pear trees and the like. Most do not. Most looked to the stars for refresh or the sun, when the land and its toil spoke to family memories of farming under duress. None, like myself, could identify more than a few edible things that grew naturally in the city, largely because they'd rarely witnessed such a spectacle. Only one could name which fish were in our rivers and lakes. None had a clear vision of what this land was like in its natural state or the plant life that abounds. All were second- or third-generation residents of the region.

Not knowing brought up issues of survival, insecurity, and the defensiveness of migrations of the past. Perhaps some knew the stories of the lands they traversed during the course of human history but not of the ones they'd arrived to in recent years. They had a relationship with the land of the American South, the Caribbean, continental Africa, and some of the stories of Indigenous wisdom from the region. In some cases they were decades or centuries removed. How did those stories and knowledge apply in the Midwest on another Indigenous land? It's not their fault, I was told. "Their" was a reference to those in their family who'd migrated. When is home ever home when there's a history of lands stolen and peoples shaken and tossed about? Is home still not home if you don't know the stories?

Simply put, knowledge of what fruits and vegetables are native to the region you live in, or which wildlife and plant life grow in neighboring lakes and rivers, was common at one point. The stories of spirits of the land informed cultures. Today this information is regarded as specialized knowledge.

This is not a local issue nor an American one solely. Many people around the world are fairly unaware of their natural ecosystems before colonization, urbanization, or the preponderance of cash crops. Many don't know the stories. Those who do know wonder how they can reroute past transgressions when the nature of greed lays such ardent tracks to co-op futures.

## Story Alignment

Although Senegal has a plethora of ethnic groups, the Lebu have been on the coastline the longest and are the purveyors of all things coastal. Life in Dakar is on the ocean. Swimming, boating, fishing, snorkeling, surfing, and body surfing are daily activities. The Lebu water spirits are the protectors of the coast and its residents. This awareness of the water spirits is carried by most in the region, whether one is Lebu or not. Many pay homage to these spirits, pouring milk in the sea or offering prayers, regardless of ethnicity. The general consensus is that the ocean is a force with a spirit that is not to be played with. The awareness of these stories plays a unique role in oceanside restoration and counteracting pollution.

The Potawatomi of the Midwest United States speak of a water panther as the spirit of Lake Michigan. Lean, quick, powerful, mighty, dangerous, and protective, it reflects the nature of this lake. The water panther frequently tussled with the hawk, the spirit of the wind, and rough ripples and crashing waves ensued. The story of the water panther isn't common knowledge cityside. Yet the hawk we knew too well. How many times had I heard the cutting wind described as the hawk, never knowing it was an ancient story? Knowing the story forged for me a deep connection, not just to the people abiding in the city, my history of migration, or the alignment of robust cultures that arrived but to the physicality of the environment itself and the people who were its caretakers for centuries. We share a story. As I visit the lake for refresh, thinking of the water panther explains so much. My reconnection with the story surfaces a renewed sense of home.

During a college winter break, I remember returning from humid Atlanta and enjoying the fervent brisk cold air whipping off Lake Michigan. Yes, I'm a person whose families hailed from much warmer climates. Yes, I am restored with the sunny, salted breeze off the Atlantic from Dakar's shore. Yes, to adapt to this northern environment, I and others who hail from warmer climates are encouraged to take 10,000 IU of vitamin D to compensate for the sun we aren't receiving. I had a family who'd thrived through many a winter in this steely city. Shivering aside, the nature of the hawk and the cultures who first told this tale were in concert with my experience. The hawk soared over skyscrapers that resembled icy popsicles and steely robots. That day, I was loving the hawk's swoop as it zipped around street corners and buildings, welcoming me with the sting of winter love.

## The Role

As a micro issue, the story of knowing the ecosystem is one of awareness. We become aware of a natural ecosystem of which we are a part. We become cognizant of the life in all things. We also become aware of how we engage with this nature system and the broader systems that order our world. Where does my trash go? How long does it take plastic to disintegrate? How do carbon emissions impact weather? These questions become more urgent and relevant when we value the story of our ecosystems.

On a larger level, our awareness may run us against bigger takes of unhinged greed. But systems are composed of people who uphold them. As Afrofuturists, or those who engage with Afro-futurist perspectives, regardless of where we find ourselves in the world, knowing the story of the land and the Indigenous people who reside on it, and valuing the story as one that informs our tomorrow, is key to the values we bring forward. We must bring the story forward. We innovate with the awareness of this story. The story makes us consciously aware of our oneness with the immediate environment across time. Whether we think of ourselves as digital nomads, are indigenous to an area, or choose to live in a region for a lifetime, it's our responsibility to increase our conscious awareness of the natural ecosystem and its story.

My neighbor is a retiree who shares vegetables from his garden. He's part of one of the communal urban farms that was part of the Afrofuturism and Climate Change tour. He's excited that younger people are enthusiastic about growing food. Recently, he was delighted to plant seeds for tomatoes with a local origin. His surprise at the taste of these grape-sized tomatoes in their red, yellow, and green hues was the story he told all summer. Engaging with the story, sharing the food, and the wisdom of the land always forges community, joy, and connection.

## Emergence

When John Jennings rebirthed scientist Al Harper as the Marvel superhero Ghost Light, in *Silver Surfer: Ghost Light*, he faced a conundrum. Harper had sacrificed his life in *Silver Surfer #5*, a comic issued in 1968, aiming to save the world from the villainous Stranger. John found a solution, with Al having a cosmic connection to nature. "Al turns his soul into matter," says Jennings. "His human body is in the ground. When he reconnects them, he turns Al's soul back into energy and this nanotech repairs his body. He comes out of the earth fully formed. This cosmic Silver Surfer flame on his grave is the power source. The cosmic flame is a cosmic energy source.

"There are billions of nanobots in his body. They can speak to various systems at the speed of light." Harper can connect to both natural and human-made systems. "He can translate what the climate is thinking. He can feel a star explode. He can tell you what an anthill is thinking."

Ghost Light has cosmic awareness. Although we may not be able to assess systems with the speed of light, we can be reborn with a conscious awareness of the stories that undergird our environment and sustain healthy futures.

## Reflection Questions

As Collins mentioned, oftentimes we have some practices that connect us with nature. Let's think upon these practices and how they speak to culture and the creation of healthy futures.

1. What recollections do you have of loved ones connecting to nature? Did you have relatives who maintained gardens? Do you have friends who observe moon cycles?

2. Do you have family stories passed down regarding honoring the land? What are they? Do you have practices that honor the environment? What are they?

3. Earlier we thought upon dancing and the elements. Is there a particular natural environment that speaks to you? Do you prefer oceans and rivers? Forest? Mountainous regions?

4. Do you know what vegetation, plants, or trees grow naturally where you currently live? Name as many as you can. Can you name plants, vegetation, or trees in your region that are not from the region where you live but grow in abundance? What are they?

5. Do you know what vegetation, plants, or trees grow naturally in places where you lived previously? Name as many as you can.

6. What stories do you know about the land you currently live on? What ancient stories do you know? What contemporary stories do you know?

7. How would you like to connect with the environment? What does a healthy environment look like?

## Exercises: Your Nature Story

1. Plucking from the realms of fantasy, sci-fi, and your wondrous life, think of a story where you and your friends have the power of conscious awareness. You have the ability to connect with natural systems and human-made ones. You can relay this story in any form you like, as a short story, a poem, a song, or a statement, among others. What is the theme of your story? What environmental or social justice issue can you address?

2. Seek out opportunities to learn more about the natural environment and Indigenous stories about the land where you're currently living. Feel free to visit farms, botanical gardens, or museums, or ask neighbors and gardeners.

# 19

# THE ART OF
# THE NONLINEAR

## The History and Future of
## Black Storytelling

AFROFUTURIST STORIES AND THEIR SPECULATIVE FICTION brethren are time and location disruptors. They embrace the nonlinear approach, one where time, space, the very nature of reality, shift at will. Nonlinear means that a narrative doesn't fall in a prescriptive order. Such works are described as nonlinear because they don't follow all the elements of a Western story format where we move sequentially through a beginning, middle, and end. The opposite of a line is a circle. Referencing our Kongo cosmogram, this circle is really a spiral. At this point, you've been immersed in the world of the spiral. You are a spiral, a storied spiral. Often, when we tell our stories, we're told that we can't tell the spiral. Share it as a line, one with a neat progression, an arc of triumph, a low point. If you can't tell this story in a line, well, delete it, or so convention would say.

## A Story's Story

Conventional storytelling goes as follows: A character wants a thing, they go through some level of turmoil to achieve it. They at some point feel this achievement is all but lost, and then they reboot, pressing the pedal to the metal to reach their end goal. Through this arc, they have some level of internal growth, either achieving the goal or not. It's sometimes referred to as the hero's journey. This form of storytelling is laid out to us as the foundation of all storytelling, from Greek myth to modern superhero. Although the character might not be a superhero per se, if you look at the heap of stories told in the pop culture, that's the arc they follow. There's nothing inherently wrong with that way of storytelling. However, it is only one way, among many, to convey meaning to a world. We like this story because it's a question of will. A single person overcomes an obstacle and finds a way. There's value in this story. We learn how to overcome obstacles. We see the value of focus, determination, and having a good friend to help us out. The challenge we face is whittled down to one person or phenomenon that can be vanquished. When we tell our stories, we sometimes use this arc, too.

How a story is told is as essential as the story itself. In some ways, they are one and the same. Whether it's the colliding realities in the HBO series *Lovecraft Country* or the world hopping in the anthology *Africa Risen*, nonlinearity is often the best way to reflect complex lives. Lives that are sometimes relegated to the unseen need another framing to tell their stories. Nonlinearity can help us tell parts of our story, the otherworldy aspects, that we sometimes overlook. In a land where assumptions about a natural order of things can keep people in a box, nonlinear stories reveal a far-reaching tapestry of who we are, who we can be.

Sheree Renée Thomas is the coeditor of *Africa Risen*, an anthology of tales from writers in Africa and its diaspora. She is also editor of the *Magazine of Fantasy & Science Fiction*. Thomas says that Afrofuturism's nonlinearity appears so often in storytelling because "it is an excellent way to create, in the reader's mind, a sense of the dissonance we experience as Black people moving in the world. It's a way to show the unreality of our reality. It's often not rational, in terms of how Black bodies are politicized. Sometimes the intersectional becomes this liminal space. There's a lot of projection." This continued push on boundaries captures the spirit of the bizarre and the baffling. Afrofuturism allows us to play with that.

It is because of this inherent nonlinearity in how many Black people talk about their own lives that Stephanie Renee Toliver wrote *Recovering Black Storytelling in Qualitative Research: Endarkened Storywork*. Noting the speculative and Afrofuturist nature in dialogue and word perceptions among everyday people, Toliver argues that it's best to capture these interviews in story form. Toliver, a researcher, gathers her interviews of varying subjects and presents them as story.

"Stories are ubiquitous, and they are powerful elements in the transformation and empowerment of communities who are constantly resisting oppression and making space to heal," she told me. "Black people have often told stories to develop knowledge, ask critical questions, and offer different perspectives. They have told stories that challenge dominant discourse to silence them. Endarkened storywork honors this history and brings Black storytelling traditions to the forefront of qualitative inquiry."

Toliver delivers her inquiry as an Afrofuturist story. The story takes place in 2085. It's a tale of the Endarkened, a people restricted from dreaming who abide in the imagination gap. Jane 9675214 seeks to lead them to a new land.

## Pairings

Lorraine O'Grady is a performance artist and writer inspired by Dadaism and surrealism. Among her prized achievements is a performance work she did as part of Harlem's annual African American parade. She and several models dressed in white and gold and, years before the internet's game-changing selfie existed, went into the crowd and held up life-sized picture frames. Audience members posed and flaunted as they were framed for O'Grady's camera. Their prized float also had a float-sized picture frame, framing the audience as it sailed down 125th street. Actress Tracee Ellis Ross, daughter of the legendary singer, later duplicated elements of the event as her evidence of camp fashion at the star-studded Met Gala.

This spectacle of performance art, too, is a story, one of people receptive to the camera's lens as they took on their inner fabulous. The characters were the community. "If pressed to describe what I do, I'd say that I am writing in space," says O'Grady. "I guess that's what comes from being trained as a writer. But I was never able to accommodate to the linearity of writing. Perhaps I'm too conscious of the stages lived through and the multiple personalities I contain," she said.[1]

Her performance work *Nefertiti/Devonia Evangeline* utilizes the idea of a diptych. A diptych is the art of placing two images together, often religious, that are fairly similar. O'Grady takes two images that don't appear to be similar, aren't similar, but are revealed to have more commonality than surface observation would reveal. Her work is designed to compel us to find relations between unlikely subjects who are juxtaposed with one another.

The *Nefertiti/Devonia Evangeline* diptych places Egyptian pharaoh Nefertiti adjacent to O'Grady's beautiful sister. O'Grady said she always thought the two looked alike. She placed images of Nefertiti's son next to that of her sister's son. O'Grady also repeated this process again, placing images of bestselling recording artist Michael Jackson next to French poet Charles Baudelaire. The *Nefertiti/Devonia Evangeline* exhibit was featured at the Brooklyn Museum's permanent Egyptian exhibit in 2021. The work disordered assumptions about who the early Egyptians resemble. The museum used O'Grady's work along with a statement that the ancient Egyptians resembled people of the Mediterranean world and African Americans today to underscore this point. Through the use of Devonia's photos, the people of Ancient Egypt come alive. There were other walls broken, too. Two women several centuries apart appeared to live lives with similar themes. The isolation of a queen or the jealousy brought on by beauty now stood as comparable experiences.

O'Grady says that *Nefertiti/Devonia Evangeline* approximates a book or "a family photo album, interlaced with personal reminiscence and ritual." The ritual element in her display was embodied by O'Grady, who performed a ceremony when the work was first displayed in 1980.

It is in ritual and story in community that Tyson Yunkaporta believes stories for the future are best preserved for the millennia. Yunkanporta, an Aboriginal scholar in Melbourne, is the founder of the Indigenous Knowledge Systems Lab at Deakin University. In Indigenous thinking, ceremony and ritual will likely outlast digital media, which Yunkaporta feels won't be around for longer than a century. In conversation with futurist Thomas Mofolo, he listened as Mofolo said that stories preserving African spirituality can live in collective gatherings.

"A good story needs to be enacted through ceremony," he says. "That's the only safe way to store data." He adds, "You need to make sure you back your shit up with intergenerational relationships within the law of the land and the spirit of the land enacted through increase ceremony. That's the stuff that will still be here in a century."[2]

In thinking about Nefertiti, it doesn't go unnoticed that the ancient Egyptians are remembered and celebrated because of the treasure trove of art and architecture left behind—most of which was covered with symbols or literal hieroglyphics telling their stories.

## Reality Shift

Some of Afrofuturism's nonlinearity is attributed to the fact that it references other ways of perceiving what's real and what isn't. In African cosmologies, the physical and spiritual worlds are linked. Writers Oghenechovwe Donald Ekpeki and Joshua Uchenna Omenga coined the term *Afropantheology* for this reason. Viewing it as an aspect of Afrofuturism, Ekpeki and Omenga assert that separating this worldview from fantasy is essential to understanding the stories.

"Every sphere of existence is connected to the other: the living to the dead, the born to the unborn, humans to the deities," the two say in their book *Between Dystopias: The Road to Afropantheology*.

"*Afropantheology* is the study of African (and African-descended) religions, gods, and the bodies of knowledge associated with them. It is a term to capture the essence of the stories in this project, and also solves the age-old problem of accurate and respectful labelling of stories based on African lore and religion." Afropantheology acknowledges the fluidity of spiritual pantheons across the African continent and seeks

> the freedom of the artist to express these stories in their original forms, unbridled by western labels and terminologies and the need for conformity to defined (often limited) literary standards. For, contrary to speculations, the relative unfamiliarity of stories reflecting African pantheons is due to the weakness of form rather than the paucity of stories. These stories have always been extant in oral forms, preserved by lore keepers whose goal was to ensure the continuity of culture rather than the fame of publication, who indeed sought no glorification outside the recognition of their fidelity in passing the stories.[3]

The telling of a story can become a quest, one that binds worlds visible and not visible. The story we tell reflects the story we are.

The film *The Gifted* toured around the world independently when it debuted in 1993. Director and writer Audrey King Lewis was exploring her own relationship to spirituality. Seeking grounding in her psychic abilities, the African American filmmaker visited elders in the Dogon tribe. Her insights inspired the film. The story follows psychic descendants of the Dogon gathered to save Earth. Aliens granted the society with psychic abilities several millennia ago to help fend off Ogo, an alien with bad intentions. Every thirty-two years, in alignment with the star Sirius B, Ogo returns to kill the psychics as he contends for power. A Black community in the American South was founded by a Dogon slave. One family in the community is targeted by Ogo, and a Dogon shaman comes to help. The beloved film baffled critics who didn't know what context to place it in.

Linear storytelling follows one hero's journey. This hero's journey is more important than all the rest. Their story is the arc. In one sense, we are the heroes of our own journey. I encourage people to think in this way to harness agency. Simultaneously, we are part of complex communities whose tales are mutually informing one another. This story is a more challenging one to share.

The Ubuntu philosophy centers "being self through others." *Ubuntu* is a Zulu word that translates to "I am because of who we are." Many of us are familiar with the adage "I think, therefore I am." However, Ubuntu philosophy says "I participate, therefore I am."

Thomas Mofolo is a champion of Ubuntu futurism. Pointing to the Black consciousness that evolved in South Africa under apartheid, he thinks of Ubuntu futurism as South Africa's Afrofuturism context. "Black consciousness today is taking on Ubuntu futurism as a new identity that takes on a lot of ideas of liberation, imagination, African spirituality, and Indigenous knowledge systems," he says. The philosophy is a "me and we and everything."

## Neptune Frost

The film *Neptune Frost* shifts storytelling by blurring the lines between tangible and ethereal worlds while kicking binary conventions out the stargazers window. Codirected by husband and wife team Saul Williams and Anisia Uzeyman, the stunning film sheds light on dreamers who find their power as they cross from Burundi into an otherworldly dimension. With e-waste camps, exploitative coltan mines, student protests, and musical communities in the backdrop, Williams and Uzeyman make social commentary about the nature of power (coltan fueled, people power, and hierarchy) while capturing the magic of Rwanda's music and landscape as the basis for an alternate dimension. In the film, Matalusa, a grief-stricken miner, and Neptune, an intersex hacker seeking safety, are among those transported into an alternate universe. The community that assembles in the new world becomes the launching pad for destabilizing technology and decolonizing systems in the Earthly one. This space where electronic goods go to die births a hacker's liberation oasis. But the story is as much about its protagonists' connection as it is the collective of otherworldly hackers dismantling Earth's problematic systems. The message of refurbishing old tech as a metaphor for discarded people finding new purpose doesn't go unnoticed.

The Ubuntu philosophy of me, we, and everything punctuates the story. As some of the newcomers question the nature of their new world, dream or reality, one asserts in song that "the future is our home. It all came from here." It's later revealed that this alternate world is Digitaria, "built by the ancestors of the stars: our past and future selves." Critic Robert Daniels was spellbound. "It's a collective dream coated in a blue lacquer dancing on the edge of something unrecognizable, something wholly transcendent. And it arrives with an exceptional display of bravura."[4]

This tale, originally designed as a graphic novel and stage play, evolved into a cinematic wonder. "The fact that it was science fiction

allowed me to push it to the extraordinary and the brilliance that I
see in it. [Rwanda] has a lot of magicality for me," says Uzeyman.
"It was the opportunity to look at it from the perspective of a child
like *Alice in Wonderland* or [from] something that's bigger than
reality. It was freeing going through the science fictional lens."[5]

In the book *The Dark Delight of Being Strange: Black Stories
of Freedom*, James B. Haile III juxtaposes real stories that feel
speculative with fictional stories that feel real. He describes it as
a book of speculative fiction and philosophical prose. Both the
fiction stories and the strange-but-true ones are in dialogue with
one another. Haile, an associate professor at the University of
Rhode Island, teaches philosophy. The only way he could reconcile these thin lines between the true and truer was to think of it
all as speculative. In one story he positions the real life of Henry
"Box" Brown, an enslaved man who mailed himself in a box to
freedom, a journey that took close to three weeks, with a fictive
story of two museum tour guides questioning how he did so. When
he reveals that Brown spent his free life as a famous, sought-after
illusionist, it puts the tried-and-true story of Brown's daring dash
to freedom in another context. But Haile wonders why we know
the story of Brown's remarkable escape to freedom but not that
of his career as a noted magician. Is the source of freedom itself
another worldly space?

> But what would it mean for Black freedom to exist on
> a dimensional plane not adjacent to white domination,
> for it to *emerge* outside of the plane of enslavement and/
> or oppression altogether? What would it mean for Black
> freedom to have another origin, another telos where its
> goal is not the usurpation or transcending of white norms,
> or worse, the assimilation *into* white norms as no-longer-
> enslaved, or as no-longer-really-Black: as in, the only way
> for Black people to be free is to no longer *be* Black? If this
> other dimensional space *were* real, what would occur in

this space? Would it still *be* freedom, or would it be something else? Something else altogether unlike any freedom we've ever known? A sense of space or time different than we've ever known? Or could possibly conceive?[6]

There's power in the story. There's power in how we tell the story. There's the in-between, the missing text or edited info given life with new context. Our own stories and those of our communities change when we tell them from other perspectives, as science fiction, when we insert missing information, rearrange the order, or shift the space in which they're told. Sometimes fiction can reveal truths in living matters.

## Reflection Questions

Let's play with nonlinear storytelling.

1.  Can you recall a story that you feel is nonlinear? Perhaps it's a film, or a poem, or a book? You can pick from any medium. What made this work of art nonlinear? How did you feel about the story?
2.  How do you think stories should be preserved? Do you like the idea of values being preserved in ceremony or ritual? What could a story ceremony look and feel like?

## Exercises: Nonlinear Memories

1.  Pick three incidents or stories in your life. You can reflect on a memory from childhood, your teen years, your adult years. Now think of a moment from your future life that reflects something you'd like to do or expect to do. The incident from your future life can include a trip you'll take or a project you'll finish. List each memory along with your future memory. List them in order of occurrence. For example, you'll list your childhood memory first and

your future memory last. Think of this as the sequence of a move. Jot down this narrative. Now reorder the memories. For example, you can put your future memory first and your childhood memory last. What themes do you see now? Has anything changed? How do you feel?

2. Watch the film *Neptune Frost*. It's a story of wonderment and insight.

# 20

# WORLD OF WORLDS

## Transforming by Sharing Stories

AFROFUTURIST STORIES ARE JOURNEYS. Some make us uncomfortable while others ignite our imaginations. While there's an art to how a story is told, perhaps what's most important is that it is shared. I remember showing my dad a copy of the graphic novel *March* based on Congressman John Lewis's life. I was curious to know how he felt about Lewis's story being told as a comic. "That doesn't matter," he said. "As long as they tell the story." Film curator Floyd Webb reasons that because stories aren't always shared collectively from generation to generation, new people are always coming across archetypes. Regardless of the medium, the lessons have an impact. At the end of the day, we all want to write our own story, fictive or otherwise.

Keem Hughley was at a crossroads. A chef in Washington, DC, he felt stifled by the restaurant business. A well-traveled young Black man adorned with tattoos, he felt hampered by the expectations of what he should and should not do as a chef. He longed to open a restaurant, but he didn't want to be confined to the culinary offerings a Black-owned restaurant was expected provide. Nor did he want to do something that was already common fare. Coming up with a concept wasn't easy. "It was very difficult for me to be truly creative in my idea, just based on the social conditions of the past 500 years . . . Every time I tried to do something different, something innate in me kept putting me back into the box."[1]

During 2020, at the pandemic's height, Hughley's life slowed down and he found himself reading about Afrofuturism. In fact, he was reading *Afrofuturism: The World of Black Sci-Fi and Fantasy Culture*. The experience would change his life. In order to change expectations of customers and to free himself, he needed to create a new story.

Hughley created the character Alonzo Bronze, a mythical eternal hailing from a locale in East Africa. The year is 1300 and Bronze is a chef who travels the world looking for spices and recipes. He shapeshifts, sometimes traveling as a bird. Bronze meets friends along the way and has adventures. Bronze settles on an island in the modern-day Caribbean. His fine cuisine is inspired by the world over. However, the temperament of the food is uniquely that of the time- and space-defying chef. This narrative gave context to the cuisine Hughley longed to provide. More than African Diasporic fusion, this cuisine would emanate from the unique perspective of a distant traveler. At the top of 2022, Hughley unveiled his creation: Bronze, the first Afrofuturist restaurant.

Located on DC's historic H Street, the contemporary design was enhanced with quaint elements of Bronze's travels. The décor included abstracted paintings of Bronze's friends and silhouettes of swans from his new island home. There were also a few Afrofuturist artifacts including books and space-tinged jazz and funk album covers. At the restaurant's entrance was a silhouette of Bronze himself.

This well-crafted story of the wanderlust chef freed Hughley from adhering to the expectations placed upon him and the limited fare he felt obligated to provide. The narrative also disrupted food time lines. Hughley could make whatever he liked. He could also present new Black cuisine as high cuisine with a fine dining legacy.

The menu reflected Hughley's, or rather Bronze's, eclectic taste. This narrative of a time travelling chef kept his diners open to new concepts with elements of the familiar. Moreover, he recruited Afro-Caribbean chef Toya Henry to help write "the food language."[2] The story is poised to be a storied cookbook and so much more.

What kinds of stories are Afrofuturists telling? At heart they are sharing tales born of liberation, whether that's a freedom from expectation or a physical freedom. Story as a liberatory tool to reconnect people with themselves in the scope of community is a constant in Afrofuturist storytelling. The story put into action helps us to see ourselves, to experience ourselves in ways that stretch our imaginations and our actions. These stories that we craft can pull from the real, the fantastic, the dream, and the aspiration. Pulling from pasts and projecting them into futures makes for great stories but also prisms to better reflect who we are and what we value.

## Ezekiel's Wheel

Playwright Addae Moon had been thinking of writing a speculative fiction work for some time. He yearned to world build from the lessons learned from the African American experience but he didn't want race to be central. "I didn't want the story to be a response to racism," he says. "I didn't want it to be a factor at all." However, Moon did want to interrogate futures and power. Moon wrote a story during the pandemic's peak. "I'm obsessed with Maroons," he said. Maroons are free communities of those who escaped slavery. "That's a side of our story that's just not told enough."

However, to survive, Maroons had to live in places that were largely inhospitable—places where no one wanted to go. In his research, Moon learned about the Great Dismal Swamp. The Great Dismal Swamp is a large swath of land, some 750 miles, that stretches from southeastern Virginia to northeastern North

Carolina. It's now believed that between 1700 and the 1860s, thousands of people may have lived there. In addition to those who escaped slavery and their descendants, Native Americans who were escaping colonialism called the Dismal home, too.

"What if our stable society was dismantled and some people returned to the Great Dismal Swamp?" Moon asked himself. The play *Ezekiel's Wheel* was the answer. The story begins with Jonathon Baker, whose family headed to the swamp when society collapsed. The story takes place some twenty years into the journey. Baker, now a leader of the community, has two adult sons. The collapsed society is now known as the Province and is ruled by swarthy leader Chancellor Bridgeport. One of Baker's sons has the gift of prophecy, and the Chancellor takes interest in him, hoping to bend his talents to meet his needs. The play is a story on the value of prophecy in unstable times. As the Chancellor and Baker debate, Afrofuturist story elements of community, choice, vision, and self-actualization come into question. "The toughest part was writing this story with all Black characters without Black and white being the tension around power," says Moon. The play's title is a reference to the Biblical story that inspired the spiritual "Ezekiel Saw the Wheel." Some have wondered if this song, first sung by the enslaved, was referencing a spaceship.

Other stories give the familiar a refresh. When Ayize Jama-Everett first decided to rewrite *The Count of Monte Cristo* as Afrofuturist, it was suggested that he put the characters in space. "There's something about outer space that gives up on Earth," says Everett. Instead, he chose to tell the story in a far-off time at what could be the world's end. Thinking of climate change, Everett set the story in a world where many of the continents we know are no more—Asia has split in two, and people are fleeing to the continent of Africa. The seafaring are the movers and shakers in this world. The Count is among them. A wedding between the Count and his great love in India is interrupted. "You have ships with solar sails that can maximize solar industry," he told me.

"You have electric eels. People are eating different types of algae. It wasn't here's the solution, but rather here's the last of the best that we have on the planet."

Is the story a warning about the perils of climate change? "I think it's a warning if you see it and decide to do something different. It's a warning if people don't want to replicate it. That's on the reader."

Although climate change is the backdrop, another question fueled the story. "What does wealth and power and privilege look like as the world is dying?" he wondered. What does power mean if a world is on its last legs? "First he has no power, then has all the power in the world," says Everett. "How does that shape who he is as a person? Hopefully, by the end of the book you get the message that all power is fleeting."

The story is reimagined with the awareness that Alexandre Dumas's father was a Black count fighting alongside Napoleon. Dumas used his father's death-defying feats as inspiration for the classic.

Even those stories which bridge our personal worlds with our imagined ones buoy us forward. These stories walk their own path. Sometimes a story can go where we think we cannot, or at least that's the premise we begin with. The telling of the story always reveals. It is the gift that keeps unfolding.

## Inner Space

Yaoundé Olu is a cartoonist who creates both fine art and comic books. An early adopter of digital art, Olu writes stories that take place in a not-so-distant world she calls inner space. In her comic *The Transformation of Threee*, released in 2007, Olu centers her world around a land called Ebixia. Populated by people with silver skin and African features, the tale follows a regretful leader whose actions contributed to the devolution of his society. In reflection he recalls meeting the mirror version of himself, one whose warning he didn't heed. "War, the necessary clash of opposites, must be transformed into warm, the complementaries," she writes in the comic.

Olu says that much of her indie comic work speaks to this idea of balance. A former science teacher, she enjoys weaving bonds of spiritual beliefs and science. She's intrigued with transforming opposites into complements. "Zero point energy is the principle of love, and zero represents the balance of all opposites," she says. The people of Ebixia migrate to their new land, New Ebixia. This principle of transforming opposites to complements reflects the community's evolution into love. Characters are often portrayed with rings of sound around them. She wrote music to the work as well.

We all have a story plucked from the realm of the fantastic or the distant future that we can tell. Let's allow ourselves to share these tales and reflect on how they transform our today and tomorrow.

## Reflection Questions

Stories are transformative. We transform ourselves by sharing our narrative.

1.  What elements of Afrofuturist and speculative stories excite you the most? You may have an affinity for the freedom themes or the superhero tropes. Why do you like these elements?
2.  What elements of Afrofuturist stories are most challenging for you? Why?
3.  What kind of story in the Afrofuturist or Black speculative realm would you like to see? Who is the main character? What is their journey? Have you seen a story similar to this before? Why do you think it should be told?

## Exercise: Storytelling

1.  Let's create a character. Let's imagine another you, a fan-
    tastic you, living a life other than the one you have now.
    This character is your doppelganger, a person who is simi-
    lar to you and abides in another dimension. Who is this
    character? Give them a name. What are their personality
    traits? What does their life look like?

2.  Describe this character's world. Perhaps you can select a
    future world you created earlier or you can make up a new
    one. Perhaps your character lives in a world much like this
    one. Describe this world. Name your world. What takes
    place there? Are there any big issues they are dealing with?
    Have they resolved any issues? Be as imaginative as you
    like.

3.  Imagine that you are your character for a moment. Pretend
    you are writing in your journal, through the character's
    eyes. Write freely. Give yourself at least ten minutes to
    write whatever comes to mind. Be sure to write from their
    perspective.

# CONCLUSION

## Star Child

ALLOW YOUR FREEDOMS TO BE as defined by the whispers of an idealized future as they are by the grit of the past. Reimagine yourself. Remix and reimagine. Allow the stories to set you free.

What is the Afrofuturism Evolution? Is it sonic journeys and escapades into protopias? Is it a ride down the imagination highway to a long lost dream? Is it a memory we can't shake—one that sticks with us long after—so long after that we know the story of the memory more than we recall the memory itself? Do we accept that we are walking characters in our own stories, in other people's narratives, swatting projections away like flies? Do we find joy in the in-betweens, morphing into a horn riff sailing between drumbeats? Do we dance ourselves out of our constrictions? Will my remixed story make me feel free?

What, I ask, are you looking to be free from? Can you identify that which keeps you not where you want to be? Do you know where you want to be? Do you dare dream and think beyond the hour when so much tossed your way says that it's about the now?

Are you uncomfortable with histories known and unknown? Does the unbridled story in nonlinear form feel like a waking dream? When people speak of futures, are you uncomfortable, still? When you look at the past, if you look at the past, do you see a future yet to be revealed? What's to be made of our tethered life? If our particles are tied to some other form in some other multiverse, am I, in some way, there too? Is the breeze I feel an ancestor ushering along? Is my noise a demand that I be heard?

Why would bells on my ankles or blue fried hair lift me so? Is my tango dance of one merely a wrestling match with my conventions? Am I forever seen as the odd one out? Is there no makeup or clothing thick enough to hide my glow? Because it's the glow we fear almost more than the exclusion. It's the glow and the inherent joy of it all that's as scary as the rejection. Yes, some Afrofuturists are wondrous at making predictions. They spot patterns, knock back opportunities like it's water with crystals in 'em. Feeling a future is the way. Do I crawl on Martian ground, eyes closed, patting my way though the new terrain? What, I ask, is the road map? Is it the archetypes of the past? Am I a bluesman wandering, using my guitar everywhere I go? Am I the DJ forever flipping through crates for the song that hasn't been sampled? Why does a dig into the past feel like raking through my subconscious? Why do unknown pasts feel so ominous?

I am both elated and nervous when I think of space travel. Is space travel only fun in my imagination? Is Earth the terrain eternally for me? We stand on rich soils older than we know. The bigness of time is too enormous to process. Yet, I know infinity. I've felt it swimming in deep lakes and lying on bluegrass, and orange sand, the yellowed sun baking my face. I felt it in the comfort of the crackling record that skips. So many technologies to learn. I am not my phone, I tell myself as I brush its screen softly. Is it the stars or the city lights that fill me with wonder? Do I know the off-hued streetlights more than the stars above? Can I see them? Why can't I see the stars? Astrophysicist Chanda Prescod-Weinstein says that we don't see our ancestors' sky. Quite literally, we can't spot it. If it was the north star I needed to get to the next protopia, could I find it without a phone app? As my future and past, the liminal and the terrestrial align, I am present but I move forward. I like the past for its lessons but I shake it off when it holds me back, back. Forward, they say. We are not robots, we are not machines, we are human in a world that's never been about mastery.

Does cooperation frighten you? Does thinking in community give you comfort or make you afraid? There are moments when we pull away and moments when we commune. Yet, as I pull away, aloneness does not contain me. Spirit guides, they say, are everywhere. They knock over books with must-read passages onto floors and kiss your cheeks when the wind blows. They show up and show out in vintage stores. What, you ask, is the point of it all? Is awareness enough? Some say we chose this life. They reason we made a pact before the before, insisting upon this very journey. They say that life in the spirit realm is awesome, but being in a body, a human one, an animal one, is worth the fight. If we are not the stories we tell ourselves or the realm of the imaginative that we so desperately need to get by, then what are we? Particles? These particles assembled for a reason. We are communing in this shared experience called life for a reason. If the reason isn't clear, then perhaps I can go back to the map to guide me.

What map, you say? Yes, we are swimming through story. Yes, we are awakening from a lucid space of story. Yes, we are creating our own narratives, cocreating them. Yes, I crave a better future and I want that better future now. Feel the future? Where is this map you speak of, the one with the archetypes, and artifacts, and ancestors, and spirit guides, and funny stories, and peppy beats? Where is this thing? Oh wait, I made it, you say? When? That journal you speak of? That's my guide? Ha, ha, ha! Do you think I'm the protagonist in *Parable of the Sower*? Ha, ha, ha! Am I, too, collecting phrases and punchlines and wisdom remembered? Ha, ha, ha! The trick's on you, that story is already written. Wait, it is already written 'cause I wrote it. It is written because I'm writing it.

Yes, well technically my journal is complete, for the moment. And technically it's already written. OK, but really, what's the point?

I am the point? I am a point, an intersection of times and spaces. I embody rhythms to chart courses for new ones. I imagine because I can. I create because I must. I expect more because to expect less doesn't make me feel on purpose.

————

You are delightful. You are a light. You are the essence of the before the before, born of a cosmic soup that says it's creation time. Through this journey together we've elongated spaces and times, soaring into inner worlds and leaping to the great beyond. We've sailed through dreamworlds, uncovered the magic of visions. We've danced, claiming a rhythm all our own. We pulled on courage to go to new spaces, alter-destinies, and the great outdoors, recognizing that our space is shared and magical. Our rhythm is our story. Our story is us. We are our story and we hold the capacity for it to change as we dart to new planets, new shared spaces, and new understandings. We are at the center of the circle and its perimeter, cheering ourselves and one another on. We recognize the connection, we embrace the spiral. We dance between the rhythm and become it because our humanness is ever expansive.

My dearest wish is that this journey at the least gives you tools to live your vibration just enough to see possibility. I truly believe that futures are waiting on us, leaning on us. Our own future selves are hoping to commune, so you can prompt another time line they can hop on for safekeeping. I sincerely wish that you bathe yourself in the Afrofuturist works of others. These visions are freedom visions. These visions are questions in self-actualization. These visons on script and canvas are punctuated with wisdom. Hopefully, you find new beauty in your own imaginative abilities. As you find your way in this lens of story, know that there are people on all sides of time and space rooting for you. You are here.

# NOTES

## 1. The O'Clock Hour: From Cultural Histories to Black Futures

1. Morena Mariah, "Afrofuture," TEDxLaçador, May 2019, https://www.ted.com/talks/morena_mariah_afrofuturo.

2. Reginald Crosley, *The Vodou Quantum Leap: Alternate Realities, Power, and Mysticism* (Llewellyn Publications, 2000), 120.

3. Milo Rigaud, *Secrets of Voodoo* (City Lights Books, 1914), 81.

## 2. Liminal Revelations: Finding Ourselves in a Liminal Period

1. Amílcar Cabral, *Return to the Source: Selected Texts of Amilcar Cabral*, expanded ed., edited by Tsenay Serequeberhan (Monthy Review Press, 2023), 66.

2. Oghenechovwe Donald Ekpeki and Joshua Uchenna Omenga, *Between Dystopias: The Road to Afropantheology* (CAEZIK SF & Fantasy, 2023), 5.

3. Neubauer Collegium for Culture and Society, "The Otolith Group," press release, University of Chicago, 2024, https://neubauercollegium

.uchicago.edu/uploads/common/Exhibitions/otolith-group/Otolith
-Group-Press-Release.pdf.

## 4. The Cry of Jazz: Unlimited Musical Improvisation in Limiting Places

1. A. B. Spellman, Larry Neal, and Amiri Baraka, eds., *The Cricket: Black Music in Evolution, 1968–69* (Blank Forms, 2022), 129.

2. Spellman et al., 120.

3. Spellman et al., 129.

## 5. Space Is the Place: Sun Ra and the Space of the Mind

1. Malidoma Patrice Somé, *The Healing Wisdom of Africa: Finding Life Purpose Through Nature, Ritual, and Community* (TarcherPerigee, 1999), 68.

## 6. Sonic Community and Being the Space: Shaping Community Spaces with Intention

1. KRS-One, *The Gospel of Hip Hop: The First Instrument* (powerHouse Books, 2009), chapter "The First Overstanding," digital ed.

## 8. The Fortitude in Optimism: The Courage to Expect More

1. Barbara Ransby, *Ella Baker & the Black Freedom Movement: A Radical Democratic Vision* (University of North Carolina Press, 2003), 7.

2. John Lewis, *Across That Bridge: A Vision for Change and the Future of America* (Hachette, 2012), 65.

3. Erin Allen, "Hazel Johnson, 'the Mother of Environmental Justice' in Chicago," *The Rundown*, WBEZ Chicago, March 13, 2024, https://

www.wbez.org/the-rundown-chicago-news-podcast/2024/03/13/hazel-johnson-the-mother-of-environmental-justice-in-chicago.

4. Lewis, *Across That Bridge*, 65–66.

5. Lewis, 207.

6. "Personal Testimonies," Fannie Lou Hamer's America, accessed November 4, 2024, https://www.fannielouhamersamerica.com/fannie-lou-hamer-resource-center/personal-testimonies.

7. Abiola Abrams, *African Goddess Initiation: Sacred Rituals for Self-Love, Prosperity, and Joy* (Hay House, 2021), 151.

8. ONE Musicfest, "Erykah Badu Explains 'Creativity Is the Absence of Fear,'" Facebook, May 17, 2016, https://www.facebook.com/watch/?v=1420835171275475.

9. Sadie Sartini Garner, review of *America the Beautiful* by Kahil El'Zabar, *Pitchfork*, November 2, 2020, https://pitchfork.com/reviews/albums/kahil-elzabar-america-the-beautiful/.

10. *Free to Dance*, in *Great Performances*, PBS, aired June 2001.

11. Katherine Dunham, *Island Possessed* (University of Chicago Press, 1994), 105.

12. Dunham, 106.

## 9. Believe a World: Imagining Our Futures

1. Nicole Mitchell Gantt, *The Mandorla Letters: For the Hopeful* (Green Lantern Press, 2022), 81.

2. Toni Morrison, interview by John Callaway, WTTW, 1977, https://interactive.wttw.com/playlist/2018/03/13/archive-toni-morrison.

3. Sienna Mayers, "8 Standout Students from the Central Saint Martins Class of 2023," *Standard*, February 22, 2023, https://www.standard.co.uk/lifestyle/fashion/central-saint-martins-ma-show-lfw-london-fashion-week-b1062086.html.

4. Ekow Eshun, *In the Black Fantastic* (MIT Press, 2022), 11.

5. Kelly Lynn Thomas, "Spitting in the Face of Empire: The Millions Interviews Nisi Shawl," *Millions*, October 2, 2017, https://themillions.com/2017/10/spitting-in-the-face-of-empire-the-millions-interviews-nisi-shawl.html.

6. Kevin Young, *The Grey Album: On the Blackness of Blackness* (Graywolf, 2012), 82.

7. Julia Peres Guimaraes, "Brazilian Afrofutures: Aquilombamento and Aesthetic Militancy as Ancestral Technologies of the Future" (thesis paper), emailed to author February 8, 2023.

8. Gantt, *Mandorla Letters*, 9.

9. Gantt, 10.

10. Gantt, 115.

## 10. The Vision: Creation, Invention, and Transformation from Visions

1. *Luaka Bop Presents: Alice Coltrane Turiyasangitananda*, developed by Eric Welles-Nystrom, edited by David McCleod and Eric Welles-Nystrom, released by Luaka Bop on YouTube, May 3, 2017, https://youtu.be/hyADcmvIbsQ.

2. Franya J. Berkman, *Monument Eternal: The Music of Alice Coltrane* (Wesleyan University Press, 2010), 3.

3. *Luaka Bop Presents*, https://youtu.be/hyADcmvIbsQ.

4. "Alice Coltrane's Legacy," John and Alice Coltrane Home official website, accessed October 10, 2024, https://thecoltranehome.org/alice-coltrane/.

5. Helena Andrews-Dyer, "How DJ D-Nice's Endlessly Spinning Journey Grew to Legendary Status," *Washington Post*, November 25, 2022, https://www.washingtonpost.com/arts-entertainment/2022/11/25/dj-d-nice-spinning-journey-quarantine-live/.

6. Jelani Cobb, "D-Nice's Club Quarantine Is What You Need," *New Yorker*, March 22, 2020, https://www.newyorker.com/culture/culture-desk/d-nices-club-quarantine-is-what-you-need.

7. Spellman et al., *Cricket*, 31.

8. Spellman et al., 34.

## 11. Notes of a Dreamer: Creating Conscious Relationships with Your Dreams

1. Somé, *Healing Wisdom of Africa*, 196.

2. Najja Parker, "Nap Ministry Redefines Resistance by Resting," *Atlanta Journal-Constitution*, February 27, 2023, https://www.ajc.com/news/martin-luther-king-jr/nap-ministry-redefines-resistance-by-resting/GJFF2TSLSRHTXHYMSN6X3K6ZO4/.

3. The Nap Ministry, "You are divine . . . ," Instagram, April 11, 2022, https://www.instagram.com/p/CcPBO2IuzBq/.

4. The Nap Ministry, "May we one day see our rest . . . ," Instagram, February 23, 2003, https://www.instagram.com/p/CpB3o49u_bU/.

5. Tricia Hersey, The Nap Ministry official website, accessed October 10, 2024, https://thenapministry.com/.

6. Mary Retta, "Welcome to Janelle Monáe's Dreamworld," *Wired*, April 26, 2022, https://www.wired.com/story/janelle-monae-afrofuturism-book-memory-librarian/.

## 12. Energy: The History and Future of Dance

1. Kiatezua Lubanzadio Luyaluka, "The Spiral as the Basic Semiotic of the Kongo Religion, the Bukongo," *Journal of Black Studies* 48, no. 1 (January 2017): 91–112, https://www.jstor.org/stable/26174215.

2. Luyaluka, "The Spiral."

3. Logan Cryer, "Art for Change: The Comic," Forman Arts Initiative, March 27, 2024, https://formanartsinitiative.org/story/art-for-change-the-comic.

4. Joanna Jowett, "Ageless: Interview with Germaine Acogny," *Yorkshire Dance*, June 6, 2022, https://yorkshiredance.com/news/ageless-interview-with-germaine-acogny.

### 13. Nature's Medicine: Movement Outdoors

1. Tommy Sutton, *Tap Along with Tommy: A Technical Guide for Tap Dance Teachers* (T. Sutton, 1986), 3.

2. Zachary Whittenburg, "Germaine Acogny, the 'Mother of Contemporary African Dance,' Continues Her Conversation with Pina Bausch," *Dance Magazine*, June 6, 2022, https://www.dancemagazine.com/germaine-acogny.

3. Jowett, "Ageless," https://yorkshiredance.com/news/ageless-interview-with-germaine-acogny.

### 14. Flow Is as Flow Does: The Life Force of Rhythm

1. Souleymane Bachir Diagne, *African Art as Philosophy: Senghor, Bergson, and the Idea of Negritude*, trans. by Chike Jeffers (Seagull Books, 2011), 77–78.

2. Diagne, 78–79.

3. Diagne, 87.

4. Diagne, 86.

### 15. A Story of Eight Counts: Polyrhythms and Defying Expectations

1. Tyler Golsen, "James Brown Explains the Origins of Funk," *Far Out*, November 24, 2021, https://faroutmagazine.co.uk/james-brown-origins-of-funk.

### 17. My Multiverse: The Multiplicity of Telling Our Own Stories

1. Chanda Prescod-Weinstein, *The Disordered Cosmos: A Journey into Dark Matter, Spacetime, and Dreams Deferred* (Bold Type Books, 2021), 67.

2. Alice Sparkly Kat, *Postcolonial Astrology: Reading the Planets Through Capital, Power, and Labor* (North Atlantic Books, 2021), 287.

## 19. The Art of the Nonlinear: The History and Future of Black Storytelling

1. Lorraine O'Grady, *Writing in Space, 1973–2019*, ed. by Aruna D'Souza (Duke University Press, 2020), 44.

2. *The Other Others*, "Ubuntu Futurism," hosted by Tyson Yunkaporta, Spotify, September 2021, https://open.spotify.com/episode/5m09VD F2oaUfDwm20LHJTj.

3. Oghenechovwe Donald Ekpeki and Joshua Uchenna Omenga, "Introduction to Afropantheology," *Public Books*, October 3, 2023, https:// www.publicbooks.org/introduction-to-afropantheology/.

4. Robert Daniels, review of *Neptune Frost*, RogerEbert.com, June 3, 2022, https://www.rogerebert.com/reviews/neptune-frost-movie -review-2022.

5. Starburst Magazine, "Saul Williams & Anisia Uzeyman About Their Afrofuturist Musical, Neptune Frost," YouTube, July 14, 2022, https:// www.youtube.com/watch?v=pugCmz55rIE.

6. James B. Haile III, *The Dark Delight of Being Strange: Black Stories of Freedom* (Columbia University Press, 2024), 5.

## 20. World of Worlds: Transforming by Sharing Stories

1. Jessica Sidman, "DC's Luxe New Afrofuturism Restaurant Is Inspired by Sci-Fi Fantasy," *Washingtonian*, January 9, 2023, https:// www.washingtonian.com/2023/01/09/dcs-luxe-new-afrofuturism -restaurant-is-inspired-by-sci-fi-fantasy.

2. Tierney Plumb, "Maketto's New H Street Sister Bronze Explores Afrofuturism Through Food," *Eater Washington DC*, April 13, 2022, https://dc.eater.com/2022/4/13/23002031/maketto-h-street-bronze -afrofuturism-coming-attractions.

# INDEX

# ABOUT THE AUTHOR

© Lauren Renner

**Ytasha L. Womack** is a filmmaker and futurist, and the author of *Afrofuturism: The World of Black Sci-Fi and Fantasy Culture*, *Post Black: How a New Generation Is Redefining African American Identity*, and *Black Panther: A Cultural Exploration*. Womack was featured in the National Museum of African American History and Culture exhibit *Afrofuturism: A History of Black Futures* as well as a contributor to the companion title released by Smithsonian Books. She has taught and lectured on Afrofuturism to audiences ranging from Carnegie Hall and the Smithsonian to Afropunk in Brooklyn and the Sonic Acts festival in Amsterdam, from Saint-Etienne School of Architecture in France to MIT Media Lab's "Beyond the Cradle" in Boston. She is the creator of the *Rayla 2212* sci-fi multimedia series, a writer-producer of the animated sky show *Niyah and the Multiverse* at the Adler Planetarium, and the coeditor of *Beats Rhymes & Life: What We Love and Hate About Hip Hop*. She lives in Chicago.